POSTMODERNISM AN
ENVIRONMENTAL (

D0083627

Environmental awareness has undoubtedly grown over the last two decades, but the actual achievements of ecological movements have been paltry. In order to explain, and to overcome, this paradoxical situation, *Postmodernism and the Environmental Crisis* examines the philosophical traditions underlying the current approaches to the ecological crisis. It is the first book to combine advanced cultural theory and environmental philosophy; the result is a radically new vision – a postmodern 'grand narrative'.

At the heart of the problem, Arran E. Gare argues, is the failure of mainstream, Marxist and postmodern approaches alike to theorize the links between the ecological crisis, the globalization of capitalism and the fragmentation and disintegration of modernist culture. A successful ecological politics needs to forge a new world-view out of the post-modernist critique of Western civilization and a global ecological perspect-ive. *Postmodernism and the Environmental Crisis* shows that this can be done and, in doing so, lays the foundations for an effective environmental movement.

This book will be vital reading for advanced students of environmental studies as well as for environmental philosophers and for all those interested in cultural and political theory.

Arran E. Gare is Senior Lecturer in Philosophy and Cultural Inquiry at Swinburne University, Australia. He is the author of *Nihilism Incorporated* and *Beyond European Civilization*.

POSTMODERNISM AND THE ENVIRONMENTAL CRISIS

Arran E. Gare

London and New York

First published 1995
by Routledge
11 New Fetter Lane, London EC4P 4EE

Simultaneously published in the USA and Canada
by Routledge
29 West 35th Street, New York, NY 10001

© 1995 Arran E. Gare

Typeset in Palatino by
Ponting–Green Publishing Services, Chesham, Bucks
Printed in Great Britain by
TJ Press Ltd, Padstow, Cornwall

British Library Cataloguing in Publication Data
A catalogue record for this book is available from
the British Library

Library of Congress Cataloging in Publication Data
A catalogue record for this book has been requested

ISBN 0–415–12478–6 (hbk)
ISBN 0–415–12479–4 (pbk)

CONTENTS

PREFACE

This book is the outcome of a continuing search for the roots of the global ecological crisis, and the cultural conditions required to overcome it. The central concern is with how increasing awareness of global ecological destruction has generated such ineffectual responses. The focus on postmodernity was provoked by the experience of taking up a teaching position at Swinburne University in Melbourne, Australia. The culture described by Fredric Jameson in *Postmodernism* was here a palpable reality. Confronting this culture both facilitated an appreciation of the work of the poststructuralists, and radically altered my assessment of the prospects of the environmental movement.

The writing of this book was assisted by a small grant from the Arts Faculty at Swinburne University, and I was encouraged in my work by the members of Swinburne's Department of Philosophy and Cultural Inquiry. However, the real source of inspiration for this work was the personality of my mother, Nene Gare, who died in May of this year. This book is dedicated to her, and what she stood for.

15 August 1994

INTRODUCTION

The postmodern scene is a panic site, just for the fun of it. And beneath the forgetting, there is only the scribbling of another Bataille, another vomiting of flavourless blood, another heterogeneity of excess to mark the upturned orb of the pineal eye. The solar anus is parodic of postmodernism, but, again, just for the fun of it.[1]

So proclaimed Arthur Kroker and David Cook in *The Postmodern Scene: Excremental Culture and Hyper-Aesthetics*, a book they claim is itself eminently postmodern.

Let there be no illusions. Taking effective action to halt massive injury to the earth's environment will require a mobilization of political will, international cooperation and sacrifice unknown except in wartime. Yet humanity is in a war right now, and it is not too draconian to call it a war for survival. It is a war in which all nations must be allies.[2]

So proclaimed Thomas A. Sancton, writing in *Time* magazine. Juxtaposing these two proclamations brings together the two issues which have evoked the most intense debates in the closing decades of the second millennium – the postmodern condition and the environmental crisis.

Reflection on the postmodern condition and reflection on the environmental crisis have much in common. They both involve efforts to understand the culture of modern civilization and how it has come to its present state. Most of those attempting to understand the postmodern condition, like those attempting to understand the roots of the environmental crisis, see Western civilization as oppressive, and are striving to create new or resurrect old ways of experiencing, thinking and living. It is arguable that the postmodern condition, associated as it is with a loss of faith in modernity, progress and enlightenment rationality, reflects people's awareness that it is just these cultural forms which are propelling humanity to self-destruction. Proponents of postmodernist politics usually endorse ecological resistance along with feminist activism as a new

1

form of politics. But the fragmentation of experience, disorientation and loss of overarching perspectives and grand narratives associated with postmodernity are threats to the efforts of environmentalists who are struggling to develop and proselytize a global perspective on environmental destruction. Clearly postmodernism and environmentalism are of great significance to each other. Yet little effort has been made to relate the discourse on postmodernity with the discourse on the environmental crisis.

The failure to relate these two discourses exemplifies the disjunction between the 'two cultures', literature and science. Reflection on the postmodern condition revolves around the study of literature and popular culture, despite the part that architectural theory and reflections on recent developments in science have played in popularizing the term 'postmodernism'. Reflection on the environmental crisis, on the other hand, has revolved around reflections on science, technology and occasionally economics. Books on postmodernism are found in bookshops on shelves devoted to the theory of literature, while books on the environment tend to be found along with books on science. Postmodernism is discussed in journals of art, literature and the media, while environmental problems are discussed mainly in journals of popular science. In this work I will show that to address properly either the issues raised by the postmodernist condition or the environmental crisis, this disjunction will have to be overcome.

Once analyses of postmodernity and modernity are conjoined with analyses of the roots of the global environmental crisis, it will become clear that what we are facing is a unique historical event. In the middle of the nineteenth century Karl Marx argued that 'only rarely and under quite special conditions is a society able to adopt a critical attitude towards itself'.[3] The situation we are in is one of those quite special conditions in which not merely a society but the whole of modern civilization is being forced to adopt a critical attitude towards itself, a critical attitude even more profound than the critique by Marx of capitalism in the nineteenth century.

The course this essay will take is first to characterize the postmodern condition, then to examine the philosophical ideas associated with it. After showing the nature of the conflict between both conservative and radical proponents and opponents of postmodern culture, these ideas will be evaluated in terms of how they illuminate the way in which environmental problems are being generated and how such problems might be surmounted. It will be argued that while the poststructuralists, the thinkers most closely aligned with postmodernism, have highlighted many of the root causes of oppression in the modern world, when measured against the environmental crisis they are totally inadequate as guides for political action or for how to live. Both revisionists of mainstream culture and

2

Marxists are more adequate to this task. Nevertheless, the poststructuralists have revealed what kind of cultural politics to avoid if the causes of
the environmental crisis are not to be reproduced by efforts to overcome
it. This analysis will reveal what is required to address the environmental
crisis: a 'postmodern' cosmology. To this end, proposals for a postmodern
science will be examined, and it will be shown how the reconception of
humanity and of its place in nature through such a science, articulated into
a new 'postmodern' grand narrative, can effect the required cultural
transformation. The essay will conclude by showing how a new ethics,
political philosophy and economics can be, and are being built upon this
grand narrative, and how they are able to provide the foundations for an
effective environmental movement.

1

WHAT IS POSTMODERNITY?

The *Modern-day Dictionary of Received Ideas* says of 'postmodernism': 'This word has no meaning. Use it as often as possible.'[1] With a few notable exceptions, cultural theorists have been following this advice. The term postmodernism has been used with astonishing frequency in a surprising variety of ways. Its popularity seems to derive from the way it can mean anything to anyone. However there is more to the proliferation of the term than this. It signifies participation in the debate about whether there has been a radical cultural transformation in the world, particularly within Western societies, and if so, whether this has been good or bad. To define the postmodern is not just to define a term. It is to characterize the present age and to assess how we should respond to it.

What then are the defining features of the present age? The most widely accepted characterization of the postmodern condition is that offered by Lyotard. It is 'the incredulity towards metanarratives';[2] that is, the incredulity to any metadiscourse which makes appeal to some grand narrative, such as the emancipation of the rational, the liberation of the exploited, or the creation of wealth, which can legitimate all particular claims to knowledge. What does this mean? The loss of credibility of grand narratives is essentially a loss of belief in 'progress'.

If this is the case, it is indeed a major cultural event. In the *History of the Idea of Progress*, Robert Nisbet convincingly argued that the whole of European civilization since the Ancient Greeks has been moved by a belief in progress. It was the Christians within the Roman Empire who gave a moral dimension to history, and defined themselves and their destiny in terms of participation in humanity's cumulative advance towards a final state of perfection. Modernity with its assumption of progress in knowledge, reason, technology, the arts and the economy, began as a secularization of Christian eschatology. The central tenets of Western civilization were merely rewritten in a new key. According to Nisbet, there have been at least five constant premises to be found in the idea of progress:

4

belief in the value of the past; conviction of the nobility, even superiority, of Western civilization; acceptance of the worth of economic and technological growth; faith in reason and in the kind of scientific and scholarly knowledge that can come from reason alone; and, finally, belief in the intrinsic importance, the ineffaceable *worth* of life on this earth.[3]

It is these premises which have lost their plausibility – at least within Western societies.

Without a belief in the future, the whole structure of Western culture falls apart. Nietzsche noted how the notion of progress first emerged, the role it has played in European civilization, and the significance of its destruction:

> From time immemorial we have ascribed the value of an action, a character, an existence, to the *intention*, the *purpose* for the sake of which one has acted or lived: the age-old idiosyncrasy finally takes a dangerous turn . . . there seems to be in preparation a universal disvaluation: 'Nothing has any meaning' . . . In accordance with this valuation, one was constrained to transfer the value of life to a 'life after death', or to the progressive development of ideas or of mankind or of the people or beyond mankind; but with that one had arrived at a *progressus in infinitum* of purposes: one was at last constrained to make a place for oneself in the 'world process' (perhaps with the dysdaemonistic perspective that it was a process into nothingness).[4]

People now appear to believe that the world process is a process into nothingness.

POSTMODERNISM, THE ENVIRONMENTAL CRISIS AND GLOBALIZATION

How could this have happened? How can the central principle which has dominated a civilization for two and a half millennia and which has inspired that civilization to dominate the world, dissolve into nothingness? While people's faith in progress has been shaken in the past, it is only in the second half of the twentieth century that disbelief in these premises has become widespread. This could only be possible in a world where there are very good reasons for ceasing to believe in such premises. What seems to have happened is that the triumph of Western civilization has revealed the hollowness of its promises. As Richard Newbold Adams summed up recent developments in Western culture:

> The nineteenth-century vision of how to make the world a better place in which to live was called 'progress.' It was a coal-fueled

ideology for a vast colonial expansion and it was crushingly discredited by World War I and the interwar era of stagnation and depression. Development is the successor to the vision of progress that accompanied the petroleum-fueled spread of industrialism in the post-World War II nationalizing. If the illusion of progress was dashed by the First World War, the 'development' illusion began to crack and fragment, on the one hand, with increasing poverty, social movements and revolts, military interventions and regional wars, and, on the other hand, environmental pollution and degradation.[5]

Of these problems it is the environmental crisis which is the most significant, because it reveals that all the suffering inflicted by Western civilization, both on its own members and on those civilizations and traditional societies it has subjugated, has been for nothing.

While the environmental crisis is the ultimate source of disorientation, this disorientation is accentuated by and resonates with the 'globalization' of economic and cultural processes. The idea of progress was very much bound up with a particular group of people identifying themselves as having advanced more than others, as being at the cutting edge of the evolution of humanity. The notion of progress was based on a hierarchical ordering of nations and races, with Europeans being at the top of the hierarchy, and 'primitives' such as Australian aboriginals being at the bottom. Such hierarchical ordering of peoples has been threatened by globalization.

Roland Robertson coined the term 'globalization' to describe a process by which the world is being integrated.[6] The conditions of this have been the spread of capitalism, Western imperialism and the development of a global media system; but the unity is a unity of a general and global agency-structure. It is associated with new forms of media, new forms of technology and new forms of management which have transformed the spatio-temporal relations within capitalism.[7] Time has conquered space. The ease with which people can now communicate over long distances, the rapidity with which people can travel and goods can be transported, has brought the affluent throughout the world into closer contact, while creating greater distances between them and the people in their geographical neighbourhood. International trade has steadily increased as a proportion of the national incomes of almost all nations. New patterns of communication within transnational business enterprises and financial organizations have reduced the autonomy of their local branches, and capital can be moved in and out of countries with astonishing speed.

Globalization has undermined state control over national economies. The growing internationalization of capital was brilliantly analysed by Stephen Hymer in the early 1970s.[8] Hymer noted the tendency for transnational corporations to grow faster than national corporations, generating a degree of capital mobility which was forcing states to compete with each other to attract capital investment. He argued that this would create a crisis in both capitalism and in the labour movement, and identified two possible paths of development. Either a new international order would be established dominated by international capital and supported by a privileged section of the working class in the advanced countries which would suppress blacks, Third World people, foreign workers, women and the aged; or a new socialist movement would emerge, which, in the attempt to gain community control over work and consumption, would struggle for national or regional self-sufficiency. Hymer thought the first path would not be taken because of the large numbers and strength of the disadvantaged groups who could only be contained with enormous brutality. It is clear that the first path has been taken, and that proponents of the second are in disarray. As Claus Offe, Scott Lash and John Urry have shown, whether national control over economic processes had been achieved from above, as in the case of Germany, or from below, as in the case of Sweden, the institutions set up to control national economies for the benefit of their members are failing.[9] The regulatory mechanisms established over economies after the Great Depression and the Second World War which resulted from it, have been steadily undermined. Effectively, this has meant a successful onslaught by oligarchical institutions against democratic institutions which were the product of centuries of popular struggles for freedom. Loss of state control over national economies has been greatest in Anglophone nations, where it was weakest in the first place, and least in Asian nations. With this loss, capital has been exported to rapidly expanding centres of economic activity in the peripheries and semi-peripheries of the world economy, which are now outcompeting the old core zone manufacturing industries of Europe and America. In these old core zones, capital freed from production and repatriated from peripheral countries has been invested unproductively in the stock market, real estate, luxury goods and the arts. Deindustrialization with high levels of unemployment has been associated with increased wealth for the wealthy and the gentrification of central city areas. As Jonathan Friedman has pointed out: 'Slumification and yuppification, the increased stratification of the "really declining" centres, is a single systemic process.'[10]

Consequently, globalization has been associated with the decline of the West and the fragmentation of Western societies. Until the last quarter of the twentieth century, the English could define themselves in opposition to and as superior to people of other European nations, as Europeans superior to Orientals, and as civilized people superior to 'primitives'.[11] North Americans' identity as a superior form of human life was developed somewhat later than the English, and has been less stable, but defining themselves in opposition to Europeans, to Latin Americans, to Asians, to blacks and to primitive tribes, white North Americans developed a strong sense of their place in the world as a nation more powerful than any other.[12] Anglophones, whether English, Americans or colonials, had come to believe that they could contain within their own discourse the discourses of everyone else, or almost everyone else, past and present. With Britain's loss of world hegemony and then economic decline and with its growing non-Caucasian population, with the USA's declining economic power relative to Japan and continental Europe and with its fastest-growing economy in California increasingly peopled by non-English speaking Latin Americans and Asians, such clear-cut identities of superiority can no longer be sustained. Anglophones are being forced to recognize themselves as just another ethnic group.[13] And other Europeans, though never as unselfconsciously ethnocentric as Anglophones, nor in such rapid decline, are also being forced to question their self-definitions relative to others.[14]

These developments have undermined national identities. To begin with, they have created a global class consisting of an international bourgeoisie and a sub-class of 'symbolic analysts' – those who make their living manipulating symbols[15] (collectively, the 'new bourgeoisie') sharing one culture with a very weak allegiance to any nation. Typically, the media magnate Rupert Murdoch simply renounced his Australian citizenship and became an American when it suited his business interests. While the process of identification with nations as 'imaginary communities'[16] has been thus weakened from above, identification has been weakened from below by assertions by ethnic minorities of cultural identity against national identity. Native Hawaiians, North American Indians and Australian Aboriginals, groups who had been defined as primitives and relics of a superseded stage of human evolution, are all rejecting the cultures which denied their present significance, and are now reviving their traditional cultures.[17] Migrants are no longer embracing the national cultures of their new homelands but are demanding that their own cultures be accorded the same respect as the native culture.[18]

It is likely that in this new global order, Westerners will no longer be the main beneficiaries of 'progress'. The future no longer belongs automatically to Caucasians, and the incredulity towards grand narratives can be partly understood as disorientation caused by this. It is the response of people of European descent to their powerlessness within the world-order created by European civilization. This disinclines them to even contemplate grand narratives, which, to have any plausibility, could only portray them as insignificant bystanders in the march of history.

CHANGING CLASS COMPOSITION AND CULTURAL CHANGE

Globalization, the disorganization of capitalism and changes in people's thinking have not taken place without resistance. These developments reflect the outcome of class struggle, a struggle which has resulted in the subordination of previously powerful classes by the new international bourgeoisie, and the expansion of a new petite bourgeoisie, a service sub-class. Class conflict has involved cultural conflict, and the emergence of a new balance of classes has been associated with new cultural configurations which have also affected the readiness of people to believe in grand narratives.

Globalization involved the breaking up of the previous balance of class relations, with the decline of the domestic bourgeoisie – those capitalists whose firms produce for the home market, of farmers, of the working class, and in most cases of the 'salariat' – salary earners.[19] The decline of the domestic bourgeoisie has not been as dramatic as one might expect, since for the most part they have either transformed themselves into members of the international bourgeoisie, or have gone bankrupt and declined into lower classes. Those remaining have been too entrenched in their traditional opposition to the working class and too small a group to develop an organized opposition to the rise of the new international bourgeoisie. They have been quietly fading away, along with farmers who are now an insignificant proportion of the population in advanced capitalist nations. The traditional working class is also shrinking. They have been fighting a rearguard action, sometimes successfully, more often, unsuccessfully. Where they have been able to maintain control over the market for labour, blue-collar workers are more affluent than ever before. However this control is being challenged from every direction. Workers in the core zones now have to compete with workers in the peripheral regions of the world-economy and with migrant workers. As a consequence, increasingly high proportions of people from working-class backgrounds are either un-employed or are engaged in casual work. The salariat, which for a long time was the fastest-growing class within Western countries, has been divided between increasingly affluent administrators and increasingly poor and insecure professionals and clerical workers. There has generally been an increase in the incomes, power and numbers of those engaged in administration relative to those salaried members of the workforce who actually provide services. Those who are engaged in providing services – teachers, academics, medical practitioners working for a salary, librarians and social workers – have suffered radical reductions in real income and conditions with reduced job security while bearing increasingly heavy loads of work. And many are being forced into the new service sub-class of the petite bourgeoisie as governments have abandoned responsibility for services to the community.

The bourgeoisie, the working class and the salariat supported different versions of the grand narrative of progress. The domestic bourgeoisie, supported by most farmers, promoted the dominant version, that capitalism based on the free market would generate increasing national wealth in the first instance, and then international wealth, rescuing all who accepted the rule of the market from poverty and oppression. This narrative had been entrenched by projecting onto nature the workings of capitalist society, so that free competition and the struggle for survival between individuals, firms and nations was seen as part of cosmic evolution.[20] The working class deviated from this model either mildly, in the case of social democrats, or more radically in the case of Marxists. However the difference was more in emphasis than in kind. For both, the development of capitalism was seen to be providing the conditions for the creation of a more benign social order in which the working class increasingly would be able to appropriate for themselves the goods produced by industrial development, and through gaining power within the institutions of the state, increasingly would become managers of the economy. The salariat did not develop an independent class consciousness and its members have been divided in their allegiances between the domestic bourgeoisie and the working class. However they have offered a distinctive colouring to the grand narratives of other classes, promoting civil liberties, education, equality between the sexes and more humanitarian treatment of people and non-human forms of life. They have been the bearers and extenders of the Enlightenment ideal of progress through reason, and as Alvin Gouldner has pointed out, they have been 'the most progressive force in modern society and . . . the centre of whatever human emancipation is possible in the foreseeable future'.[21] The decline of all these classes has involved their cultural subordination as well as their political and economic subordination. The narratives by which they had previously defined themselves and their role in history have been undermined.

THE NEW INTERNATIONAL BOURGEOISIE

While undermining the grand narratives legitimating old class identities, the new international bourgeoisie has not replaced these with a new grand narrative – or at least not one that can be appropriated, or even argued against, by others. The new international bourgeoisie is the class responsible for the transformation of the world-system. While capitalism is less organized at the national level, it is becoming more organized at an international level.[22] The new international bourgeoisie are the agents of the new transnational organization of capitalism, bringing to fulfilment the grand narrative underlying capitalism. The achievement and maintenance of their power has been possible through developments in communications, and to a considerable extent through the control of mass media which has been the site of unprecedented corporate activity in recent decades. This has been associated with massive expenditure by large, mainly transnational, business corporations on public relations, promoting the economic policies favourable to their expansion.[23] However, by far the biggest factor in their domination is their ability to circumvent efforts by national governments to regulate them, to organize enterprises and projects at an unprecedented level of complexity. Since they have been able to move money and capital around the globe and force state governments to compete with each other to serve their interests – in order to attract or retain investment – it has not been a major concern for members of this class to justify the power they have gained.

This does not mean that the new bourgeoisie are devoid of beliefs about the nature of the world and their place within it. They assume a modern, refined version of the mechanical world-view and of Darwinism.[24] However, unlike the Darwinian grand narrative of the old bourgeoisie, there is no presumption that what is evolving is improving the lot of humanity at large. In place of matter in motion, the world is seen in terms of information; and instead of life being seen as a struggle between individuals, nations and races, life is seen as a struggle between information-processing systems. The evolution of humanity is seen to be leading us into the 'technotronic age'.[25] While this conception of the world is more broadly articulated through information theory, socio-biology and a psychology which now represents people as information-processing 'cyborgs', the ideological spearhead of this class is post-Keynesian neo-classical economics. This is characterized not only by monetarism, rational expectations theory and supply-side economics, the ideological weapons of the New Right in their struggle to dismantle social welfare provisions and institutions and to promote the deregulation of markets and reduction of trade barriers, but also by the rapid expansion of econometrics and computer modelling, and the transformation of economics from a science primarily concerned with guiding political policy-making to a science concerned to guide investment decisions by financiers.[26] The rise of the new class has been associated with the rise in status of economics, business studies and information science to the dominant intellectual positions within universities and government bureaucracies – and the devaluing of everything which does not serve as an instrument of the international economy.[27]

What is conspicuously lacking in this configuration of beliefs is any direction, any point to it all. For the new bourgeoisie there is nothing but power for the sake of power, control, for the sake of control, and conspicuous consumption on a massive scale. The telos of the grand narrative guiding their actions is already realized. As Francis Fukuyama, a deputy director of the US State Department's Policy Planning Staff, argued, history has come to an end.[28] Many members of this class are engaged in finance, design, marketing and purchasing.[29] They are the 'paper entrepreneurialists'. As such they are responsible for the massive redistributions of income from the poor to the wealthy, both within and between countries, disrupting the economic life of businesses and nations, particularly Anglophone and Third World nations.[30] Their entry into the mass media and book publishing and distribution has been associated almost uniformly with the decline in standards of newspapers, television and books, and the disruption and impoverishment of education and cultural life. Their domination of world agriculture is impoverishing farmers in the affluent nations, is starving to death some twelve million people each year in Third World countries – more than were being killed each year during the Second World War, and is permanently destroying agricultural land at a rate which promises a catastrophe unparalleled in human history.[31] This class is contributing nothing to human welfare, and their attitude to this is summed up in the words of an economist writing in *Business and Society Review*: 'Suppose that, as a result of using up all the world's resources, human life did come to an end. So what?'[32]

CLASS CONFLICT AND CULTURAL POLITICS

To say that the rise of the new bourgeoisie was associated with the discrediting of the narratives of progress of the defeated classes does not explain this cultural transformation. The transformation suggests cultural conflict, but the question is whether this conflict was a mere by-product of the demise of the old classes, the condition of their demise or something more complex. That cultural politics was insignificant in determining events is highly plausible. The growing powerlessness of the old bourgeoisie and the old working class itself would be enough to undermine the confidence of their members in narratives defining and celebrating their destiny as primary agents of history. The development of transnational corporations and of the new bourgeoisie, once this had reached a certain stage, was inexorable. The new bourgeoisie did not need to engage in a great deal of cultural politics in order to have their way once they were in a position to undermine the economies of nations. In place of legitimation through grand narratives the new bourgeoisie could threaten governments with the withdrawal of capital, and rely on a population seduced into almost total market dependence by the products of global capitalism to remove any government which did not bow to such threats. The uniformity with which the states of Western nations lost control over their economies suggests that changes in culture were of little importance in this transformation.

However, the success of Asian nations has been largely due to the ability of Asian states to retain control over their economies.[33] Such control *was* possible, and if it was not maintained or re-established within the affluent nations of the West, one must ask, why? It is here that the role of culture and cultural politics becomes evident. However the dynamics of cultures is extremely complex. It is too simple to account for the cultural transformations of the West as the result of strategy of a class to establish cultural hegemony over society. These can only be understood by taking into account the unintended effects of social and economic processes, the ways in which social changes affecting the way people live have affected their ways of thinking, the ways in which individual members of classes responded to their situations, as well as the more deliberate efforts to control people's thinking. In the cultural conflict between classes, it is the culture of the 'new petite bourgeoisie' which has played the greatest part in determining the outcome. And it is in the analysis of cultural transformations within and brought about by the new petite bourgeoisie that most of the other features of postmodern culture become intelligible.

To begin with, what needs to be explained is the lack of resolution of the domestic bourgeoisie to protect its own interests, and then the inability of the working class to mobilize effectively as a class to meet the threat to its welfare. What globalization and the rise of the new international bourgeoisie seems to have revealed is how the unity within these two classes had been undermined in Western societies. This is not to say that there was no unity at all. Members of the bourgeoisie generally recognized their unity in their interests as employers in opposition to the working class, and members of the working class recognized their unity in their interests as employees struggling for better wages in opposition to employers. However, there was little more holding them together as classes than this. In the face of a threat coming from an entirely different direction the old bourgeoisie could only attack the wages and conditions of the working class. Under this attack the last element of working-class identity dissolved with the shift from national bargaining to enterprise-level bargaining. As politicians elected by the working class consistently acted against their interests, members of the working class have increasingly turned to racist ideologies to protect themselves.

What was responsible for the weakness of these old classes? One of the most profound analyses of the cultural dimension of the class struggle has been provided by Pierre Bourdieu. Bourdieu argues that each class and class fraction has a particular 'habitus', an embodied set of classificatory schemes underpinning consciousness and language through which people orient themselves. The first principle of such classifications is based on the high versus low opposition, which is elaborated into such distinctions as 'noble' and 'ignoble', the 'élite' and the 'masses', and the second on the light versus heavy opposition, which is elaborated in pre-modern societies into such distinctions as that between warriors and clerics. Such classificatory schemes are at the same time, for the people who embody them, systems of ultimate values which are experienced viscerally as tastes and distastes. There are continual struggles between groups to impose those taxonomies most favourable to their own characteristics, that is, their own habitus, on other groups and on the whole of society. Bourdieu's analysis can be utilized to explain how narratives come to be disbelieved. The narratives by which people define themselves should not be thought of only as tales produced and recited. They are embodied as orientations to the world, its past, its present and its future.[34] Such embodied narratives embody the taxonomies described by Bourdieu. The struggles between groups to impose their habitus will also be a struggle to impose a particular narrative as the correct interpretation and evaluation of the present situation, of what has happened in the past and what ends should be realized in the future. Success by one group in such a struggle will involve people of a rival group coming to experience themselves in terms of the taxonomies of the victorious group, and re-evaluating their position in history accordingly. This will often involve their ceasing to experience themselves as agents of history, and coming to experience history as having a dynamics beyond their ideals and goals. If the old classes are weak and are no longer able to function as agents, this suggests that another class has successfully imposed its habitus on their members, and they are no longer able to see themselves in terms of a coherent narrative as playing a leading role in history.

In the case of the subordination of the domestic bourgeoisie, globalization must be understood as the disintegration of taxonomies, projects and ideals centring around symbols exalting 'the nation', and their reconstitution around the international economy and its symbols. Henceforth 'success' must be success on the international stage. Success at a local level is drained of significance, particularly if the local market is protected by tariffs. How has this subordination occurred? How did the old symbols lose their meaning? Direct contact through a shared social milieu with the form of life of members of the new international bourgeoisie, with their 'Californian' style – eschewing national symbols and partaking of an international symbol market, may have played a part. However, the images promoted in the public relations of businesses and business organizations and celebrated in the mass media, now largely under the control of the new bourgeoisie,[35] and the complex economic theories and models of the economy produced by academics and touted by politicians are more likely to be responsible for undermining the old habitus.

The cultural subordination of the working class was more complex. It was effected through the transformation of capitalism from a system in which people gained their identity through participation in production processes, that is, in terms of their job or trade, to a system in which people gain their identity through consumption. As in the case with the old bourgeoisie, old habituses and the narratives with which they were associated have been undermined by images projected by the mass media. However the impact of the mass media has not been uniform. A new habitus has been imposed on the general population, initially by affecting a small number of people, and then by reinforcing the habitus of such people at the expense of those more resistant to mass media images. For the most part, it has been the 'middle class' which has been influenced directly by the mass media, and the rest of the population has then succumbed to the influence of the middle class.

THE EVOLUTION OF THE MIDDLE CLASS

The 'middle class', that is, members of the salariat, lawyers, doctors and other professionals, scientists, various kinds of artists and intellectuals as well as shopkeepers and small businessmen, has a long history. Its career as a component of capitalism goes back to its origins in the sixteenth and seventeenth centuries. This class absorbed artisans, former peasants, descendants of the aristocracy and the bourgeoisie, and people rising from the working class. For the most part they were imbued with a strong work ethic and had a high regard for education, and these were central to their identity. They were associated with Protestantism, or with 'protestant' elements within Catholicism. The lower middle class defined themselves primarily as upholders of a severe morality and work discipline in opposition to the working class, while the upper middle class defined themselves as upholders of culture and higher values in opposition to the bourgeoisie. As the middle class began to expand towards the end of the nineteenth century, its habitus began to change. The early stages of this change, along with the causes of it, have been charted by Daniel Bell.[36]

According to Bell, American capitalism was established on the basis of an ascetic Protestant ethic. This ethic was sustained by the small towns in which most of the population lived. However towards the end of the nineteenth century, more and more people began to live in big cities, freeing them from the small-town pressures to social conformity. Mass consumption, made possible by new developments in technology – cars which made it possible for people to get away from their local communities, radio and film which brought new ideas and models to conform to, advertising which continually pressed people to consume the latest products, and then the introduction of television – dissolved local cultures and created a common culture committed to social and personal transformation. The virtues endorsed by Protestantism had no place within this common culture which was concerned not with how to work and achieve, but how to spend and enjoy.

Artists and writers promoted this transformation, and in so doing

15

undermined their own position in society. Bell accepts the argument of Lionel Trilling that:

> Any historian of literature of the modern age will take virtually for granted the adversary intention, that characterizes modern writing – he will perceive its clear purpose of detaching the reader from the habits of thought and feeling that the larger culture imposes, of giving him a ground and a vantage point from which to judge and condemn, and perhaps revise, the culture that produced him.[37]

According to Bell, it is the culture of Protestant asceticism that has been most under attack. Responding to the new awareness of motion and speed, light and sound which came from communication and transport, and from a new self-consciousness generated by the loss of religious certitude, artists adopted a stance of unyielding rage against the official order. In doing so they attacked all forms of external constraint, and more particularly, all forms of self-discipline. In place of religion and morality, in place of restraint and planning for the future, modernists proposed an aesthetic justification of life – to free people to create works of art, to create themselves as works of art. While it was not the intention of the modernists to reduce works of art to objects of consumption, such a reduction was the inevitable outcome of their attacks on self-discipline and moral constraint.[38] To the postmodernist successors of modernist artists, '[i]mpulse and pleasure alone are real and life-affirming; all else is neurosis and death. In a literal sense, reason is the enemy and the desires of the body the truth. Objective consciousness defrauds, and only emotion is meaningful.'[39] Modernist artists and writers are no longer significant in society, are no longer seen as the harbingers of a new order. They have won. They have transformed culture, or played a major part in its transformation, and there is nothing left for them to do. This has devalued works of art and literature. They are now *consumed*. As Hannah Arendt argued, mass society now 'wants not culture, but entertainment, and the wares offered by the entertainment industry are indeed consumed by society just as are any other consumer good'.[40]

Bell's analysis accords with, and is supported by, radical cultural theorists such as Jean Baudrillard, Mark Poster and Neil Postman. These theorists have been particularly concerned with the impact of changing media: the displacement of the print medium by electronic media. That different media have the potential to profoundly transform the way people think and construct their identities is made plausible by studies which have revealed the effects of writing and print on oral cultures. Walter Ong has shown how the whole development of Western philosophy, the capacity for abstract thinking, for constructing definitions, for entertaining abstract notions of justice, for formal logic and for introspection were all effects of literacy.[41] Literacy fundamentally changed the way people related to themselves, to each other, to their society and to nature, and made possible new kinds of social organization. The invention of print furthered this transformation. Mark Poster, following Marshall McLuhan and Jean Baudrillard, has argued that television is having an effect just as dramatic:

> The language/practice of TV absorbs the functions of culture to a greater degree than face-to-face conversations or print and its discursive effect is to constitute subjects differently from speech or print. Speech constitutes subjects as members of a community by solidifying the ties between individuals. Print constitutes subjects as rational, autonomous egos, as stable interpreters of culture who, in isolation, make logical connections from linear symbols. Media language – contextless, monologic, self-referential – invites the recipient to play with the process of self-constitution, continuously to remake the self in 'conversation' with differing modes of discourse. Since no one who knows the recipient is speaking to them and since there is no clearly determinate referential world outside the broadcast to provide a standard against which to evaluate the flow of meanings, the subject has no defined identity as a pole of conversation.[42]

Television has disorganized people's experience so they can no longer relate their own lives and experiences to the world which television reveals to them, or situate themselves as having a place in this world. As Neil Postman put it, television has created 'a neighbourhood of strangers and pointless quantity; a world of fragments and discontinuities'.[43] To relate to the world through television amounts to 'amusing ourselves to death'. It is the middle class which has been most significantly affected by this.

THE NEW SERVICE SUB-CLASS

The salariat and the professions expanded rapidly through the 1950s and 1960s in virtually every Western society. Although they did not develop an independent class consciousness there was some effort made in this direction in the late 1960s. Young members of the middle class developed a radical opposition to the ideology of the national bourgeoisie, to an intellectual culture subordinated to the capitalist economy and its state and military system. This was the New Left. However in their rejection of prevailing culture, and faced with the massive power of an expanding capitalist economy and its political institutions, most of the New Left opted for a life of hedonism and self-indulgence.[44] This failure heralded the rise of the New Right, attacks on the welfare state and the decline of the salariat as a class, and correspondingly, the rise of a new fraction of the petite bourgeoisie, the service sub-class.

The new service sub-class consists of people engaged in presentation and representation, and in providing symbolic goods and services.[45] It includes not only people engaged in advertising and public relations, but also those engaged in providing medical and social assistance (in day-care centres, drug-abuse centres, race relations centres, marriage guidance bureaus, etc.), and those involved in direct production and organization (as with youth leaders, untenured tutors, radio and TV producers and presenters, magazine journalists). It is made up of people who rejected the self-discipline required of the salariat and professionals, or people who strove for, then failed to succeed in the traditional professions. These people have developed a habitus totally at variance with the habitus of the old middle class. People in the new sub-class are often engaged in efforts to *create* jobs suitable to their ambitions through professionalization strategies and through efforts to legitimate new licences and certifications. This often involves promoting a 'therapeutic morality' as a legitimating ideology. They often succeed, despite their deficient 'cultural capital', by creating and selling new products, and by accumulating the 'social capital' of new contacts. In promoting themselves, this new cultural petite bourgeoisie encourage symbolic rehabilitation projects, giving cultural objects such as jazz and cinema a new status. Sharing the internationalist consumer tastes of the new bourgeoisie, celebrating consumption as the end of life, they have intruded into and increasingly subverted the hegemony of both the old bourgeoisie and the working class together with the patterns of classifications which had crystallized out of the confrontation between them, and subverted the emerging class consciousness of the salariat.

Members of this new sub-class are characterized by their 'decentred identities'.[46] Even when they are economically successful, they seldom identify with the occupations through which they make their living. Such decentred identities first emerged in Britain among the working-class young in the 1950s, and only developed among middle-class youth in the 1960s.[47] In both cases what made such identities possible was the extension of the period of 'liminality' between childhood, when people are constrained by their parents, and their absorption into responsible adult roles. The occupations of the new sub-class effectively extended this liminality into adulthood. During this period of liminality, they are socially atomized, and this dissolves any buffering between them and the definitions of reality produced by the mass media.

Television has been the most important mass medium in creating the postmodern habitus. Not only has the very nature of the medium influenced people's thinking, ways of relating to others and self-conceptions, but television has assaulted the boundaries between the 'frontstage' and 'backstage' of fictional and non-fictional figures; it has given people greater access to information, augmenting their knowledge relative to authorities, and allowed people to see a far greater variety of forms of life than previously possible. It has encouraged a scepticism about any particular form of life, while encouraging experimentation with life forms. Taking their conceptions of themselves as open to modification, manipulation and transformation, there is a continual social construction or borrowing, legitimating and internalization of new expressive symbolic formulations. As Bourdieu observed of such people:

> [T]heir life-style and ethical and political positions are based on a rejection of everything in themselves which is finite, definite, final ... that is, a refusal to be pinned down in a particular site ... Classified, déclassé, aspiring to a higher class, they see themselves as unclassifiable, 'excluded', 'dropped out', 'marginal', anything rather than categorized, assigned to a class, a determinate place in social space.[48]

Often presenting themselves as radicals, members of this sub-class have directed protest away from concern with economic and political justice into expressive forms which have no political effect. They are concerned primarily with the existential and psycho-social meaning of people's lives. Recent social movements have had as their central concern the construction, interpretation and dissemination of new ideological models to facilitate the construction of more gratifying personal identities. This contrasts radically with feudal societies where honour required individuals to identify with and act according to their position in society, and to modernity in which individuals were expected to develop an identity which would remain relatively permanent from adolescence to old age and respect was paid to those who refused to modify their behaviour to accord with structural and situational contingencies. In the postmodern period, personal identity has become fluid as people transform themselves throughout their lives as they move from situation to situation. Identities are defined primarily through emotional responses to the world. Self-definition has been divorced from either cosmology or history, and from efforts to uphold values and realize goals defined as objectively more worthwhile than others. In place of social movements organized by an ideology designed to orient people for effective action, postmodern societies are characterized by 'ideological primary groups', informal, unstructured collectivities which meet to discuss in a supportive, permissive context, common personal problems, feelings and experiences. New identities, which acquit individuals of responsibility for their problems, are constructed through such shared emotions. Members of these groups are made aware that institutional and role constraints are socially constructed structures which can be dismantled as easily as they were built, that all perspectives and viewpoints are relative, and that therefore the only absolutes, the only objectives worth striving for, which are possible of attainment, are within oneself. The effect of this, as John Marx has noted, is that postmodern societies are characterized on the one hand by 'the bewildering rapid rates of change in the symbolic meanings, models, and interpretations that constitute the domain of expressive culture', and on the other by 'the stability, rigidity, and resilience to change of its basic institutional designs, structural patterns, and role-status relations'.[49]

The success with which they have imposed their habitus on others has largely dissolved not only nationalist bourgeois culture, but also the working-class culture which gave this class a sense of solidarity and which enabled them to act as an effective political movement. How has this been achieved? The culture of the new service class is centred on consumption and social discrimination rather than production and creativity. Post-modern culture does not unite people. It divides people. Through post-modern discourses, people struggle to define themselves as significant by struggling to define others as insignificant. Members of the new petite bourgeoisie have either risen from the working class or descended from the salariat or the old bourgeoisie, and look down upon all of these. They also have little regard for the asceticism, dedication and work ethic of the old intelligentsia. Obversely, they laud the cosmopolitanism and style of the new international bourgeoisie.

More importantly, the new international bourgeoisie has promoted the habitus of the new service class through their control of television stations, newspapers, journals, publishing companies and chains of bookstores, and virtually transforming the way the media is run.[50] This association between the new sub-classes is not one of alignment. It amounts to the successful hegemony of the new bourgeoisie which has been able to subvert the efforts of both the Old Left and the New Left to transform society by promoting the hedonistic forms of life of those who failed or refused to enter the salariat or professions. Media moguls and other members of the international bourgeoisie have selectively empowered those members of the new petite bourgeoisie promoting postmodern culture – supporting the integration of the aesthetic into the marketing of commodities in advertising, design and architecture, and the reduction of all cultural activity not immediately associated with the marketing of commodities to entertainment, or if this is not debasing enough, to 'amusements'. It is under these circumstances that there has been a dissolution of a privileged discourse, a situation in which discourses struggle to legitimatize them-selves as privileged forms – not by rational argument but by the sort of promotion used to establish fashions in clothing.

THE INTELLIGENTSIA

While postmodernism has been most used to characterize new develop-ments in architecture, literature, film and art, its greatest impact is on the culture of intellectuals whose very existence is based on the assumption that culture is not merely relative, that there is a 'high culture' and that progress can be made in understanding, ways of living and social organization. The very existence of intellectuals is constituted by the ability of its members to uphold the reality of grand narratives which defines them as a vanguard. The Enlightenment attack on the cultural hegemony of the Church inaugurated a relatively unstructured élite of artists, writers and intellectuals who strove to replace the clergy as the ultimate arbiters in matters of belief, value and taste. In the nineteenth and twentieth centuries, universities and related research organizations became the institutional base for this Enlightenment élite, and intellectuals and cultural movements have had to gain recognition from such institutions in order to gain recognition of their credentials. These institutions are now losing their legitimacy.

The first cultural fields to be undermined were those based or anchored in the humanities departments of universities. Portents of the crisis in the humanities have been with us for some time. It was diagnosed in 1964 by Ernest Gellner, and his observations are so pertinent to understanding what is now called the postmodern condition that what he wrote then is worth quoting at length:

> Language is the tool of trade of the humanist intellectual, but it is far more than that. Language . . . *is* culture. . . . The humanist intellectual is, essentially, an expert on the written word. . . . A literate society possesses a firmer backbone through time than does an illiterate one. It is at least potentially capable of consistency. The literate intellectuals become the guardians and interpreters of that which is more than transient, and sometimes its authors. This role was one they once filled with pride. . . . But this sense of pride is conditional on the fulfilment of the central task of this estate, which cannot but be one thing – the guardianship or the search for truth. If this is gone, only a shell remains. . . . The question now is: how seriously does one now take the *cognitive* equipment of the *clerk*? The answer is, alas: not very much. . . . The deprivation of the humanist intellectual of his full cognitive status has happened fairly recently. Signs and portents, in philosophy and elsewhere, can be traced very far back: but as a general and widely half-recognized phenomenon, it is very new, and has occurred within this century, and almost within the last few decades. The magnitude and profundity of this social revolution can scarcely be exaggerated.[51]

While this state of affairs was brought about by the loss of monopoly on literacy, there was still the assumption that literacy was important. With the rise of electronic media, the value of literacy itself is being brought into question. The position of humanist intellectuals is now even more precarious.

Philosophers have responded to this crisis in a number of ways. In the early years of the twentieth century efforts were made to legitimatize philosophy by either defending the claims to knowledge of science, or, in the case of phenomenologists, by claiming to be a science. However little consensus was achieved, at least, not for more than a few years. Philosophy was characterized by revolutions in quick succession. With each revolution the previously reigning school of thought was condemned totally. There was no need for philosophers to concern themselves with the long history of their discipline, or even with what contemporary philosophers were doing in other countries. Philosophy had been effectively reduced to a sequence of academic parlour games, with the quest for wisdom virtually abandoned. Philosophy has since dissolved into a multiplicity of sub-disciplines, and schools of thought have multiplied at such a rate that they no longer succeed each other – they coexist. With rare exceptions – mostly German philosophers or philosophers aligned with German philosophy – these schools do not contend with each other; they dismiss each other. Anglo-American analytical philosophy specializing in language, logic and computer models of the mind justifies itself by providing the means to develop new computer languages. Philosophy is taught in universities by anthologizing authors into snippets, and by fragmenting systems into piecemeal treatments of particular problems to fit in with the current sub-disciplinary boundaries, enabling people to avoid any confrontation between the systematic claims of great thinkers and their own ethical, political, religious or cosmological beliefs. Addressing the American Philosophical Association in 1987, Alasdair MacIntyre characterized the state of modern philosophy:

> [I]n modern academic philosophy no issue, or almost no issue, is ever conclusively settled. . . . [There is] no shared understanding of what philosophical rationality consists in. . . . Academic philosophy thus no longer provides the socially prescribed arena within which and by appeal to which systematic beliefs of various kinds, including political beliefs, are accorded or denied their title to rational justi-fication. And its piecemeal character, its selective history and its inability to bring any issue of importance to agreed resolution all combine to make it intelligible that this should be so. . . . [Philosophy] is, in the main a harmless, decorative activity, education in which is widely believed to benefit by exercising and extending capacities for orderly argument, so qualifying those who study it to join the line of lemmings entering law school or business school. The professor of philosophy . . . stands to the contemporary bourgeoisie much as the dancing master stood to the nobility of the *ancien régime*. The dancing master taught the eighteenth-century expensively brought up young how to have supple limbs, the philosophy professor teaches their twentieth-century successors how to have supple minds.[52]

It is hardly surprising in these circumstances that philosophers have come to seriously doubt whether the subject can continue as a discipline,[53] and Richard Rorty, attacking philosophers' traditional concern with epistemology, has aligned himself with postmodernism and called for the reduction of philosophy to edifying discourse, to keeping the conversation going.[54]

The crisis in the humanities has been even more profoundly manifest in the study of literature. The study of vernacular literature began in Britain in the radical academies in the nineteenth century as an alternative to the Greek and Latin classics as a means to instil morality into students. It was promoted by Matthew Arnold and John Stuart Mill as a means to civilize the middle classes in place of religious indoctrination. In this way a new discipline emerged which spread through the universities, and soon began to displace the classics as a means of defining the cultural élite. F.R. Leavis, who retired from Cambridge in 1962 after twenty-five years of extolling the Great Tradition of literature, represented the high point in the history of this tradition. By the end of his career, the study of literature was facing two crises. The first, superficial crisis was that the study of literature did not make anything explode or travel faster, and the powers of the time were not interested in much else. Second, and more fundamentally, the claim that literature civilized people and enhanced the quality of life came to be seriously doubted. Such doubt disoriented academics in the discipline, and brought into question the category of literature itself.[55] In response to this, members of English departments intensified their interest in literary theory, turning to structuralist semiotics in an effort to turn the study of literature into a science. This effort was shortlived. Importing from France the deconstructionist techniques developed by the poststructuralists, academics confronting an influx of students from the new petite bourgeoisie contemptuous of 'high' culture have capitulated, aligning themselves with popular culture against any effort to privilege one form of writing over another. The study of literature is now being transformed into cultural studies, extended to deal not only with popular fiction, but also songs, films, television and radio, and its proponents are engaged in a programme of debunking the pretensions of high culture.

While the humanities appear to have succumbed to a joint assault by science and popular culture, it might still be claimed that science, the greatest intellectual achievement and ultimate point of reference of modernity, retains its privileged status. In the nineteenth century, science was differentiated from philosophy, and a number of thinkers struggled mightily to create a new priesthood of scientists in place of priests, and to reorganize education around science.[56] They were astonishingly successful. The demise of the humanities could be regarded as the final triumph of science. Surely it must now be recognized by everyone that scientists have access to truth in a way which privileges them over the pretensions of the humanities and makes them invulnerable to challenges from popular culture? In the last resort, doesn't almost everyone turn to scientific experts to resolve disputes?

Until very recently this was the case. But that scientists have some sure-fire way to the truth has been severely questioned. The efforts of logical positivists to draw a sharp distinction between science and non-science and to equate this with the distinction between knowledge and emotional expression, came under attack. The first opponents of logical positivism were merely trying to develop a more adequate notion of rationality to account for the complexity of science – and in some cases, to allow that ethics and aesthetics could also be rational. However the outcome of this attack was a general debunking of science, which came to be equated with ideology or religion. Paul Feyerabend, arguing that science, with its claims to cognitive superiority and its hierarchical organization, had become a threat to democracy, quoted with approval Bakunin's warning against 'the reign of scientific intelligence, the most autocratic, despotic, arrogant and elitist of all regimes'.[57] Feminists then equated science with the ideology of patriarchy. Science has now lost its place at the centre of the education curriculum, and in the USA religious views about life must be taught alongside scientific views. Young people no longer look to science for their conception of the world, and it can no longer be assumed that science is the reference point for understanding society's conception of its place in the cosmos. A National Science Foundation survey in the USA found that only 45 per cent of Americans understand that the earth moves around the sun each year.[58]

This is not to say that the funding of science or the number of scientists has declined. In the USA and elsewhere both have increased dramatically. But almost all of what is now called science is merely well-organized research for the development of technology. Science is financed to augment military might or to produce saleable commodities. Research funds are allocated by states or corporations according to their potential to augment political and economic power, and any research sectors unable to show how they can contribute to such power are doomed. As David Dickson pointed out in his recent study of science: 'The notion of scientists as independent scholars, motivated solely by a thirst for knowledge and unconcerned about the eventual utility of their results, has been banished for good.'[59] 'Scientific experts' still play a part in society. To give credence to any significant political action, especially where technology is concerned, it is necessary to refer to scientific experts. However scientific experts and the knowledge required to justify the views they are supporting are available to anyone with enough money. As Jean-François Lyotard argued: 'No money, no proof – and that means no verification of statements and no truth. The games of scientific language become the games of the rich, in which whoever is wealthiest has the best chance of being right.'[60]

On any technological matter which becomes a political issue there will almost always be found scientific experts on both sides of the debate, with the majority of them being on the side with the most money. This prostitution by 'scientific experts' of their expertise has severely devalued their currency.

Associated with these developments universities are being fundamentally transformed. Thoroughly corrupted by the 'publish or perish' syndrome and by the pressure to lower standards to accommodate the higher proportion of young people going on to higher education, they are being reduced to extensions of high schools and technical colleges, valued by governments only insofar as they provide people with vocational training or produce technological knowledge, and by students only to increase their earning power. Arts and science faculties have lost status within universities – with good reason.[61] For the most part, undergraduate courses in arts faculties are being reduced to a form of entertainment and courses taught in the science faculties have been regeared to produce technicians. Within the arts faculties careerists have excluded or marginalized people driven by a quest for understanding; while as Paul Feyerabend noted of the science faculties: 'Most scientists today are devoid of ideas, full of fear, intent on producing some paltry result so that they can add to the flood of inane papers that now constitutes "scientific progress" in many areas.'[62]

There are perhaps still two domains which have not been undermined by popular culture. Despite some efforts to gain democratic control over technology, it remains out of reach of the lay-person. The development of technology appears as a law unto itself to which the rest of society must adapt. More significantly, economics has not merely maintained, but increased its autonomy from popular culture. Until fairly recently people who were not economists were quite prepared to argue against the assumptions and prescriptions of economists. Now, while they might complain about economic conditions, reasoned disagreement with economic experts has almost disappeared, and those few economists who oppose mainstream economics have no audience apart from each other. The 'educated public' willing to think about such issues is dissolving. With the field to themselves, economists, with the support of the international bourgeoisie, have been able to dominate politics throughout the Western world, and in most of the remainder. Despite the incredulity towards all grand narratives, the grand narrative of economic progress as defined by economists has retained its dominating influence as a guide for political action by default.

In this environment public intellectuals have all but disappeared. Today there are no intellectuals with the standing among the general public enjoyed by John Dewey, Niels Bohr, Albert Einstein, Bertrand Russell or

Jean-Paul Sartre.[63] In the USA the few remaining public intellectuals are now over 60. Few academics today are intellectuals.

THE DECENTRING OF CULTURE

The environmental crisis, globalization, the decline of the West, and Anglophone countries in particular, the decline of the old classes and the rise of new classes, the eclipse of print media by electronic media and the collapse of the intelligentsia have all contributed to creating an incredulity towards grand narratives. But this incredulity can now be seen as only the most obvious manifestation of what amounts to a fundamental cultural transformation, a decentring of culture. The decline of academia, and along with it, those whose credentials or 'cultural capital' had been legitimated by it, has left cultural production (outside technology and economic theory) without any organization. The 'cultural fields' which had slowly developed during the eighteenth, nineteenth and early twentieth centuries, transforming conflict between participants from a struggle between friends and foes to a struggle to ascertain truth and falsehood, have been dissolved. So, as Jim Collins has argued:

> 'culture' no longer can be conceived as a Grand Hotel, as a totalizable system that somehow orchestrates all cultural production and reception according to one master system. Both insist, implicitly or explicitly, that what we consider 'our culture' has become *discourse-sensitive*, that how we conceptualize that culture depends upon discourses which construct it in conflicting, often contradictory ways, according to interests and values of those discourses as they struggle to legitimatize themselves as privileged forms of representations.[64]

Without an existing hierarchical order of established discourses and without universally accepted canons by which participants in cultural life can define their works, supportively or oppositionally, these can no longer be understood diachronically as responses to and efforts to go beyond established predecessors. First and foremost they must be defined and understood in relation to synchronic tensions, fragmented mass consciousness and multiple *zeitgeists*. While modernist texts, whether scientific, historical or literary, constructed a dialogic relation to previous texts in order to reject them as outmoded, postmodernist texts construct a *polylogic* relation to a multiplicity of 'already saids', in such a way that the relationship between past and present coding is based on interaction and transformation rather than outright rejection. This further justifies the appellation 'postmodern' as something radically different from the 'modern', and which prevents the postmodern being presented diachronically as simply that which succeeds the 'modern', which would make it another phase of modernity. As Andreas Huyssen has argued:

> Postmodernism at its deepest level represents not just another crisis within the perpetual cycle of boom and bust, exhaustion and renewal, which has characterized the trajectory of modern culture. It rather represents a new type of crisis *of* that modernist culture itself.[65]

The decentring of culture has changed the nature of cultural productions. Postmodernism has frequently been identified with 'double coding', whereby cultural products communicate with two or more different audiences – the general population and an élite.[66] Having to recognize the demise of a homogeneous audience, or a structured, clearly delineated set of audiences whereby any cultural production could easily be situated in relation to a master code, producers of texts – books, buildings, works of art or whatever – must take into account that different audiences will understand and evaluate works according to different and often irreconcilable assumptions. Texts must now be self-referential and relate themselves to other texts in order to position themselves within the different fields of discourse. But since these fields of discourse are themselves without any definite organization, texts must strive to create a model of these fields of discourse in order to impose some organization on them and achieve some control over the way they are received by audiences. Consequently no issue of any complexity can be dealt with by postmodern texts.

Such imperatives account at least in part for the different relationship to reality in postmodern texts. Modernist texts often highlighted the differences between perspectives on reality, and in doing so, undermined the sense of identity based on each perspective. The intention, whether reactionary or revolutionary, was radical – to pave the way for a more adequate grasp of reality and a more authentic identity. Postmodernist texts construct different realities, thereby undermining the sense of there being a privileged reality, or the sense of reality as such. The assumption of a reality which can be interpreted or misinterpreted, against which claims to knowledge can be measured, is itself brought into question, thereby acknowledging the validity of multiple sub-cultures and reaffirming the identities they construct – as much as any identity can be affirmed when no sub-culture is held to be more valid than any other. The notion that some people or some cultural productions are more authentic than others is rejected. With this decentring of culture, people have been deprived of the fixed reference points by which they previously oriented themselves. What they took to be unvarying components of their experience are no longer taken as natural facts of life, but as social constructs. As Katherine Hayles has pointed out, language, context, space and time, and selfhood no long appear 'natural'. They have been 'de-natured'.[67]

To begin with, language has lost its transparent relation to the world. It can no longer be seen to be referring in any straightforward sense to an independent reality. As Jean Baudrillard argues, signs now float free of referents, and people now consume signs.[68] Advertisers do not describe the functions of their products, but, drawing on Watsonian or Freudian psychology, attempt to create images, and people buy the images. At the same time the boundaries between advertising, art and reporting have become blurred. Art has been incorporated into advertising, and politicians no longer depend upon arguments to justify their programmes, but advertise to sell themselves, their platforms and the views about reality required to justify these. Television stations sell their news broadcasts with television personalities, who, as symbols, are regarded as more important than the news stories they recount. Television broadcasts are not accepted as reality, but as models, as simulations of reality which people in turn simulate, and then become models themselves to be simulated on the mass media, creating a hyper-reality without referent or authentic origins. This blurs the boundaries between the products of culture and everyday life. Advertisements have colonized social life to define reality and its significance, while at the same time reality has been depreciated and reduced to the status of a social product. The world of advertisements has become more real than the world of everyday life, and people in everyday life must strive to imitate the world created by advertisements to be acknowledged as significant, to be taken as a meaningful part of reality.

Contexts of communication also have lost their quality of being a naturally fixed background. With the development of media technology, messages have been separated from their contexts, and information, 'understandable in itself', has supplanted stories, both told and written, undermining the legitimacy of personal experience.[69] This decontextualization of messages has led to its reconceptualization as such through information theory so that it has come to appear natural to conceive of messages in this way. This has engendered a new form of social engineering, 'context control', through which advertisers, politicians, press barons and editors set out to influence the way messages are received by audiences. The effect of such developments on people's social experience is profound. Split between what Marshall McLuhan referred to as the global village created by the mass media and the intimate family circle, people live without a common context of shared activities and experiences to unite the different communities of discourse within which they participate, and the global village itself is fragmented. Video art can be taken as an attempt to come to terms with this destruction of context. As Katherine Hayles wrote of watching MTV:

> Turn it on. What do you see? Perhaps demon-like creatures dancing; then a cut to cows grazing in a meadow, in the midst of which a

28

singer with blue hair suddenly appears; then another cut to cars engulfed in flames. In such videos, the images and medium collaborate to create a technological demonstration that any text can be embedded in any context. What are these videos telling us, if not that the disappearance of a stable, universal context is *the context* for postmodern culture?[70]

With the denaturing of contexts, space and time have also been denatured.[71] Once originality was regarded as important. Originality implies an origin at some place and at some time. With the decontextualization of information, with the capacity for indefinite transformations and recombinations and reproductions of information, the notion of something being an original no longer makes sense. When things no longer have a place of origin, what do space and time mean? When music is produced by mixing sounds recorded at different places, films and television stories are produced by splicing film taken at diverse times in diverse places, when styles are taken from their original context and reproduced indefinitely with or without changes, when almost identical fast-food shops, motels and hotels are reproduced throughout the world, when imitations are imitated and claimed to be better than the originals, what does location in space mean? At the same time, television has extended people's spatial horizons, creating the global village; but in the process it has stressed impact at the expense of meaning, destroyed perspective and left people feeling helpless in relation to an undifferentiated mass of problems totally beyond their control. Rather than space being the ultimate reference point, spaces are produced with such bewildering complexity that they defy efforts by individuals to orient themselves within them. As Fredric Jameson has argued: 'postmodern hyperspace – has finally succeeded in transcending the capacities of the individual human body to locate itself, to organize its immediate surroundings perceptually, and cognitively to map its position on a mappable external world'.[72]

Correspondingly, time has lost its meaning. Just as spatiality is extended but disorganized, so is temporality. People become aware of past forms of life and styles in the present, but the present is no longer interpreted as the outcome of the past, nor in relation to the future. People no longer orient themselves through intergenerational narratives. So while styles of the past are more than ever deployed in the present, people have almost lost their sense of history. Popular culture changes so quickly that to be current one must be futuristic, because to be merely current is already to be out of date. The future is already used up before it arrives. The present is then almost immediately relegated into a distant past where its significance is denied, where it is 'derealized'. Through such derealization, society has lost or abandoned its capacity to retain its own past. The sense of time derives from change against a constant background. But if there is no constant background to serve as a reference point for appreciating changes, time itself ceases to exist as a background against which life can be organized. 'Time' dissolves into disconnected intervals.

This undermines even the possibility of people establishing stable identities, and denatures the experience of being a stable subject. There is an absence in people of a sense of personal history, of a sense of their lives as unfinished stories worth struggling to complete, integrated into the stories of their families, their communities, the organizations within which they work and their society. Such an absence goes to the heart of modern culture, since it involves the dissolution of what since the seventeenth century it meant to be a person.[73] Thus it has been noted by Christopher Lasch that people nowadays take one day at a time, that selfhood, 'which implies a personal history, friends, family, a sense of place' becomes 'a kind of luxury, out of place in an age of impending austerity'.[74] Fredric Jameson, who is at pains to dissociate himself from Lasch, offers a similar, if more refined diagnosis of postmodern human existence. Following Lacan, he argues

> that personal identity is itself the effect of a certain temporal unification of past and future with the present before me; and second, that such active temporal unification is itself a function of language, or better still, of the sentence, as it moves along its hermeneutic circle through time.

From this he concluded: 'If we are unable to unify the past, present and future of the sentence, then we are similarly unable to unify the past, present and future of our own biographical experience or psychic life.'[75] When personal identity has dissolved, then also has the idea of a constant human nature underlying the variety of human modes of existence. It is then no longer possible to talk of human nature being suppressed, distorted or unrealized. There can only be differences, differences in each individual, different individuals and different societies.

This dissolution of the human subject is associated with not only the breakdown of grand narratives, but of all narratives. The linearity of narratives presupposes temporal development as people constitute themselves as identities through change. It also presupposes an indeterminate future that is made determinate in the present. In a postmodern world there is no place for the slow struggle to find and live one's destiny which is the core of narratives, whether these are lived or recounted. This underlies some of the most distinctive features of postmodernism. As Fredric Jameson pointed out:

> If, indeed the subject has lost its capacity actively to extend its pro-tensions and re-tensions across the temporal manifold, and to organize its past and future into coherent experience, it becomes

difficult ... to see how the cultural productions of such a subject could result in anything but 'heaps of fragments' and in a practice of the randomly heterogeneous and fragmentary and the aleatory ... precisely some of the privileged terms in which postmodernist cultural production has been analysed and even defended.[76]

Correspondingly there is a shift from a 'discursive' sensibility to a 'figurative' sensibility, that is, a shift from a sensibility which gives priority to words to a sensibility which gives priority to images, from one which gives a high value to formalisms to one which acclaims the banalities of everyday life, from one which promotes rationalism to one which contests it, from one which operates by distancing the spectator from the cultural object to one which operates through the unmediated investment of desire in the cultural object. Surfaces are celebrated, and the distinctions between essence and appearance, true and false consciousness, authentic and inauthentic, as well as the distinction between the signifier and the signified, are rejected. All these changes are associated with the shift from what Freud referred to as secondary process, that is, the struggle to come to grips with reality, to primary process, the working out of desire.[77]

THE SIGNIFICANCE OF POSTMODERN CULTURE

The decline of grand narratives corresponds to the rise of popular culture; but it is not any popular culture. The cultures of non-Europeans, of rural societies and of the working class have seldom been more effectively silenced; at best, these have been reduced to a spectacle. It is the consumerist culture of the new service class of advanced capitalist countries as fostered by the new international bourgeoisie which has come to prevail. Members of this new petite bourgeoisie have failed to gain any significant political power while having gained considerable symbolic power, 'the power of constructing reality ... which tends to establish ... the immediate meaning of the world'.[78] They have acquired the power to impose their habitus upon others – so long as this serves the interests of the international bourgeoisie.

The rise and success of the new petite bourgeoisie was complementary to, and in part was the condition for the rise of the new international bourgeoisie. The political failure of the salariat as a class was an almost inevitable concomitant of the emergence of the new international order and the rise of the new international bourgeoisie, since there is very little room for local political or economic power in a world dominated by transnational corporations and financial institutions. The failure of the New Left can at least in part be accounted for in terms of the immense power of international capitalism which they would have had to surmount. It can also be accounted for by the incapacity of the New Left, confronted by the environmental crisis, to envisage a realistic alternative future. But the seductiveness of a consumerist lifestyle made possible within advanced capitalist countries was also a factor. In a world where the products of people's labour had been to reproduce and reinforce a system which had subjugated most of the world's population and wrecked most of the world's environment, being self-indulgent and promoting self-indulgence in others was seen by many as the only way to resist the system.

Using the slogan 'the personal is the political' to identify such self-indulgence with political activity, a new petit bourgeois 'intelligentsia' emerged to identify entertainment with culture and psychotherapy with intellectual life. Pierre Bourdieu has described the members of this intelligentsia:

> Guided by their anti-institutional temperament and the concern to escape everything redolent of competitions, hierarchies and classifications and, above all, of scholastic classifications, hierarchies of knowledge, theoretical abstractions or technical competences, these new intellectuals are inventing an art of living which provides them with the gratifications and prestige of the intellectual at the least cost; in the name of the fight against 'taboos' and the liquidation of 'complexes' they adopt the most external and most easily borrowed aspects of the intellectual life-style, liberated manners, cosmetic or sartorial outrages, emancipated poses and postures, and systematically apply the cultivated disposition to not-yet-legitimate culture (cinema, strip cartoons, the underground), to every-day life (street art), the personal sphere (sexuality, cosmetics, child-rearing, leisure) and the existential (the relation to nature, love, death).[79]

Bourdieu went on to wonder whether 'the ethic of liberation is not in the process of supplying the economy with the perfect consumer whom economic theory has always dreamed of'.[80] Not only are such people intent on consuming the latest things, but as consumers they have isolated themselves from the constraints of collective memories and expectations which in the past had insulated people from the images of the high life produced by the mass media.

With an oppositional stance people could identify and exalt themselves as heroic opponents of the established order; without it, people could only define themselves in opposition to each other. It is to maintain exclusiveness, to present themselves as better than others while living powerless but self-indulgent lives, that people now consume symbols.[81] With postmodern cultural practices, symbols are severed from their association with ways of living. Groups differentiate themselves through selective appropriation of aspects of other cultures without concern for the forms of life of which they were part. Original artists, architects and writers are no longer necessary, or even useful. As people appropriate the outward characteristics of intellectuals to consume the status accorded intellectual life, people behave like artists to consume the mystique associated with creativity, or like political radicals to consume the aura of revolutionary traditions. Similarly they eat at sushi bars, dress like peasants or meditate like Indian holy men. But always with a difference – they imbue their simulations with more style than the originals. Postmodern people are poseurs who assume superiority over the people they pose as; and the originals are devalued in the process. Eventually, as simulations are simulated, simulation becomes the whole of symbolic reality and symbols outside this realm are finally drained of significance, along with the forms of life with which they were associated.[82]

This brings us to the central feature of postmodern culture, the lack in people of a sense of personal history, the dissolution of time into disconnected intervals, and again, the incredulity towards grand narratives. At the root of this fragmentation is the disempowerment of people, and associated with this, the breakdown of genuine praxis. The associated severance of culture from the quest for an orientation for action and an orientation to live by associated with the consumer orientation of postmodernity accounts for the characteristic depthlessness of the postmodern sensibility, the celebration of surfaces, the rejection of the distinctions between essence and appearance, between true and false consciousness, between authentic and inauthentic and between the signifier and the signified. For people striving to orient themselves for political praxis some consensus must be achieved on the nature of the world and on what are the ultimate goals worth striving for. Such people must make distinctions between what is true and what is false, and have means for adjudicating between conflicting beliefs in this regard. This must lead to reflection, and through this, efforts to create a master discourse which can relate and mediate between all other discourses. And it is not only Hegelians who have concluded that the quest for this inevitably forces people to struggle for a totalizing perspective, and ultimately for a grand historical narrative in terms of which all other such perspectives can be comprehended and evaluated. As one of the world's leading analytical philosophers, Hilary Putnam, recently argued:

> I am saying that theory of truth presupposes theory of rationality which in turn presupposes our theory of the good. 'Theory of the good', however, is not only programmatic, but is itself dependent upon assumptions about human nature, about society, about the universe (including theological and metaphysical assumptions).[83]

The more democratic a society, the less social order is based on force, fraud and manipulation, the greater the importance of arguments and therefore of totalizing perspectives and grand narratives. It is impossible for people engaged in political action to avoid making provisional commitments to one metanarrative or another, no matter how inadequate the alternatives, and to define their stand-point in relation to institutions of power, to people with power, and to their decisions and actions, in terms of such a metanarrative. It is through defining their place in the world in this way that people acquire a strong sense of history; of their place in history, of the past and the problems inherited from it and of the possibilities of overcoming these problems in the future. Postmodern culture is the culture of a society in which politics has become a farce, where rational critique and protest have become impossible.

The postmodernist response to this is to make a virtue of and celebrate disorientation, the absence of any fixed reference points, the impossibility of representing the world, the breakdown of narrative coherence and the absence of authenticity in a social and economic order in which disorientation and authenticity have become almost impossible. The commodification of life, depersonalization (the death of the subject) and the derealization of experience are savoured rather than struggled against, an attitude expressed in postmodern architecture, in art, and particularly in video art, which Jameson argues is the privileged index of the postmodern era.[84] While the modernists acclaimed the passionate engagement of individuals who refused to compromise their convictions, postmodernists laud the cool detachment of cynical opportunists who are able to exploit each situation as it comes.[85] But there is more than mere detachment in the postmodernist response to new circumstances. After having failed to gain political power, these people have come to embrace their lack of power to avoid taking responsiblility for their complicity in the destructive effects of a global capitalist economy. As Henry Kariel noted:

> For postmodernists, it is simply too late to oppose the momentum of industrial society. They merely resolve to stay alert and cool in its midst. Consciously complying and yet far from docile, they chronicle, amplify, augment it. They judge it as little as it judges itself. Determined to assail nothing, they are passionately impassive.[86]

Decrying the quest for political power as the problem, they have handed over responsibility for their fate, and the fate of the world environment, to the economic rationalists, to the new international bourgeoisie and the international market. By embracing and celebrating their disorientation and powerlessness, they are abasing themselves before the unrepresentable power of the new global economy and the new information technology which makes this system possible, a system which now has the power through its environmental destructiveness to destroy the whole of humanity; as once people abased themselves before the uncontrollable and unfathomable forces of nature whose power they were dependent upon for survival.[87]

Given this characterization of postmodern culture, its association with

34

the rise of the New Right, with the age of Thatcher, Reagan and Bush, becomes intelligible. Postmodernists, often assuming the posture of radicals, have not only disguised the lack of opposition to the rise of the New Right and to the globalization of capitalism, but have played a major part in undermining opposition to it. Ostensibly radical social movements, infiltrated or dominated by postmodern thinking and postmodern personalities, have done almost nothing to advance their causes. Hence we have the paradox of a large environmental movement with unabated environmental destruction.

But there is more to postmodern culture than the pseudo-radicalism and political ineffectuality of a section of the lower middle class. Through its refusal or inability to adopt earlier cultural forms, the practices of the new service sub-class have exposed as social constructs the basic framework of assumptions on which Western civilization has been based. We now live in one of those rare instances in which it has become possible to fully understand the nature and limitations of the whole of European civilization.

2

POSTMODERNISM AND POSTSTRUCTURALISM

The thinkers who have responded most vigorously to the crisis of European civilization, who have spoken for postmodernism or been appropriated and popularized by postmodernists, are the French 'poststructuralists'.[1] The best known of these: Barthes, Lacan, Foucault, Derrida, Lyotard, Baudrillard, Deleuze and Guattari, are, or were, a group of Parisian intellectuals who, from marginal positions within the French educational establishment, succeeded in displacing the Marxists and the structuralists as the dominant group of philosophers and literary and social theorists in France.[2] Some poststructuralists were reacting against and trying to overcome the limitations of structuralism, the systematic attempt to carry out Saussure's proposal to develop on the foundation of his linguistic theory a general science of signs; however, poststructuralism is generally related to earlier traditions of thought in a much more complex way. Poststructuralism is not just another fashion in French philosophy. In reacting against structuralism, poststructuralists have attacked the attempt to reduce the world to an object of analysis. This rejection of 'objectivism' has not been a return to the subject-centred philosophy of the Hegelian or Marxist existentialist phenomenologists, the target of the structuralists, but has involved a questioning of the subject/object dichotomy which underlay not only the opposition between phenomenology and structuralism, but at least since the seventeenth century, most of European culture. And this questioning of European culture has not stopped with questioning this crucial opposition. It has led to a questioning of every aspect of Western civilization from its origins in Ancient Greek and Hebraic thought to the most recent developments in European and American culture. In particular, the tendency to identify European notions of rationality with universal truth has been questioned.[3] While this furthers the work of the structuralist Lévi-Strauss, it continues more profoundly the work of Nietzsche and Heidegger, and poststructuralism is only fully intelligible in relation to their ideas. In fact what is most significant about the poststructuralists is that they have revived and sustained interest in these philosophers, who can be regarded as the true originators of postmodernism.[4]

In this chapter I will show how poststructuralists share assumptions which enable their ideas and arguments to be situated within one of the two main traditions of thought which emerged within Germany in the nineteenth century. Aligning themselves with Nietzsche and Heidegger, they have taken a stance against Hegel and the Hegelian celebration of the progress of reason. However, the poststructuralists are aligned with the Hegelians as part of a broader tradition, which began with Giambattista Vico, of opposition to the Cartesian tradition of thought on which science and the mainstream of modernity have been based; the tradition which engendered the articulation of culture into separate cognitive, normative and expressive components. To stress the dominance of the Cartesian tradition, particularly in Anglophone countries, and to show that this is the ultimate foe of both Hegel and Nietzsche, I will present Hegelian and Nietzschean traditions of thought as different branches of the Vicovian tradition.

Attempting to understand poststructuralists in this way encounters a problem. To situate poststructuralists historically and to interpret their ideas accordingly is to oppose the ideas being examined. Poststructuralists celebrate diversity and reject efforts to see unity in this diversity and to see later ideas as developments of earlier ideas. To claim in one's writing to capture the essence of the diverse texts of a single writer is problematic enough. To represent the texts of diverse thinkers over several centuries as stages in the career of a unitary idea is the kind of fixation of meaning which calls for deconstruction. Nevertheless, such 'misreadings' of texts can facilitate their comprehension.

VICO AND CARTESIAN PHILOSOPHY

In the seventeenth century, the efforts of the Moderns to leave behind the wisdom of the Ancients received its most forceful expression in the philosophy of Descartes. Descartes claimed to have formulated and systematized a new method for acquiring knowledge in place of the authority of tradition, dogma, faith, superstition and prejudice. Modelled on mathematical thinking, this new method was combined with the rejection of dialectical thought as a means of reasoning from reputable opinions to conclusions, the rejection of the use of metaphor and other rhetorical devices and the rejection of the claims of history and historical narratives to knowledge. It presented a picture of the natural world as a single system which could be described and explained by rational principles, and while conceiving of minds as thinking substances radically disjoined from the extended matter of the physical world, at least implicitly claimed that society and people's lives should be organized in the light such rational principles. Elaborated by Hobbes, Newton and Locke, this picture provided the impetus for the Enlightenment, the quest to bring all beliefs before the bar of reason and to create a rational society accordingly.[5] The idea of humans as complex machines, society as a social contract between egoistic individuals, utilitarianism, mainstream economic theory and psychology, are all aspects of this world-orientation, and products of this project to order society rationally.[6]

Giambattista Vico (1668–1744) was the first and one of the greatest ever opponents of the philosophy of the Modernists. He opposed the dismissal of dialectical thinking, of metaphor and rhetoric, of history, of tradition and of imagination, and rejected the attempt to organize society in accordance with abstract principles. By rejecting the view of society as an atomistic collection of mechanical egoists and characterizing minds as the product of culture he was, and remains, one of the great defenders of the humanities. In opposition to Descartes' science of nature and his conception of the mind as a thinking substance, Vico claimed to have created a New Science of the socio-historical world, and argued for the superiority of the kind of knowledge attainable through this science over any knowledge which could be gained of nature. It is only what we have made that we can truly know, that is, know 'from the inside' rather than the outside.[7] Mathematics is transparent to us because it is a human construction. It is possible for us to know works of art, political schemes, legal systems and history, to understand motives, purposes, ambitions, hopes, jealousies, outlooks and visions of reality for the same reason. We can grasp the thoughts, the attitudes, the beliefs, the worlds of thought and feeling of societies dead and gone through language, myths and rites, that is, through institutional behaviour. Language in particular was regarded by Vico as a key to the entire mental, social and cultural life of societies. We think in symbols, and ideas are inseparable from the symbols by which they are expressed. We can infer mental processes from words and the way they are used, for 'genius is the product of language, not language of genius'.[8] We are able to enter the mentality of people very different from our own because we possess the faculty of *fantasia* – imagination – which allows us to appreciate more than one way of categorizing reality. By contrast, it is only possible to describe nature, to predict how it will behave in different situations and relationships, not to know why it behaves as it does – something only God, the creator of nature, can know.

At the same time Vico attacked Descartes' quest for perfect, incorrigible, timeless truths which could be expressed in universally intelligible symbols available to everyone, at any time, in any circumstance. In its place he proposed a 'genetic' approach to knowledge, arguing that the validity of all true knowledge, even that of mathematics and logic, can only be demonstrated by showing how it has been created. Natural law theorists and social contract theorists have gone radically astray in striving to demonstrate the ethical basis of law through abstract reasoning based on some postulated eternal human nature, since human nature is a process continually transforming itself, and so is constantly generating new needs and new categories of thought and action. Modern law, together with such concepts as justice, rights and obligations, is the outcome of a long history of cultural evolution, and the validity, the value and prospects of law and the ethical claims based upon them can only be determined through the study of their historical background and genesis. For Vico, notions such as 'obedience to universal reason', the 'social contract' or the 'calculation of self-interest' are implausible myths, merely the refuge of ignorance.

More broadly, Vico began the schism between thinkers for whom the primary concern is with the specific and the unique, and those in the Cartesian tradition whose concern is with the repetitive and the universal. This opposition is correlated with concern for the concrete rather than the abstract, with change and perpetual movement rather than rest, with the inner rather than the outer aspect of reality, with quality rather than quantity, with what is culture-bound rather than with timeless principles, and with mental strife and self-transformation rather than with the possibility, or even desirability of eternal peace, order, harmony and the satisfaction of all rational human wishes. However Vico did not totally reject the concerns of Cartesian thinkers. He allowed them a legitimate, though subordinate place; but a place which can only be justified historically.

History itself was seen to be governed by God's providence. Providence shapes people's lives, often against their conscious purposes. It is through the unintended effects of people's desires, goals and actions as they engage with the external world and with each other, that providence operates.[9] Providence leads 'nations' or civilizations to develop through three stages, each being a development of and revolt against its predecessor. These were characterized as the age of gods, the age of heroes and the age of men, and were seen by Vico to correspond to the psychological stages individuals in the modern world go through in their own mental development.

Each age has its own type of government, language, religion, art, custom and law. Vico argued that the people of the first age are savages dominated by their senses. Having powerful imaginations but being weak at reasoning, they think in images rather than concepts, and have a poetic or creative nature. Their language begins as a divine mental language operating through mute religious acts and divine ceremonies in which actual things, such as thunder or the entrails of animals, are designated to stand for or signify other things resembling them. The first characters used in writing are hieroglyphs or pictorial representations. These are imaginative or 'poetic' universals rather than universals created through genera made by abstraction. Such people produce poetry rather than prose. Terrified by nature, in awe of a power greater than themselves, they create gods, assigning these to physical things, and then live in fear of their creations without recognizing them as such. Only this fear tames their fierceness and savage egotism and allows them to unite for self-protection, to create the terrifying discipline and to enforce the absolute obedience necessary for their survival. Their customs are then tinged with religion and piety, and law is conceived of as divine, as depending on the gods. Governments are theocratic, people believing that everything is commanded by the gods. Outside this realm there is no security, and men attacked by other men stronger than themselves seek protection and are given it by the 'fathers' at the price of becoming slaves or clients.

This inaugurates the age of heroes in which oligarchies of harsh and avaricious masters, believing themselves to be of divine origin, rule over serfs and slaves. Typical figures of heroic ages were Achilles, 'who referred every right to the tip of his spear'[10] and Brutus, who killed his sons. While being prepared for heroic action, such men are devoid of any sense of mercy and are dominated by avarice, arrogance and cruelty. In the age of heroes language is rich in similes and metaphors – not because people are concerned to embellish their utterances through such linguistic devices, but because this is the only way of ordering, connecting and conveying what they sense. Such people create myths, described by Vico as 'civil histories of the first people, who were poets'.[11] Myths were interpreted by Vico as expressing social struggles and conflicts, these often being of a class nature. Myths are the natural mode of expression of the collective imagination of people who lack the differentiation of genres characteristic of modernity. It is important to recognize that it is not possible for people living in this age to distance themselves from these myths, to ask whether they are fictions or true representations of reality. Such mythology legitimates a framework of divine, imprescriptible laws, a cruel discipline imposed by society's rulers on their subjects. Jurisprudence looks to civil equity or reasons of state. The rights of people are thought to be set forth within words, and the cruelties of the system are borne because people think their laws are naturally this way. Liberties fought for within this framework are liberties for rulers against usurpers and despots, not liberty for servants and dependants. However, the existence of such framework provides the conditions for plebeians, who have become dissatisfied with their inferior status which has debarred them from such rights of their masters as inheritance, legal succession, legal marriage and the like, to struggle for such civil and religious rights.

This leads to the age of men, in which plutocracy and meritocracy succeed oligarchy, which in turn tends to break down before the demands for popular sovereignty. The rule of democratic justice is established with its accompaniment of free discussion, legal arguments, prose, rationalism and science. Metaphor in language is eclipsed by literal or 'epistolary' language based on abstract genera, and by a phonetic alphabet and conventional signs invented and altered at will; a 'language of which men are absolute lords . . . a language whereby the people may fix the meaning of the laws by which the nobles as well as the plebs are bound'.[12] Jurisprudence centres on the principle of natural equity according to which people for their own good demand universal laws, and laws are required to pay attention to the least details of matters calling for equal equity. All this is accompanied by the unrestricted questioning of received values, that is, by philosophy and criticism, which in the end undermines the accepted structure of society. Individualism grows until the ties that unite the mass of the people are dissolved, leading to the destruction of unifying faith and the disintegration of the state. Civic virtue melts away to be replaced with lawlessness and arbitrary violence.

At this stage society may be reintegrated and rejuvenated either by a strong individual or through conquest by more vigorous societies which are at an earlier stage of development. However if the rot is too deep and there are no societies to conquer it, the nation collapses into a second barbarism, a barbarism of senility rather than of youth, of reflection rather than of the senses. Rotting in that ultimate of civil disease,

> peoples, like so many beasts, have fallen into the custom of each man thinking only of his own private interests and have reached the extreme of delicacy, or better of pride, in which like wild animals they bristle and lash out at the slightest displeasure. Thus no matter how great the throng and press of their bodies, they live like wild beasts in a deep solitude of spirit and will, scarcely any two being able to agree since each follows his own pleasure and caprice.[13]

This is associated with a new form of savagery, not the gentle savagery of the first barbarism against which one could take flight, but a base savagery of premeditated malice in which, under soft words, people plot against the life and fortune of friends and intimates.

It is difficult to estimate how much influence Vico had on subsequent thinkers because similar ideas were developed independently, particularly by Herder in Germany and then by a number of German thinkers. However, once ideas similar to Vico's had been developed in Germany, Vico's ideas were appreciated, and appear to have exerted some direct influence, and it is in terms of Vico's ideas that it is possible to understand the main lines of German philosophy in the nineteenth century. Vico did not evaluate different stages in history since to do so it would have been necessary to invoke absolute values. Hegel and Marx can be understood as the main proponents of the view that the kind of cultural history described by Vico could be understood as progress, as the realization of rationality and freedom, while Nietzsche and Heidegger can be understood as the main proponents of the view that Vico's cultural history is best understood as the description of a slide from the age of gods and the age of heroes into decadence and nihilism.

VICO AND HEGEL

Unlike Vico's philosophy of history, Hegel's philosophy of history is part of a total philosophical system.[14] In accordance with the tradition of radical neo-Platonism which goes back to John Scotus Eriugena in the ninth century, Hegel identified the cosmos with God or spirit.[15] The differentiation of the cosmos, the positing of nature and the creation of humanity, was seen as part of the process by which spirit reveals itself to itself, a process in which humanity plays the leading role. The whole of world history was interpreted as the process of humanity transcending nature, developing individual self-consciousness and the institutions which would enable some people, that is, philosophers, to gain an unobstructed view of the totality, to reveal the rationality implicit within nature and within history, and thereby to see that the ultimate end of nature and of history is the world spirit's achievement of this self-consciousness. Within this scheme Hegel strove to give a place to the specific, to the concrete, to change, to the 'inner' aspect of reality and to mental strife and self-transformation, but ultimately subordinated these to the universal. As Hegel put it: 'Philosophy is timeless comprehension, of time too and of all things generally in their eternal mode.'[16]

As with Vico, historical development was not seen as an organized or orchestrated phenomenon. It was seen as the outcome of socially situated individuals driven by their passions to respond to the problems of their times. What Vico called providence, Hegel referred to as 'the cunning of reason' which 'sets the passions to work for itself'.[17] However, the account of world history given by Hegel, drawing on ideas from both Herder and Kant, was somewhat more complex than that given by Vico. For Hegel, as for Herder, each nation or civilization is united and inspired by a principle, and its collapse follows the realization of this principle in forms of life and institutions and in art, religion and philosophy. And following Kant, Hegel held that human freedom is rational self-determination, and represented history as the development of such rationality. However for Hegel, people are not fully conscious of the rationality which moves them. The passion driving individuals was interpreted as the unity of individual character and the universal, the divine element in humans, and Hegel identified this element as '*Reason*, or, insofar as it has activity and power of self-determination, as *Freedom*'.[18] So where Vico described history as a cyclical process in which nations pass through a succession of stages, Hegel combined an account of the development of nations as cyclical with a view of history as a whole as a linear development. Each nation was seen to have its own rise and fall, much as Vico described, but some later nations were seen to be able to build on the achievements of their predecessors, to then overcome their limitations to embody in their institutions greater degrees of reason or freedom, the condition for the achievement of the full self-consciousness of spirit. This development was best described by Hegel in his introduction to the *Philosophy of History*:

> [W]orld history is the manifestation of the Divine, the absolute process of Spirit in its highest forms. It is this development wherein it achieves its truth and consciousness of itself. The products of its stages are the world-historical national spirits, the definiteness of their moral life, their constitution, art, religion, and science. . . . This development implies a gradual progress, a series of ever more concrete differentiations, as involved in the concept of freedom. . . . [E]ach stage, being different from the other, has its definite, peculiar principle. Such a principle is in history the differentiation of Spirit; it is a particular national spirit. This principle defines the common features of its religion, its political constitution, its morality, its system of law, its mores, even its science, art, and technical skill. . . . The principles of the national spirits progressing through a necessary succession of stages are only moments of the one universal Spirit which through them elevates and completes itself into a self-comprehending *totality*.[19]

The emergence and gradual development of forms of life and consciousness, of political institutions or the state, of artistic, religious and philosophical ideas, successively acknowledging the significance and rights of broader and broader strata of the population, is represented as the march of reason through history.

For Hegel one of the most significant stages in the development of forms of life and consciousness is that typified by the emergence of Christianity in an 'age of heroes'. His analysis of this in terms of the dialectic of recognition, the dialectic of labour and the dialectic of representation grants a major role to the weak and defeated in the spirit's advance towards full self-consciousness.[20] Hegel argued that self-consciousness can only be achieved when desire is oriented towards another desiring subject, that true self-consciousness is dependent upon the mutual recognition of consciousnesses. But such mutual recognition is only achieved through a series of defective relationships between people. The first stage in this series is characterized by a struggle in which one group, the masters (essentially, Vico's heroes), subordinate another, the slaves. The triumphant masters force the slaves to recognize and subordinate themselves to their will. In this way the masters should be successful in their struggle for recognition. However in reducing slaves to things and treating them as instruments, the recognition they obtain is deprived of any significance. The slaves on the other hand can see in their masters something to aspire to. But beyond this, the slaves in constant fear of death are shaken from concern with their particular existence to take the point of view of the universal, and at the same time, in being forced to work for their masters, gain mastery over nature and impress themselves upon it. By creating a standing reflection of themselves as universal beings, the slaves become such beings and gain self-substantiation in a way which is denied to the masters, whose relationship to nature is mediated by the slaves. In this way the universality of the ego and freedom of all is first recognized, although at this stage only in an ideal, that is, alienated form. Hegel traced the development of consciousness from this first stage through various defective forms until true reciprocity is achieved, and people have come to identify themselves with the universal and thereby achieved freedom in their everyday lives.

Such transformations in subjective spirit and consciousness were seen by Hegel to be conjoined with developments of political institutions, notably the state, that is, of objective spirit, in which through history this freedom has come to be concretely realized. In Oriental societies only one person, the emperor, was recognized as free. In Ancient societies, Greece and Rome, only some were recognized as free. The concrete embodiment of universal freedom for everyone is finally effected in the modern constitutional monarchy in which universal recognition and freedom of the individual is institutionalized. The development of objective spirit provides the conditions for the development of absolute spirit. The development from people's original immersion in the senses to conceptual thinking was interpreted by Hegel in accordance with Plato's theory of knowledge as a struggle first to rise above the visible realm of images and physical objects, of illusion and belief, to the intelligible realm of ideas which are known, first through mathematical reasoning and then ultimately through dialectics. This was associated with a scheme in which art was held in relatively low estimation as a moment or stage in the development of absolute spirit, to be followed by revealed religion and then philosophy. And the most important part of philosophy is the *logic*, the systematic deduction of categories covering all aspects of reality. For Hegel, as for Plato, the end point of such intellectual development is the achievement of a comprehensive grasp of the rational structure of the world, the idea – the ideal union of objective reality in its essential features with the human world of thought. But Hegel also included the history of spirit in this world, and the end point of this history is the self-consciousness of spirit. The spirit's comprehensive grasp of all reality, including its own history and self-consciousness, is achieved in the concept, the most general and most concrete act of thinking, hence the most philosophical, building upon and standing at the apex of the activities of sensing, imagining, opining and calculating.

VICO AND MARX

The most important Hegelian was Marx. Marx's thought evolved through a number of stages, and never achieved the consistency of Hegel's philosophy. His inconsistencies have generated a diversity of Marxisms elaborating on various aspects of his work. However these inconsistencies can be ignored for our purposes. What is important is that Marx accepted Hegel's arguments that the social is ontologically prior to the individual, that the individual emerges through culturally constituted social relations. His distinctive contribution to the Hegelian tradition was to have focused on the social relations associated with the dialectic of labour, showing their transformations through history and how these transformations underlie other social and cultural transformations, and in terms of this, to have analysed the origins and self-reproducing and self-destructive dynamics of the capitalist socio-economic formation. For Marx, history is the development of the productive powers of humans and their transformation of nature for human ends. This has involved the emergence of class societies and the subjugation of those engaged in production by the ruling class of each socio-economic formation. Instead of liberating humanity, the development of these productive powers has been associated with increasing domination and exploitation of the workers, which has reached its highest point in capitalist societies.

Within this mode of production, categories such as 'commodity', 'money', 'labour' and 'capital' have become the 'forms of existence'. All the world has been staked out as property, and labourers, deprived of access to the means of production, are forced to sell the only property they have left, their labour power, as a commodity to get the money needed to buy the products they have made, while capitalists, owning the means of production as constant capital, buy labour power or variable capital to produce commodities for the market in order to make a profit to buy more capital. In this process, not only commodities but also the relations of production are produced and reproduced, including the relationship between the capitalist and the labourer. Capitalists and labourers are equally the products of this process. The artificial nature of property, of the expropriation of workers from the means of production, of the treatment of labour-power as a commodity, of capital and of money itself are disguised and made to appear as the natural order of things; as though individuals, pre-existing social relations, are freely exchanging their labour or products for money to their mutual advantage. This is reinforced by the elaboration of a mechanical view of nature and of people, so nature appears as devoid of significance except insofar as it can be transformed for human purposes, and people are represented as Hobbesian mechanical egoists moved only by their appetites and aversions to truck, barter and exchange.

Of all socio-economic formations, this is the most dynamic, since the ruling class, in order to maintain their social position, are forced to reinvest their capital in search of more capital, to develop technology and expand the means of production. However, in augmenting their own position, individual capitalists are undermining the entire formation. In defeating their rivals and concentrating wealth in their own hands, they are reducing the size of the ruling class, and in developing the means of production they are reducing the role of labourers who are essential actors in the cycle of production and consumption through which capital is realized. At the same time they are cultivating a disciplined and increasingly educated class of workers who are being placed in a position where they will be able to seize and manage the means of production for their own ends. With the communist society which will result from this the mystifications of all class societies will be revealed and the full potentialities of humans realized.

VICO AND NIETZSCHE

Nietzsche is the most forceful representative of those thinkers who believe that Hegel's project failed, that what he was trying to defend is indefensible.[21] In place of Hegel's characterization of the development from the age of heroes to the age of men as progress towards greater rationality and freedom, Nietzsche characterized it as a journey into nihilism.

What is the cause of this nihilism? It is the failure of the whole project of philosophy, a project which culminated in Hegel's metaphysics, which leads to the devaluation of the world. As he put it:

> The feeling of valuelessness was reached with the realization that the overall character of existence may not be interpreted by means of the concept of 'aim,' the concept of 'unity,' or the concept of 'truth.' . . . Briefly: the categories 'aim,' 'unity,' 'being' which we used to project some value into the he world – we *pull out* again; so the world looks *valueless*.[22]

However the project of philosophy was itself seen as an expression of the logic of European civilization. Where Hegel had seen in Christianity a major advance in the spirit's coming to consciousness of itself, Nietzsche saw in Christianity a religion of the weak expressing *ressentiment* at the power of the masters. It is not that Nietzsche rejected Hegel's analysis of the genesis of greater self-consciousness and the transcendence of ego-centricity in the slave; but for Nietzsche it was precisely this which was so disastrous and which led to the effort to put meaning into the world through philosophy rather than creating it through living. And the development of morality and the democratization of political institutions, what Hegel had seen as the concrete realization of reason and freedom, Nietzsche saw as nothing but the triumph of the ignoble, resentful masses over the nobility who had been able to create value in their lives. What is necessary is a revaluation of all values, a return to the unselfconscious affirmation of life characteristic of an heroic aristocracy.

Nietzsche's philosophy is thus the more extreme of the oppositional stances to the Cartesian tradition of thought. He was interested in change, in the particular, and in conflict and strife. He totally rejected the quest for a transcendent perspective beyond the world of becoming, from which a unified perspective on the world could be gained, as a delusion, and with this, the effort to create a coherent system of thought. The will to system is the will to self-deception. There is no reason to believe that all valid insights will cohere. Accordingly, Nietzsche adopted an aphoristic style of writing and experimented with different genres. His whole outlook is inimical to the neat summarization of his ideas, since summarization implies a unified perspective which can be adumbrated, precisely the view Nietzsche was attacking. But while Nietzsche's ideas might not form into a totally coherent system, there are a number of central ideas which do cohere, which 'hang together', and these can be adumbrated and their relationship to each other shown. These ideas reveal the affinity between Nietzsche and Vico.

To begin with, Nietzsche affirmed the reality of becoming, criticizing the traditional fixation on being as an attack on life itself. As he wrote in *Twilight of the Idols* of the idiosyncrasies of philosophers:

> There is their lack of historical sense, their hatred of even the idea of becoming, their Egyptianism. They think they are doing a thing *honour* when they dehistoricise it, *sub specie aeterni* – when they make a mummy of it. All that philosophers have handled for millennia has been conceptual mummies; nothing actual has escaped their hands alive. They kill, they stuff, when they worship, these conceptual idolaters – they become a mortal danger to everything when they worship. Death, change, age, as well as procreation and growth, are for them objections – refutations even. What is, does not *become*; what becomes *is* not. . . . Now they all believe, even to the point of despair, in that which is.[23]

This rejection of becoming is responsible for the second idiosyncrasy of philosophers, that of 'mistaking the last for the first'.

> They put that which comes at the end . . . the 'highest concepts', that is to say the most general, the emptiest concepts, the last fumes of evaporating reality, at the beginning *as* the beginning. It is again only the expression of their way of doing reverence: the higher must not be *allowed* to grow out of the lower, must not be *allowed* to have grown at all. . . . All supreme values are of the first rank, all the supreme concepts – that which is, the unconditioned, the good, the true, the

47

perfect – all that cannot have become, *must* therefore be *causa sui*. . . .
That mankind should have taken seriously the brainsick fancies of
morbid cobweb-spinners! – And it has paid dearly for doing so![24]

But if we invert the order, if we take what is first as first, what do we have?
The will to power, which Nietzsche takes to be the principal feature of all
existence, inanimate, animate and human.[25] This assumption underlies all
other aspects of Nietzsche's thought.

The will is not something that can be represented. Nietzsche argued:
'Linguistic means of expression are useless for expressing "becoming".'[26]
The will reveals itself through its symptoms. For Nietzsche, what is most
important is whether symptoms are produced by active forces or reactive
forces. His analysis of the nihilism of European civilization is based on
this. European civilization is sick because it is dominated by reactive
forces. The Homeric Greeks were active. The 'Hellenic will' was a
'mastering unity' through which the Greeks achieved a 'unifying mastery
of their drives', of their knowledge drive in philosophy, of their ecstasy
and the formal drive in art, and of their *eros* in *agape*.[27] 'Good' (*agathos*)
was used by these masters to approve the lives they led. They meant by
it what is noble, mighty, high-placed and high-minded. Contra Hegel,
Nietzsche argued that the masters did not need recognition from anyone
to define and ascribe value to themselves. Their mode of existence was
such that they were able to evaluate, and thereby, create value. By contrast
the Christians were reactive. It is slaves who, incapable of ascribing value
to and thinking well of themselves, feel compelled to define themselves
in opposition to others and through the opinion others have of them.[28] It
is this reactive will which turns life against itself, appropriating the
language of the masters and using it against them, condemning nobility
as evil while praising themselves, their responsibility, conscience and
abnegation, as good. The 'fully emancipated man, master of his will, who
dares make promises', the responsible person, was shown by Nietzsche
to be the outcome of 'brutality, tyranny, and stupidity . . . of custom and
the straightjacket' through which people were rendered 'regular, uniform,
equal among equals, calculable'.[29] It is this slave mentality which needs
external supports for its sense of value, which tries to find a moral order
in the world or in institutions, and which, failing to do so, collapses into
nihilism.

This turning of the will to power against life is manifest in science:

Has not man's determination to belittle himself developed apace
precisely since Copernicus? . . . Ever since Copernicus man has been
rolling down an incline, faster and faster, away from the centre –
whither? . . . All science . . . is now determined to talk man out of his
former respect for himself, as though that respect had been nothing
but a bizarre presumption.[30]

Nietzsche set out to reveal the roots of this trend in untenable conceptions of knowledge and truth, that is, of knowledge as correspondence with reality and truth as descriptive adequacy. Conceiving of knowledge in this way generates the typical 'knowers' or 'lovers of truth', people who fancy themselves confronting an independently real world, which, by a determined effort to throw off illusion and by using sense and reason, they can know just as it is and describe it so that representations of it correspond exactly and in every detail to the things themselves; and who then become sceptics as they realize this ideal is unattainable.

Against these conceptions of knowledge and truth, Nietzsche argued that knowledge is a process of accommodating ourselves to the world and the world to us, that truths are humanly constructed instruments designed for human purposes. Knowledge which is of any use to people 'involves the *identification of things which are not the same, of things which are only similar*',[31] that is, the use of metaphor. Accordingly, Nietzsche argued: 'The drive toward the formation of metaphors is the fundamental human drive, which one cannot for a single instant dispense with in thought, for one would thereby dispense with man himself.'[32] Knowing is based on operations which are usually dismissed as rhetorical tropes: on transferring things from one sphere to an entirely different sphere (metaphor), confusing a thing with its attributes (metonymy), taking a part for the whole or the whole for a part (synecdoche) and on illicit generalizations. Concepts are formed by equating unequal things, and then overlooking what is individual and actual. Words become concepts when they no longer refer to any one particular but fit countless more or less similar instances:

> In order to think and infer it is necessary to assume beings: logic handles only formulas for what remains the same. That is why this assumption would not be a proof of reality: 'beings' are part of our perspective.... The fictitious world of subject, substance, 'reason,' etc., is needed—: there is in us a power to order, simplify, falsify, artificially distinguish.... What then is truth? A movable host of metaphors, metonymies, and anthropomorphisms: in short, a sum of human relations which have been poetically and rhetorically intensified, transferred, and embellished, and which, after long usage, seem to a people to be fixed, canonical, and binding. Truths are illusions which we have forgotten are illusions; they are metaphors that have become worn out and have been drained of sensuous force, coins which have lost their embossing and are now considered as metal and no longer as coins.[33]

Nietzsche's theory of knowledge and his analysis of science were closely tied to his theory of language. To be truthful, he argued, is to employ the generally accepted, the most familiar metaphors, and it is language which legislates which metaphors are taken to be appropriate in each circumstance: 'The spiritual activity of millennia is deposited in language',[34] and it is the 'legislation of language' which 'establishes the first laws of truth'.[35] It is language which then leads us to conceive of the world the way we do:

> The separation of the 'deed' from the 'doer,' of the event from someone who produces events, of the process from a something that is not process but enduring, substance, thing, body, soul, etc. – the attempt to comprehend an event as a sort of shifting and place-changing on the part of a 'being,' of something constant: this ancient mythology established the belief in 'cause and effect' after it had found a firm form in the functions of language and grammar.[36]

Science is the extension of the labour of language in the construction of a great, rigidly regular edifice of concepts. '[S]cience works unceasingly on this great columbarium of concepts, the graveyard of perceptions.'[37] It takes to extremes the tendency to deny life by refusing to acknowledge the reality of difference. The centrality to science of logical identity, mathematical equality and physical equilibrium expresses this mania, which can only depreciate life and promise it death, as in the heat death of the universe postulated by thermodynamics. But what do we achieve in science? '[O]ne is obliged to understand all motion, all "appearances," all "laws," only as symptoms of an inner event and to employ man as an analogy to this end.'[38] We simply find in nature what we project onto it.

To overcome nihilism it is necessary to return to the celebration of active forces, characteristic of the Ancient Greeks, to a will which affirms life. It is art which displays the unity of style, the harmonious manifoldness which was characteristic of Ancient Greek culture – and of any real culture, which, according to Nietzsche, the modern world lacks. Art presents beautiful illusions which are affirmed as illusions, deceptions which are accepted as deceptions. Unlike mythology, art shares the commitment to honesty of science, but it is more honest than science because it recognizes and accepts the ultimacy of illusion, which, by being treated as illusion, can be dealt with creatively. Art also makes possible once again good will towards appearances. The only criterion that can now count for us is the aesthetic criterion. What is required is a new kind of philosophy which is art as well as knowledge. Thus, Nietzsche defined his life project in *The Struggle Between Science and Wisdom*:

> My general task: to show how life, philosophy, and art can have a more profound and congenial relationship to each other, in such a way that philosophy is not superficial and the life of the philosopher does not become mendacious.[39]

VICO AND HEIDEGGER

Heidegger's work can be understood as an attempt to carry through this project even more radically than had Nietzsche, whose conception of life as 'will to power' was, according to Heidegger, still only an answer to the question 'What is Being?' posed as 'What is the being of the entity?'[40] Heidegger saw the primary characteristic of the modern age as 'the loss of the gods', where 'the gods have fled' and the relation to the gods has been 'changed into mere "religious experience"'.[41] Essentially Heidegger was concerned to take us back before the age of heroes to the age of gods, although this was not understood by him in the way Vico had represented it.

Heidegger's philosophy is essentially an effort to treat the temporality of being as presencing, and through this, by showing how the nature of presencing has been denied, to reveal the roots of the nihilism of modernity. In his seminal work *Being and Time*, he defined his project as treating the 'question of Being', and mapped out two distinct tasks requiring two parts: first, 'the Interpretation of *Dasein* in terms of temporality, and the explication of time as the transcendental horizon for the question of Being' and second, to map out the 'basic features of a phenomenological destruction of the history of ontology, with the problematic of Temporality as our clue'.[42] Only part of the first task was attempted in *Being and Time*, a preliminary analysis of *Dasein* (there-being – which in German means 'existence', or more specifically, 'human being') and an analysis of *Dasein* and temporality. The analysis of time and Being and the 'destruction' of the history of ontology, that is, the dismantling of the structural layers of Western civilization to see how it has been constituted, to show how Being as the self-revealing or self-manifesting of beings has been forgotten through a fixation on beings as entities, was left for the future.

However, in his 'Letter on Humanism' Heidegger distanced himself from existentialist philosophy and affirmed his more basic concern with Being. For Heidegger *Dasein* is only comprehensible in relation to Being: 'As ek-sisting, man sustains Da-sein in that he takes the *Da*, the lighting [or clearing] of Being, into "care". But Da-sein itself occurs essentially as "thrown". It unfolds essentially in the throw of Being as the fateful sending.'[43] The essay also signalled the central place he had come to give the study of language in his analysis of Being and the 'destruction' of the history of ontology. Heidegger tried to show how, since Plato, Being has come to be forgotten so we no longer dwell in the world in a way that the meaning of Being is revealed to us. He argued that the fusion of Christian theology with Greek metaphysics in Roman society involved a radical transformation of Greek thought, infusing it with the engineering mentality of the Romans. This change occurred with the translation of Greek words into Latin. '*Roman thought takes over the Greek words without a corresponding, equally authentic experience of what they say, without the Greek word.* The rootlessness of Western thought begins with this translation.'[44] As the early Greeks understood it, *physis* is the event of self-emergence, as when a bud bursts forth into a flower, and the appearing, shining forth or presencing of an entity. The Romans translated *physis* as *natura* which, although it has its etymological roots in the notion of being born, was understood in terms of what is produced, caused or created. While the Greeks began the process of conceiving of Being as an underlying and constantly present 'ground' of the presencing of things, it was the Romans who conceived of this ground as that which produces things. Thus 'being' itself was reduced to the status of a superior kind of entity which produces the world, and the world came to be seen as the totality of all created beings, as composites of form and matter bearing various traits which are ready at hand for use. Western civilization comes to be dominated by metaphysics, by 'onto-theo-logy' (identifying being, God and reason) through which all particular beings are conceived as merely products of some ultimate ground:

> Philosophy is metaphysics. Metaphysics thinks beings as a whole – the world, man, God – with respect to Being, with respect to the belonging together of beings in Being. . . . For since the beginning of philosophy and with that beginning, the Being of beings has showed itself as the ground (*arche*, *aiton*, principle). The ground is that from which beings as such are what they are in their becoming, perishing, and persisting as something that can be known, handled, and worked upon. . . . [T]he ground has the character of grounding as the ontic causation of the real, as the transcendental making possible of the objectivity of objects, as the dialectical mediation of the movement of the absolute Spirit and of the historical process of production, as the will to power positing values.[45]

Descartes' philosophy is the culmination of onto-theology. For Descartes, it is reason which is the ground for reality and truth. It is in Descartes that we have the beginning of subjectivism, where the subject is conceived of as the self-determining, as certain of itself, and as that which knows and places value on an objective world. This is associated with the idea of truth not as revelation but as adequate representation of reality or world-picture, that is, the world conceived and grasped as a picture. As Heidegger pointed out, the notion of representation is redolent of domination: 'Representing is making-stand-over-against, an objectifying that goes forward and masters. In this way representing drives everything together into the unity of that which is thus given the character of object.'[46] The subject representing the world reduces the world to a collection of calculable, controllable objects. In this way onto-theology engendered modern science.

Heidegger noted that the development of science within the field opened by philosophy had already begun in Ancient Greece, and that even at this stage the different sciences had established their independence from philosophy. This development is in full swing today in 'all regions of beings' and, Heidegger argued, this is not the 'mere dissolution of philosophy', but 'is precisely its completion'. The independence of psychology, sociology, anthropology, symbolic logic and semantics illustrate this. And

> [n]o prophecy is necessary to recognize that the sciences now establishing themselves will soon be determined and steered by the new fundamental science which is called cybernetics. . . . For it is the theory of the steering of the possible planning and arrangement of human labour. Cybernetics transforms language into an exchange of news. The arts become regulated-regulating instruments of information.[47]

Science, and most importantly, modern science as it was inaugurated by Descartes, manifests the orientation of the onto-theological philosophy which engendered it. It is the expansion of a technological orientation which reduces the world to manipulable objects. The use of mathematics and the design of experiments are such as to reveal the world only insofar as it is controllable:

> Modern science's way of representing pursues and entraps nature as a calculable coherence of forces. Modern physics is not experimental because it applies apparatus to the questioning of nature. The reverse is true. Because physics, indeed already as pure theory, sets nature up to exhibit itself as a coherence of forces calculable in advance, it orders its experiments precisely for the purpose of asking whether and how nature reports itself when set up in this way.[48]

While initially this technological character was confined to the natural world, it is now coming to dominate the human world. The almighty subject liberated from all constraints in Descartes' philosophy, has become itself an object of control:

> In the planetary imperialism of technologically organized man, the subjectivism of man attains its acme, from which point it will descend to the level of organized uniformity and there firmly establish itself. This uniformity becomes the surest instrument of total, i.e., technological, rule over the earth. The modern freedom of subjectivity vanishes totally in the objectivity commensurate with it.[49]

So what is the outcome of the completion of philosophy in its dissolution?

> The end of philosophy proves to be the triumph of the manipulable arrangement of a scientific-technological world and of the social order proper to this world. The end of philosophy means the

53

beginning of the world civilization based upon Western European thinking.[50]

If onto-theology, and following it, science, is an orientation which reduces the world to an ordered totality of objects to be used, what is technology? In 'The question concerning technology' Heidegger questions the common conception of technology as the human activity of positing of ends and procuring and utilizing the means to them. If technology is looked upon as an instrument, we will remain transfixed by the will to master it. But it is only because we are in the sway of onto-theology, and of Roman misappropriations of Greek language, that this way of thinking about technology prevails. According to Heidegger, Aristotle's notion of causation is misinterpreted as that which brings something about. Rather, Aristotle's four 'causes' are the ways of being responsible for something else, for bringing something into appearance. The principal characteristic of being responsible is starting something on its way to arrival. The Greek word *aitia* which the Romans translated as *causa* is thus better translated as 'occasion'. Occasioning by which what is not present is brought to presence, that is, the bringing forth into presence, was for the Greeks, *poiesis*. *Aletheia*, which the Romans translated as *veritas*, truth understood as the correctness of an idea, was for the Greeks the bringing forth from concealment to unconcealment, revealing. The arising of something from out of itself, the highest form of poiesis, is *physis*. *Techne*, which included the activities and skills of the mind and the fine arts as well as of the craftsman, is a secondary kind of bringing forth, of poiesis, and is thereby a mode of *aletheuein*. As Heidegger put it:

> Technology is no mere means. It is a way of revealing. . . . It reveals whatever does not bring itself forth and does not yet lie here before us, whatever can look and turn out now one way and now another. . . . Technology is a mode of revealing. Technology comes to presence in the realm where revealing and unconcealment take place, where *aletheia*, truth, happens.[51]

Modern technology is also a revealing, but it only reveals the world as a collection of objects to be controlled. As Heidegger argued:

> Only when we allow our attention to rest on this fundamental characteristic does that which is new in modern technology show itself to us. And yet the revealing that holds sway throughout modern technology does not unfold into a bringing-forth in the sense of *poiesis*. The revealing that rules in modern technology is a challenging, which puts to nature the unreasonable demand that it

54

supply energy that can be extracted and stored as such. . . . The work of the peasant does not challenge the soil of the field. In the sowing of the grain it places the seed in the keeping of the forces of growth and watches over its increase. But meanwhile even the cultivation of the field has come under the grip of another kind of setting-in-order, which *sets* upon nature. It sets upon it in the sense of challenging it. Agriculture is now the mechanized food industry. Air is now set upon to yield nitrogen, the earth to yield ore, ore to yield uranium, for example; uranium is set upon to yield atomic energy, which can be released either for destruction or for peaceful use. . . . Unlocking, transforming, storing, distributing, and switching about are ways of revealing. But the revealing never simply comes to an end. Neither does it run off into the indeterminate. The revealing reveals to itself its own manifoldly interlocking paths, through revealing their course. The regulating itself is, for its part, everywhere secured. Regulating and securing even become the chief characteristics of the challenging revealing.[52]

Heidegger accepted Nietzsche's characterization of the role language has played in orienting us towards the world's domination and constituting us as subjects over against the world, but thought this characterization valid only for the modern world. However he considered it 'an open question whether the nature of Western language is in itself marked with the exclusive brand of metaphysics, and thus marked permanently by onto-theo-logic, or whether these languages offer other possibilities of utterance'.[53] The languages of Western civilization were thus conceived of as degenerate. Language is 'the house of the truth of Being', but has surrendered itself 'to our mere willing and trafficking as an instrument of domination over beings'.[54] As a consequence, all we are left with is a will to will and an ever-expanding urge to planetary domination. Until his death in 1976, Heidegger devoted himself to reviving the way of thinking of the pre-Socratic Greeks for whom '[t]hat which is, is that which arises and opens itself, which, as what presences, comes upon man as the one who presences, i.e., comes upon the one who himself opens himself to what presences in that he apprehends it'.[55]

THE POSTSTRUCTURALISTS

The poststructuralists can be interpreted and evaluated as contributors to the Nietzschean/Heideggerian branch of the Vicovian tradition of thought, carrying on the task Nietzsche and Heidegger set themselves and building on their insights. In carrying on this task they have defined themselves in opposition to, yet have drawn upon the insights of the Hegelian tradition of thought as this was developed in France under the influence of the Russian émigré Alexandre Kojève, on structuralist semiotics and on

Freudian psychoanalysis.[56] However I will not examine in any detail the relationship between poststructuralists and these thinkers, nor will I discuss the work of all poststructuralists, the whole of the work of any poststructuralist or the differences and complex relationships between different poststructuralists. There are many excellent commentaries which already do all these things. For present purposes the most useful way to consider the ideas of the poststructuralists, and the more recent thinkers they have been influenced by, is in terms of where they have further advanced the insights of Nietzsche and Heidegger, where they have revealed problems in the Hegelian tradition of thought, and more broadly, where they have furthered the Vicovian opposition to the Cartesian tradition of thought. This most clearly reveals the achievements of the poststructuralists and the relationship between poststructuralism and postmodernism.

Poststructuralists have been and are developing the Hegelian thesis that humans are creating themselves through culture, reformulating this in the light of Nietzschean criticisms of Hegel. Kojève, whose ideas dominated French intellectual life after the Second World War, had presented Hegel's dialectic as the history of successive forms of consciousness, and interpreted Hegel's spirit as 'in reality nothing but the negating (i.e. creative) Action realized by Man in the given World'.[57] French phenomenology and Marxism were both subordinated to this Hegelian historicism. While Lacan and Foucault were among the first to react against the pan-rationalism of this vision of history and humanity, they were both concerned with the nature and development of forms of consciousness and with the social formation of subjects in a way which would have been inconceivable except as a revision of Hegelianism. Foucault designated himself an historian of systems of thought, and his notion of power operating through people to generate new forms of power without their intending this effect is a transmutation of Hegel's notion of the 'cunning of reason' which guarantees, despite people's intentions, that their actions ultimately contribute to progress.[58] Similarly, Derrida's analysis of the interrelationship between concepts and their constitutive role in society and Lyotard's analysis of the role of narratives in the constitution of the state, while developed in opposition to Hegelian thought, preserve Hegelian assumptions and insights, despite the hostility of these thinkers to the very idea of dialectical *aufheben*.

Poststructuralists have advanced Nietzsche's insights on the importance of language in culture by drawing on structuralist semiology and Heidegger's philosophy. Durkheim had argued for the reality of systems of collective representations, while Saussure had analysed language as an objective reality by taking a cross-section through time, abstracting it from speech and then treating language as a system of signs. He argued on this basis that a sign does not simply refer to a thing. It is a 'mysterious union' of a sound or acoustic image and a thought or concept, both of which are in principle exchangeable for other sounds or concepts. Signs are significant by virtue of the total system within which they function, both at the level of acoustic image where what matters is not the sound as such but the acoustic differences which allow a word to be distinguished from other words, and at the level of concepts which are always defined by differential relations with other concepts. Conceiving of signs in this way paved the way for a new science of semiology in which all collective representations could be analysed as parts of systems of signs with characteristic patterns of binary oppositions. This was the project carried through first by the formalists in Russia and Czechoslovakia, and then by the structuralists in France. Combining Durkheim's anthropology and Saussurian semiology, Claude Lévi-Strauss argued that society is an *ensemble* of symbolic systems, in the first rank of which are language, marriage rules, economic relations, art, science and religion; that 'meaning' is secondary and derivative, the result of a combination of elements which are not themselves significant; and that matrimonial exchange, as a system of symbolic exchanges, is the foundation of human society. Poststructuralists, most of whom had welcomed the attack by structuralists on the centrality of the subject in existentialist phenomenology, have defined their own position by rejecting the structuralist aim of constructing combinatorial systems in terms of which all possible valid signs or sign combinations could be deduced, and by reintroducing a temporal dimension into the analysis of sign production. More significantly, they have rejected the assumption of a stand-point outside all sign systems from which these systems could be studied and analysed in a detached way. While this turn was taken by many under the influence of the Russian literary theorist, Mikhail Bakhtin, who had been introduced into French intellectual life by Julia Kristeva and Tzvetan Todorov, the most important break with structuralism has occurred among those influenced by the later work of Heidegger.

LANGUAGE: DERRIDA

One of the most profound of the French poststructuralists to draw inspiration from Nietzsche and from Heidegger's 'destruction' of the history of ontology or metaphysics, his analysis of the relation between the rise of a domineering attitude towards the world and rationality and his philosophy of language, is Jacques Derrida.[59] Derrida has been concerned to criticize metaphysics, specifically what he refers to as 'logocentric metaphysics', the quest for an origin or foundation in truth, reason or the '*logos*'; and the 'metaphysics of presence' – taking what is claimed to be present or immediately given: the subject, objects of thought, what is perceived, concepts or propositional assertions, as such an origin or foundation. For Derrida, even Heidegger is guilty of striving for a foundation in what is immediately and self-evidently present.[60] Derrida has striven to show how what appears to be given and self-evident is generated by and dependent upon language and other systems of signs. To develop this notion, Derrida accepted Saussure's arguments that signs only have significance as parts of systems; but he attacked Saussure for subordinating the signifier to what it signifies. If the presence of a sign is only possible by virtue of its relations with other absent signs, then it is inconsistent of Saussure to allow this sign to have reference to an 'immediate presence of thought' outside the play of difference. He also rejected Saussure's abstraction of sign systems from the temporal process of signifying. Following Nietzsche and Heidegger, Derrida argued that the play of difference must be temporal as well as spatial, and introduced the term *'différance'*, implying both 'differ' and 'defer', to deal with this. *'Différance'* is *'sameness* which is not *identical* . . . referring to differing, *both* as spacing/temporalizing and as the movement that structures every dissociation.'[61] On this basis he argued

> [t]hat the play of differences supposes, in effect, syntheses and referrals which forbid at any moment, or in any sense, that a simple element be *present* in and of itself, referring only to itself. . . . [N]o element can function as a sign without referring to another element which itself is not simply present. This interweaving results in each 'element' . . . being constituted on the basis of a trace within it of the other elements of the chain or system. This interweaving, this textile, is the *text* produced only in the transformation of another text. . . . There are only, everywhere, differences and traces of traces.[62]

Consequently for Derrida 'there is no extratext. . . . There is nothing before the text; there is no pretext that is not already text.'[63] That is, there is nothing beyond the text which can be taken as an absolute point of reference. The world itself is, as Nietzsche suggested in 'On truth and lies in a nonmoral sense', an unstable foundation of 'running water'.

According to Derrida, the deepest desire of the Western philosophic tradition, that is, the tradition of metaphysics, has been to deny all this, to find some fixed, permanent centre, a transcendental signifier which will give meaning to all other signs. It has tried to freeze the play of *différance* in Platonic Forms, in God, in clear and distinct ideas, in material substance, in the transcendental ego, in Absolute knowledge, in Man or in the logical essence of language. To reveal what is being denied and to expose the arbitrary nature of all such efforts is what Derrida calls, following Heidegger's call for a 'destruction' of the history of ontology (onto-theology), 'deconstruction'.[64] Derrida argues that in each attempt to fix the play of *différance*, a binary opposition is assumed, one term of which is taken to be prior to and superior to the other.[65] The second term is made out to be derivative, accidental and unimportant in relation to the first, which is taken either as an ideal limit or the central concept of a metaphysical system. The second terms are then either effaced or repressed. This repression takes place because the second terms – abnormal, parasitical, void, non-literal, non-ideal, absence, difference, falsity, undecidability – suggest the breakup of the values assured by the first term – normal, standard, fulfilled, literal, ideal, presence, identity, truth, knowability conceived of as conscious mastery. In this way metaphysics establishes ethical-ontological hierarchies based on subordination. These hierarchies are embedded in everyday language, which according to Derrida 'is the language of Western metaphysics, and it carries with it not only a considerable number of presuppositions of all types, but also presuppositions inseparable from metaphysics, which, although little attended to, are knotted into a system'.[66] Derrida deconstructs ideal limits and the central concepts of metaphysical systems by showing how what is excluded as secondary and derivative is in fact at least as primordial and general as the metaphysical original. For instance, difference is not derived from identity, it makes identity possible, and in doing so makes impossible a pure identity, an identity exempt from differential relations. Deconstruction reveals a root system beneath metaphysics which never touches ground, exposing the arbitrary nature of what have been taken as absolutes. It reveals that 'transcendental essences', which have been taken as absolute points of reference, are abitrary signifiers arrested from the chain of signifiers and privileged, or made to seem 'natural' by a power group, thereby freezing the play of differences and imposing a fixed structure and hierarchy on society. In this way, Derrida argues, deconstruction provides 'a way of taking a position, in its work of analysis, concerning the political and institutional structures that make possible and govern our practice, our competences, our performances'.[67] Most importantly, by subverting the fixation of meaning which legitimizes exclusive groups, it enables those who have been suppressed and marginalized by Western civilization – the colonized, women, those outside the academies, to be heard.

THE EGO AND THE SUBJECT: LACAN

Along with their work on language, poststructuralists have further developed Nietzsche's thesis that personal identity is an illusion created by language. Derrida himself contributed to this, arguing that

[t]he subject, and first of all the conscious and speaking subject, depends upon the system of differences and the movement of *différance*, that the subject is not present, nor above all present to itself before *différance*, that the subject is constituted only in being divided from itself, in becoming space, in temporalizing, in deferral.[68]

However, the most comprehensive effort to analyse the linguistic constitution of the subject through a poststructuralist theory of language has been made by the Freudian psychoanalyst, Jacques Lacan.[69]

Initially Lacan attempted to reinterpret Freud's ideas in terms of Hegel's theory of the development of self-consciousness through the dialectic of recognition, differing from Hegel only in giving absolute priority to language in achieving such recognition. Speech, Lacan argued in early papers, is always a pact, an accord; in order for two subjects to name the same object they must recognize each other as recognizing the same object. But Lacan came to see this analysis as inadequate; it implies subjects with pre-linguistic intentions. His rejection of this was associated with the development of a much more complex theory of the formation of both the ego and the subject, which he had come to differentiate from each other. The ego is engendered in very young children before they learn to speak through misrecognizing themselves in images and then identifying themselves with these images. This is what Lacan called the 'mirror phase' of development. This sets the stage for a life-time of ego-building through identification with various images which then make up the 'imaginary', the world of images, conscious or unconscious, perceived or imagined. This is the birthplace of the narcissistic 'ideal ego'. The mirror phase is followed by the Oedipal stage in which the individual enters the symbolic order, the order of language and other sign systems; and it is this entrance which constitutes the child as a subject. In characterizing the symbolic order, Lacan followed Lévi-Strauss. Language is the primordial law which, by defining the kinship relations which regulate marriage ties, superimposes the kingdom of culture on that of nature. According to Lacan, the child in entering the symbolic order is given a name and becomes someone, but at the same time is bound for life to the law, or the symbolic father (the phallus) insofar as he signifies this law. Most significantly, the child is prohibited from sexual union with the mother.

In his characterization of the symbolic order Lacan went beyond structuralist analyses. He accepted the structuralist notion that signifiers are related as substitutions or combinations, as metaphors or metonymies, or what Lévi-Strauss referred to as 'paradigmatic transformations' and 'syntagmatic chains'; and following Roman Jakobson he interpreted in these terms the concepts of 'condensation' and 'displacement' used by Freud to analyse dreams. However, Lacan denied that the unity of signification could be resolved into a 'pure indication of the real', arguing that it 'always resolves back to another signification'.[70] The real, for Lacan, is the 'impossible', that before which the imaginary falters and the symbolic stumbles – in other words, what Nietzsche thought of as the unrepresentable becoming. The signified is then not the reality which is referred to, nor the meaning communicated by language, but, as for Derrida, 'the diachronic set of concretely pronounced discourses'.[71]

Meaning, then, cannot be objectified, but is characterized by a fundamental elusiveness and unpredictability.

It is through this conception of the symbolic order that Lacan re-interpreted Freud's more basic concepts. Most importantly he offered a new account of the unconscious. In the struggle for recognition, for a confirming image in the response of the other which will reinforce our ego, we find that we can never gain a definitive grasp of who the other subject truly is. Subjects are separated from each other by a wall of language which makes it impossible to discount the possibility that the other is dis-simulating. To highlight this, Lacan drew a distinction between the 'other' of imaginary identification and the 'Other', the third term beyond I and thou (he, she, it) interposed between subjects by language, the medium of intersubjectivity which confronts us as radically different from ourselves, although we are dependent upon it. This Other not only disrupts the initial dyad but rules it, making it impossible for the dialectic of recognition to ever come to rest in an equilibrium of mutual acknowledgement in which people's self-conception would coincide with their intersubjective position.

It is because this equilibrium is impossible that desire is generated. Desire is the mobile and unmappable excess of demand for love, that is, for the recognition of one's needs from the other, over and above the appetite for satisfaction. As Lacan put it, 'desire is neither the appetite for satisfaction, nor the demand for love, but the difference that results from the subtraction of the first from the second, the phenomenon of splitting (*Spaltung*)'.[72] The unconscious is formed through the splitting of the subject between such demand and need. But this means that the un-conscious is 'the discourse of the Other', that is, 'that part of the concrete discourse, in so far as it is transindividual, that is not at the disposal of the subject in re-establishing the continuity of his discourse'.[73]

In this way Nietzsche's conception of the subject as an effect of language is affirmed against both the Cartesian or Kantian notion of the subject as the ego which exists, acts and speaks as a self-subsistent entity, and against the Hegelian notion of the subject which is culturally formed but achieves freedom through taking a position within culture and society. According to Lacan,

> Symbols . . . envelop the life of man in a network so total that they
> join together, before he comes into the world, those who are going
> to engender him 'by flesh and blood', so that they bring to his birth
> . . . the shape of his destiny.[74]

It is not the ego but the structure of the chain of signifiers which is constitutive of experience, of why subjects construe situations the way they do and act this way or that; and at the same time this structure governs whatever may be made present of the subject.[75] As Lacan put it: 'There where it was just now, there where it was for a while, between an extinction that is still glowing and a birth that is retarded, "I" can come into being and disappear from what I say.'[76] This subject exists as a subject of desire, as excluded from, while being represented in the signifying chain. Its identity is the effect of the temporal unification of the past and the future with the present brought about by the movement from signifier to signifier in a chain of signifiers.[77]

NARRATIVES: BARTHES, RICOEUR AND LYOTARD

The granting of a central place in culture and the constitution of the subject to language and to chains of signifiers inevitably led to an interest in the more complex levels or organization of signifiers beyond sentences, that is, in the organization of discourse, the most important kind of which is narrative. For those dominated by the analytico-referential view of language, narratives are nothing more than convenient ways of organizing statements about the world. The structuralists, notably Jakobson, Benveniste, Greimas, Todorov and the early Barthes rejected this, arguing for the reality of a level of organization which must be understood in its own terms. Concern with this created a new discipline, 'narratology'.[78] As narratives became an object of study their pervasiveness immediately became apparent. As soon as people become capable of monologue (an ability posterior to dialogue), they begin constructing and making sense of the world through narratives. As Roland Barthes noted:

> The narratives of the world are numberless . . . narrative is present in myth, legend, fable, tale, novella, epic, history, tragedy, drama, comedy, mime, painting . . . stained glass windows, cinema, comics, news item, conversation. . . . [N]arrative is international, trans-historical, transcultural: it is simply there, like life itself.[79]

Narratology seemed to hold the key to the organizational principles of culture.

Structuralist narratology involved analysing narratives into elements and exploring their combinations.[80] In the case of Lévi-Strauss and Greimas, a distinction was drawn between surface and deep narrative structure. While the surface structure was seen to be syntagmatic, governed by temporal and causal principles, the deep structure was seen to be paradigmatic, based on static logical relations among the elements. The aim of analyses of the deep structure was to account for narrative time, the 'chronological illusion', in terms of an atemporal matrix structure. Narrative was seen as a communication, requiring a donor and a receiver, and structuralists examined the variety of relationships between the real author, the implied author, the narrator, the narratee, the implied reader and the real reader. In general, the real author and the real reader were left out of the analysis. In this way narratology conformed to the ideal of an objective science in which the discourse of the investigators was treated as something unproblematically separate from the object of study.

Poststructuralist narratologists attacked the assumptions underlying all aspects of the structuralist approach. To begin with, following immediately from poststructuralist arguments against structuralist linguistics, poststructuralists abandoned the project of accounting for the temporality of narratives through synchronic analyses of their elements and principles of combination. As both Derrida and Lacan argued, the generation of meaning is an essentially temporal process. Narrative is irreducibly temporal. The conception of language as communication was then criticized for simply assuming pre-formed subjects. According to poststructuralists, language sets up the positions of the 'I' and 'you', which are necessary for communication to take place, within the narration. In Lacan's formulation, the positions of narration, such as 'I' and 'you', are anchored by desire, which curbs the infinite temporal regress opened by *différance*.[81] Narratives are not simply produced and received by subjects, but are temporal processes which constitute subjects as the condition of relating the narrative into a whole. This is the case not only for the reader, but also for the writer – and in fact the distinction between the writer and reader is questionable, as writers cannot write without reading their own texts, and each reader must in some sense 'rewrite' the text in reading it. As Barthes argued in an essay signalling his shift from structuralism to poststructuralism,

> the author is never more than the instance of writing, just as *I* is nothing other than the instance saying *I*: language knows a 'subject', not a 'person', and this subject, empty outside of the very enunciation which defines it, suffices to make language 'hold together', suffices, that is to say, to exhaust it.[82]

Barthes concluded from this rejection of the notion of pre-existing subjects that a narrative cannot be conceived of as having a single meaning, the 'message' of the author-God, but is 'a multidimensional space in which a variety of writings, none of them original, blend and clash'.[83] The truth of writing is that

> the writer can only imitate a gesture that is always anterior, never original. His only power is to mix writings, to counter the ones with the others, in such a way as never to rest on any one of them.[84]

In place of the message conveyed by the author, the focus of analysis was shifted to the text which, as opposed to a work, is held in language, only exists in the movement of a discourse and is experienced only in the act of production.[85] There can be no objective science of narratives since there is no metalanguage or metadiscourse from which an exposition about the nature of texts could be generated which is not itself another text in a chain of texts. As Barthes put it:

> [T]he discourse on the text should itself be nothing other than text, research, textual activity, since the Text is that *social* space which leaves no language safe, outside, nor any subject of the enunciation in position as judge, master, analyst, confessor, decoder.[86]

Poststructuralists conceived the relationship between life and narratives as being much closer than had the structuralists. In his 'Introduction to the structural analysis of narratives', Barthes had argued that

> [n]arration can only receive its meaning from the world which makes use of it: beyond the narrational level begins the world, other systems (social, economic, ideological) whose terms are no longer simply narratives but elements of a different substance (historical facts, determinations, behaviours, etc.).[87]

However from a poststructuralist perspective, life itself is a text, and people's lives are lived stories. According to Paul Ricoeur, who has shared the same intellectual milieu as the poststructuralists, there are three forms of mimesis in, or aspects to, narrative.[88] First, life itself is an inchoate narrative. It is for this reason that we have a pre-understanding of what human action is, of its semantics, its symbolism, its temporality. The second aspect involves the representation of action according to specific rules of emplotment, that is, the making of a structure to interpret and organize this pre-understanding. Through the activity of emplotment a quasi-world of action and characters is generated. The third aspect is the reception of this representation. People are provided with the means to think about the way they live and to appropriate the new structure to organize their own actions and lives. Taking a more negative view, Barthes suggested that as writers simply mix writings, replace signs in an endless chain of signifiers, so do people live their lives. '[L]ife never does more than imitate the book, and the book itself is only a tissue of signs, an imitation that is lost, infinitely deferred', he argued in 'Death of the author'.[89] So it is with the subject, which, deriving its coherence from the narrative of the unfinished biography it lives, is never able to finally define itself as a unity.

Barthes went on to suggest, following Freud and Lacan, that the lives of people in Western civilization, and correspondingly, the stories they have constructed, have been Oedipal narratives. These symbolize entry into and coming to terms with the constraints imposed by culture, the symbolic order, constraints upheld by the father which destroy the male child's unity with his mother and force him to make his way in the world outside the family, to struggle for a replacement for the mother, and then to strive to understand the origins of his existence and the limits to what he can achieve. He ended his book *The Pleasure of the Text* reflecting on the pervasiveness of this theme: 'Doesn't every narrative lead back to Oedipus? Isn't storytelling always a way of searching for one's origin, speaking one's conflicts with the Law, entering into the dialectic of tenderness and hatred?'[90] It is through such narratives that gender relations are defined and constituted. But it is not only narratives about individual lives that are Oedipal narratives in this way. The archetypal Christian Judaic narrative of the fall and the coming redemption, the Hegelian narrative of world history as the struggle by the self-dirempting world-spirit to gain consciousness of itself and its purpose, and thereby to regain its original unity and the Marxist conception of history as the self-formation of humanity through alienation, reification, class division and class conflict, in which the secret of history will be fully revealed at its end when humanity will once again become a unified community, are Oedipal narratives on a grand scale.

While poststructuralist feminists such as Cixous, Irigaray and Kristeva have striven to overcome the domination of society by Oedipal narratives in their efforts to transform gender relations, Lyotard has been particularly concerned to oppose grand narratives as an effort 'to organize the multitude of events that come to us from the world, both the human and the non-human world, by subsuming them beneath the idea of a universal history of humanity'.[91] In attacking these narratives Lyotard has pointed out the significance of narratives for society. Just as personal identity, however spurious, is defined through the narratives of biographies, so social groups, societies as a whole, and Western civilization itself are constituted through narratives. To highlight the way in which narratives function and the distinctive nature of grand narratives, Lyotard described the role of storytelling among the Cashinahua:

> In order to hear these stories, one must have been named.... By putting the names into stories, narration protects the rigid designators of a common identity from the events of the 'now', and from the dangers of what follows on from it. ... [B]y repeating that story, the community reassures itself as to the permanence and legitimacy of its world of names in virtue of the recurrence of the world in its stories.[92]

People are given authority to tell stories by the stories they tell, and the scraps of life which cannot be integrated into the stories are sacrificed. Thus a self-enclosed culture is created. 'Narrative is authority itself. It authorizes an unbreakable *we*, outside of which there can only be *they*.'[93] Grand narratives are the opposite of such culturally closed narratives. They are cosmopolitical, designed to transcend all particular cultural identities to create a universal civic identity. But by what authority do the people who tell these stories make these claims? They are told by an avant-garde who believe they pre-figure today the free humanity of tomorrow; but there is no evidence that their narratives have been or will be heeded by others. More importantly, such narratives further the elevation of discourse over experience and figure, they are part of

> the penumbra which, after Plato, speech has thrown like a grey veil over the sensible, which has been constantly thematized as less-than-being, and whose side has very rarely truly been taken, taken in truth, since it was understood that this was the side of falsity, of scepticism, of the rhetorician, the painter, the *condottiere*, the libertine, the materialist.[94]

The civilization in which we live has no unity, and the representation of it as otherwise amounts to little more than a grab for power, or the defence of power already gained, by a privileged few. It supports the linguistic terrorism which denies a voice to all those (particularly people from non-European cultures) who cannot reduce the complexity of their experiences and desires to the language of bureaucracies. In opposition to such grand narratives, Lyotard valorizes local narratives and art, which undercut such universalizing tendencies and which reveal the unsuppressible gap between the intelligible and the sensible.

DISCURSIVE FORMATIONS – DISCOURSE AND POWER: FOUCAULT

In the study of language, subjects and narratives, few poststructuralists have paid specific attention to the power relations and institutional contexts of social interactions. Michel Foucault's work is the most important exception in this regard. Throughout his life Foucault strove to extend Nietzsche's analysis of how the will to power has turned against itself to constrain people and their lives by showing how discourse operates in relation to non-discursive practices and social formations. Like Nietzsche, Foucault was even more fundamentally opposed to the Cartesian tradition of thought than the Hegelian tradition, and he extended Nietzsche's critique of science to the human sciences, revealing the inseparability of knowledge and power. He focused on the transition from traditional to modern industrial societies to reveal the emergence, consolidation and expansion of administrative apparatuses of control over the social world in order to bring into question the totalizing perspective of Marxism and the evaluative concepts of the Enlightenment, notably rationality, truth and the subject, by which people in the modern world have celebrated the social order they have created.

Most of the themes which were developed in later works were already present in Foucault's first book, *Madness and Civilization: A History of Insanity in the Age of Reason*. In this, Foucault examined the confinement of the mad, and the vicissitudes of their confinement. He showed how in 1657 this confinement transformed the category of madness, reducing it to the underside of the triumph of reason, in opposition to which reason was defined. At the same time madness became a spectacle 'under the eyes of reason that no longer felt any relation to it. . . . Madness had become a thing to be looked at.'[95] This was regarded as of major importance by Foucault, who, following Heidegger and Merleau-Ponty, noted that in the seventeenth century, with the demise of the medieval cosmology, reason had come to be identified with sight, with clear and distinct ideas and with what can be observed, and that other sensory modalities were correspondingly devalued as sources of knowledge. Such reason was then seen to be closely associated with keeping things, and particularly people, under observation.[96] Keeping those designated as mad under observation was seen as part of a more general development within society of keeping everyone under surveillance in order to discipline, moralize and homogenize them. The apparent liberation of the mad which occurred in 1794 with the birth of the asylum, while appearing to be a triumph of a more humane attitude to the mad, was simply a consolidation of this development. Two of Foucault's later works, *The Birth of the Clinic* and *Discipline and Punish* were even more emphatic in pointing out the role of observation in producing disciplined bodies. Foucault showed how it was these new forms of institutionalized observation and disciplinary practices within asylums, clinics and prisons which generated the discourse of the social sciences. As he put it in *Discipline and Punish*, 'that moment when the sciences of man become possible is the moment when a new technology of power and a new political anatomy of the body were implemented'.[97] Social sciences have their roots in the drive to dominate and control people.

Such developments were not conceived of in the manner of a grand strategy for the ruling class to control the population. The discursive formations which have emerged since the seventeenth century were seen by Foucault to have their own dynamics. Claims to knowledge made within such discursive formations have to be understood in relation to a set of background assumptions or rules which determine the range of objects of knowledge, concepts, methodological resources and the theoretical formulations available.[98] These underlie institutional practices and the organization of these practices. Thus, Foucault had to 'recognize that clinical discourse was just as much a group of hypotheses about life and death, of ethical choices, of therapeutic decisions, of institutional regulations, of teaching models, as a group of descriptions'.[99] To understand knowledge claims it is necessary to take into account who has the right to make statements, from what site these statements emanate, and what position the subject of discourse occupies. In the context of clinics,

[m]edical statements cannot come from anybody; their value, efficacy, even their therapeutic powers, and, generally speaking, their existence as medical statements cannot be dissociated from the

statutorily defined person who has the right to make them, and to claim for them the power to overcome suffering and death.[100]

But then it is necessary to investigate how people come to be defined as having the right to make statements. As he pointed out, 'The status of doctor involves criteria of competence and knowledge; institutions, systems, pedagogic norms; legal conditions that give the right . . . to practice and to extend one's knowledge'.[101]

It was extended reflection on these issues which led Foucault to theorize more carefully the relationship between knowledge and power, and the association between knowledge-power and domination through the control of people's bodies and through constituting them as subjects. He defined his basic thesis in *Discipline and Punish*: '[P]ower produces knowledge . . . power and knowledge directly imply one another . . . there is no power relation without the correlative constitution of a field of knowledge, nor any knowledge that does not presuppose and constitute at the same time power relations.'[102] On this basis he argued that 'the subject who knows, the objects to be known and the modalities of knowledge must be regarded as so many effects of these fundamental implications of power-knowledge and their historical transformations'.[103] However, Foucault's concern was not just with the power–knowledge relationship by itself, but with its role in society. Taking up the Nietzschean thesis that a reflexive relation to the self and the inculcation of an internalized moral control of behaviour can only develop through threats and violence, he showed how people have been dominated and made predictable by being constituted as individuals through such power–knowledge relations. *Discipline and Punish* shows how subjects are constituted not merely through language, but through the disciplining of people's bodies by keeping them under surveillance. Describing the effect of the architecture of the Panopticon, the prison proposed by Bentham which Foucault took to be representative of a society of surveillance, he argued:

> He who is subjected to a field of visibility, and who knows it, assumes responsibility for the constraints of power; he makes them play spontaneously upon himself; he inscribes in himself the power relation in which he simultaneously plays both roles; he becomes the principle of his own subjection.[104]

It is this which produces the modern soul, whether this be called psyche, subjectivity, personality or consciousness. This soul is

> produced permanently around, on, within the body by the functioning of a power that is exercised on those one supervises, trains and corrects, over madmen, children at home and at school, the colonized, over those who are stuck at a machine and supervised for the rest of their lives.[105]

In his last work, *The History of Sexuality*, Foucault showed how sexuality has been promoted to the centrestage of society, how behind the façade of sexual repression, discourses on sex have proliferated, and sexuality has been continually aroused. Such discourses have individualized people through the confession, which began in the Middle Ages and has been intensified ever since. Today,

> [o]ne confesses in public and in private, to one's parents, one's educators, one's doctor, to those one loves; one admits to oneself, in pleasure and in pain, things it would be impossible to tell anyone else, the things people write books about. One confesses – or is forced to confess. When it is not spontaneous or dictated by some internal imperative, the confession is wrung from a person by violence or threat. . . . Western man has become a confessing animal.[106]

This has created in people the illusion of an inner mental life which must be continually examined and monitored, which, combined with the deployment of images of normality, has made for an unparalleled control by society over its members. Sex has been constructed and elevated over the soul, over love, to become the ultimate value, almost more important than life itself. Desire for it, to have access to it, to discover it and to liberate it has attached to each person the injunction to track along the paths laid out by society and to place oneself, one's body, in the grip of its power.

SYSTEMATIZING POSTSTRUCTURALISM: DELEUZE AND GUATTARI

Despite the hostility to systematic thought manifested by the post-structuralists, it could be argued that their main achievement is to have systematized Nietzsche's insights. The presentation of their work as elaborations of Nietzsche's philosophy, informed by Heidegger's effort to go beyond Nietzsche and assimilating ideas from the Hegelians against whom they were reacting, reveals its systematic nature. But it is still necessary to acknowledge their attacks on the way culture has been systematized in the past. What they have shown is the need for a new way of organizing ideas which does not lead to the exclusion of or denial of significance to the 'other', as modernist grand narratives have character-istically tended to do. Gilles Deleuze in association with Félix Guattari has gone furthest in elaborating a new kind of systematicity.

Deleuze is the most thoroughly Nietzschean of the poststructuralists, defending Nietzsche as a consistent philosopher who was attempting to complete Kant's project for a critical philosophy by directing criticism against the traditional principles of Western rationality, to replace Hegel's dialectics of the negation of the negation with a philosophy of affirma-tion, and most fundamentally, to overturn the Platonism of European thought with its celebration of eternal forms and its denigration of the changing sensible world by a philosophy of becoming based on a physics of force.[107] Rejecting the anti-naturalism of other poststructuralists, Deleuze has embraced Nietzsche's physicalism, and drawn on the ideas of the Stoics, on the philosophies of Lucretius, Spinoza and of Bergson, and on various developments within science and mathematics to elaborate a Nietzschean philosophy of nature. Among these sources, Bergson, with his defence of intuition, different orders of duration, multiplicity and creative becoming, has been the most important, and Deleuze has called for a return to Bergson, for 'a renewal or an extension of his project today, in relation to the transformations of life and society, in parallel with the transformations of science'.[108] Deleuze's philosophy has been characterized as 'The New Bergsonism'.[109]

Along with Guattari, Deleuze has attempted to fulfil this project by developing a new way of writing free from old organizational forms. They have described Nietzsche's thought as nomadic, and have attempted to emulate this nomadism, characterizing their major work, *A Thousand Plateaus*, as the opposite of a history, as a 'nomadology'. Each issue investigated breaks old disciplinary boundaries without imposing new fixed boundaries. Instead, new configurations of ideas are structured in improvisatory conformity to the constraints of the issue at hand. In this sense each of the fifteen chapters of the book is a 'plateau' with its own themes and concepts, interrelated with those of other plateaus without being integrable into an abstract system or 'plateau of plateaus'. The writers inform the reader that the chapters can be read in any order. But this does not mean that there is no ordered relation between all these different plateaus. Rather than an 'arborescent' system, the kind of system conforming to the model of a tree in which branches all stem from a central trunk, that is, where all truths are ultimately derived from a single principle, there is a 'rhizome' system, comparable to the root systems of bulbs and tubers, in which any point can be connected to any other point. Western thought and Western reality have been dominated by the tree. Biology, theology, ontology, philosophy and history are all organized as trees. History is always written from the sedentary point of view in the name of a unitary state apparatus which is itself organized as a tree with a central structure controlling a multiplicity of sub-structures. By contrast the rhizome is neither one nor a multiple, but is composed of dimensions, or directions in motion:

> In contrast to centred (even polycentric) systems with hierarchic modes of communication and pre-established paths, the rhizome is an acentred, non-hierarchical, non-signifying system without a general and without an organizing memory or central autonomon, defined solely by a circulation of states.[110]

This rhizomic organization of their thought is conjoined with a call for a new kind of politics, a 'nomadic politics' in place of 'the politics of the sedentary'. In *Anti-Oedipus* Deleuze and Guattari strove to undermine the Oedipal narrative and the psychological structures associated with the subordination of the organism's libido to the symbolic order of culture, characterizing this as the constitution of the mind into a mini-state morally unified into the state of society. Equating libidinal energy with the Nietzschean will to power, they sought to discover flows of desire which have not been reduced to Oedipal codes, opposing these to the kind identified by Lacan. They then attacked psychoanalysts as 'technicians of desire' along with what Foucault called 'the sad militants, the terrorists of theory, those who would preserve the pure order of politics and political discourse. Bureaucrats of the revolution and civil servants of Truth.'[111] However their main target has been fascism, not just as a political movement, but the fascism in us all, the fascism which leads us to love power and to desire our own repression, to subordinate ourselves to the state. Deleuze and Guattari are striving to free politics from totalizing paranoia, to withdraw allegiance from the old categories of the negative (law, limit, lack, castration) and to affirm what is positive, 'difference over uniformity, flows over unities, mobile arrangements over systems', to develop 'action, thought, and desires by proliferation, juxtaposition, and disjunction, and not by subdivision and pyramidal hierarchization'.[112] Accordingly they have formulated a conception of political action based on the metaphor of grass:

> Here in the West, the tree has implanted itself in our bodies, rigidifying and stratifying even the sexes. We have lost the rhizome, or the grass. Henry Miller: 'China is the weed in the human cabbage patch. . . . The weed is the Nemesis of human endeavour. . . . Of all the imaginary existences we attribute to plant, beast and star the weed leads the most satisfactory life of all. True, the weed produces no lilies, no battleships, no Sermons on the Mount. . . . Eventually the weed gets the upper hand. Eventually things fall back into a state of China. This condition is usually referred to by historians as the Dark Age. Grass is the only way out.'[113]

The relationship between postmodernism and poststructuralism is ambiguous. Lyotard can be regarded as both a poststructuralist and a proponent of postmodernist cultural trends, but most of the other post-structuralists have been either uninterested in or unsympathetic to post-modern culture. However the appropriation of their ideas by those hailing the postmodern condition as liberation from an oppressive culture reveals the affinity of poststructuralist thought with postmodernism. The work of Deleuze and Guattari is the highest expression and the most positive contribution of the postmodernist spirit.

OPPOSITION TO POSTSTRUCTURALISM

The main opposition to poststructuralist thought comes from Marxists belonging to the Hegelian tradition of anti-Cartesianism.[114] Those committed to the Cartesian tradition such as Anglo-American analytical philosophers, while being hostile to poststructuralism, seldom engage with it.[115] Marxists who have criticized poststructuralism are almost all intellectual descendants of the Frankfurt Institute for Social Research. The importance of this school of thought lies in its association with the reinterpretation of Marx's ideas in the 1920s and 1930s through Hegelian philosophy, through Max Weber's Nietzschean critique of rationality, through Heidegger's philosophy (in the case of Herbert Marcuse) and through Freudian psychology. Members of the school were particularly concerned with ideology, with mass culture and with the psychological characteristics which led to sympathy with authoritarian governments. This means that the Frankfurt Institute philosophers were already responding to the galaxy of ideas and problems from which poststructuralism emerged some thirty years later. They had already assimilated Nietzsche's ideas, and in most cases, no longer assumed the necessity of rational progress in history. But while French poststructuralists aligned themselves with Nietzsche in opposition to Hegel and the Hegelians, and opposed any notion of rational progress and any effort to achieve a comprehensive perspective on the world, members of the Frankfurt school and those influenced by them have ultimately set themselves in opposition to Nietzsche and have taken up Hegel's project of defending a broader notion of rationality, developing a comprehensive perspective on the world, and committed themselves to furthering the project of modernity.[116]

I will not directly review the debates between poststructuralists and Marxists. Instead, I will review efforts to address the environmental crisis, and Marxist and postmodernist ideas will then be evaluated in terms of how they orient people in relation to this crisis, how they enable the problems to be defined and their causes to be understood, and how they orient or fail to orient people for effective action to deal with these problems. To begin with I will consider the problem of defining the environmental crisis as such and consider the kinds of responses to the crisis generated by mainstream culture, that is, the culture permeated and dominated by Cartesian or Hobbesian thought, the main target of both Marxists and poststructuralists, and then examine first the Marxist critique of this, and then the postmodernist critique of both mainstream and Marxist environmentalism. This will be the subject of the next chapter.

3

POSTSTRUCTURALISM, MARXISM AND THE ENVIRONMENT

In the introduction to this book an article was quoted which spoke of massive injury to the earth's environment and claimed that humanity is in a war for survival, a war in which all nations must be allies. This implies that gaining universal recognition of a global environmental crisis is straightforward, and that there should be little difficulty in achieving universal consensus about its severity and significance. However the notion of a global environmental crisis is a social construct. To talk of 'massive injury to the environment', holes in the ozone layer, the rising level of carbon dioxide in the atmosphere and the possible effects of this on average global temperatures, to consider the total amount of land devoted to agriculture or covered by closed forests and to calculate the rate at which these are decreasing, to talk of resources and to measure the rate at which stocks are being depleted, is to invoke complex frameworks of concepts based on metaphors negotiated and sustained by practices of investigation which are themselves sustained by a large number of institutions of research, communication and administration, which are in turn sustained by political and economic institutions and processes of different kinds at local, national and global levels. As yet, there is no definitive social construct of the environmental crisis. The mass media presents one image of the global environmental crisis, scientific journals another, while economics journals scarcely recognize any but minor problems which can be solved by the proper functioning of the market. Scientists, economists and business leaders in the USA have dismissed environmentalists as cranks, while many political leaders in Third World countries see the claims of environmentalists as nothing more than an effort to prevent Third World countries sharing the benefits of industrialization. The majority of the world's population have no conception of a global environmental crisis at all. So how does one evaluate and respond to the claim that there is massive injury to the earth's environment and that humanity is in a war for survival, a war in which all nations must be allies?

There is no neutral way to answer this question. From the perspective

73

of mainstream culture it is a matter of investigating the evidence, of considering the possibility that more research is required, and then compiling more evidence until an objective answer can be reached and appropriate action decided upon. From the perspective of Marxists, to ensure that a judgement valid for the whole of humanity is obtained, it is necessary to take into account the pervading influence of class interests and, more fundamentally, the categories mediating social and economic relations. This is usually assumed to be a judgement made from the perspective of the universally oppressed class, the proletariat. However, poststructuralists are suspicious of all such globalizing claims and are more concerned to deconstruct all claims to a privileged stand-point. To gain any perspective on the environmental crisis, and to evaluate these different responses, all that can be done is to examine and then contrast the various stances on the issue.

MAINSTREAM CULTURE AND THE ENVIRONMENTAL CRISIS

Defining and evaluating the 'mainstream' approach to the environmental crisis is the most problematic. Even allowing the possibility of examining all the evidence to reach an objective conclusion does not guarantee a univocal answer to the question of whether there is a global environmental crisis. In *Ecological Communication*, Niklas Luhmann has argued against even the possibility of 'society' representing itself to itself and then defining problems for the whole of society. He argued that environmental problems are defined differently by the different function systems which make up society, that economics, law, science, politics, religion and education each have their own way of coding the world, and therefore their own way of defining environmental problems and responding to them.[1] If this is correct, then it is impossible to talk about *the* mainstream response to the global environmental crisis. While this argument has something to commend it, not every function system has equal power in society, and the way each function system codes the world is not unrelated to the way all other function systems code the world. One does not have to be a Marxist to recognize that it is the dynamism of the economy which has the most power to determine the direction of modern societies and the economy is the system to which all other function systems are constrained to adapt, and that it is what is defined as an economic problem which comes closest to defining what are taken to be the problems and goals of society as a whole. And the science of economics is so imperialistic that those engaged in studying other 'systems' are struggling to preserve their autonomy.[2]

Not only is economics the most influential and prestigious of the human sciences, expressing the perspective and assuming the coding of the most

74

powerful system of society, it is the social science most fully based on Cartesian forms of thought. Economics has its origins in efforts by Hobbes, Locke and Adam Smith to develop a conception of society on the model of physics, and the neo-classical economists or marginalists, Jevons, Walras and Menger, continued this project in the late nineteenth century.[3] The mainstream of twentieth-century economics is firmly based in this tradition. Following Hobbes, the economy is represented as analogous to a mechanical body in which money, equated with blood, distributes nutrients to the different parts and components of the system. To be understood, the whole must be analysed into its constituents, that is, economic actors, and explained in terms of them, that is, their quest to maximize their satisfaction and minimize their dissatisfaction. The model of explanation is a deductive system of mathematically expressible laws which, from a limited number of assumptions about the elementary constituents of the system, enables prediction of the functioning of the whole system, and of the effects of any interventions in the system.

Until very recently mainstream economics has been virtually blind to the environment. While Hobbes, as the founder of modern economics, saw the social body as being dependent on the fruits of the land, a view which was accepted by the Physiocrats in France, Smith developed Locke's labour theory of value and almost excluded from consideration the contribution of land to the wealth of nations. With the marginalists, all value was defined in terms of subjective preferences and exchanges within the market. As Dieter Groh and Rolf-Peter Sieferle have noted, with this development, '[e]conomic theory had ... been so particularized and instrumentalized that economic reality had taken on an appearance making industrial progress seem independent of any natural limit and essentially endless'.[4] This is the view which still prevails among economists. The winner of the 1987 Nobel Prize for economics, Robert Solow of MIT argued: 'The world can, in effect, get along without natural resources, so exhaustion is just an event, not a catastrophe.'[5]

However, with the commotion about environmental destruction, some mainstream economists have been addressing themselves to environmental problems, and environmental economics has become one of the fastest growing areas of economic science.[6] Some of this work is devoted to minimizing environmental concerns. Writing in *The Economist*, Professor William D. Nordhaus of Yale University argued that environmental destruction is of little significance:

> Greenhouse warming would have little effect on America's national output. About 3% of American GNP originates in climate-sensitive sectors such as farming and forestry. Another 10% comes from sectors only modestly sensitive – energy, water systems, property and construction. Far the largest, 87%, comes from sectors, including

most services, that are negligibly affected by climate change. . . . In sum, the impacts of climate change on developed countries are likely to be small, probably amounting to less than 1% of national income over the next half-century.[7]

Other economists are less sanguine. Following the central place given to the concept 'sustainable development' in *Our Common Future*, the report of the World Commission on Environment and Development chaired by Gro Brundtland, they have attempted to reformulate and utilize neo-classical economics to define sustainable paths of economic development. Typical of the work being produced by such economists is a report by David Pearce and others of 'The London Environmental Conference Economics Centre', *Blueprint for a Green Economy*.[8]

According to this report, the aim of environmental economics is to give increased emphasis to natural, built and cultural environments, to short- to medium-term *and* to long-term horizons, and to intra- and intergeneration equity, both within countries and between richer and poorer countries. In order to achieve this, a distinction is drawn between economic growth (increasing real GNP per capita), the traditional measure of economic performance, and economic development, which is conceived to have a much broader meaning, taking into account not only 'utility' which individuals experience, but also freedoms (including freedom from ignorance, poverty and squalor) and people's self-esteem and self-respect. It is taking these into account which makes imperative the appreciation of the direct and indirect contributions of natural and built environments, and which requires some measure of wealth, and more specifically, of natural capital stock, in order to properly evaluate economic performance. Sustainable economic development requires the maintenance of natural capital stock without this being achieved by depleting the stock of other countries. Such maintenance is best understood in terms of constancy of the economic value of the stock. Judging the sustainability of economic development therefore requires some way of measuring natural capital stocks, some way of accounting to monitor these stocks and some way of appraising capital investment projects which takes into account their impact on natural stocks. Then it is necessary to work out how to ensure that people make the best decisions, that is, the decisions which contribute most to economic development.

It is argued that the best way of estimating the value of the environment is by putting a monetary value on it, that is, by seeing what people are willing to pay to preserve it. While it is acknowledged that some things, for instance human life, cannot be evaluated in this way, it is argued that except for such rare cases, willingness to pay is a measure of the degree of people's concern for the environment. This is not meant to imply that value is nothing but a matter of subjective preference. Pearce and his colleagues allow that total economic value consists of user values, option values *and* intrinsic or existence values, the 'value that resides "in" something but which is captured by people through their preferences in the form of non-use value'.[9] Estimating value in monetary terms allows comparison between different benefits, and also has the advantage that values are expressed in terms that voters, politicians and civil servants are used to, and in a form which allows the techniques of cost-benefit analysis to be used to weigh up the advantages and disadvantages of decisions. A variety of techniques can be used to estimate monetary value, the most important of which is the 'contingent valuation method' which consists in asking people what they are willing to pay for a benefit and/or what compensation they would accept to tolerate a cost. It is also necessary to have an accounting system to effectively manage the environment, a system which gives a profile of the stocks available at a particular time, shows what uses are being made of stocks, and which, by ensuring that stock accounts and flow accounts are consistent, makes it possible to derive the balance sheet of any year from the balance sheet of the previous year together with the flow accounts of that year. While there are different ways of accounting for stocks, Pearce and his colleagues recommend monetary rather than physical accounting.

It is self-evident that sets of projects or programmes of governments should be assessed and put into effect in accordance with the objectives of society, and if the main objective of society is sustainable development and the value of the environment can be measured, then it should be a straightforward matter to take the environment into account in assessments. However in the private sector projects will be evaluated according to shareholder's perspectives. It is generally argued by environmental economists, including Pearce and his colleagues, that divergence between public and private interest can be minimized through regulation, and that the most effective form of regulation is the use of market incentives to reward private interests for acting in the public interest. Economists have such a high regard for the power of the market mechanism to achieve the best allocation of resources that they often call for the privatization of public property to ensure its proper conservation.[10] Where the free operation of the market results in prices which do not reflect true social costs of production and use, this can be rectified. For instance markets can compel those who pollute to pay, either by setting standards, by setting charges or taxes on the polluting product, or, and this is the favoured option of economists, by issuing pollution permits which will restrict pollution to tolerable levels, and then allowing these permits to be traded.[11] The use of carbon can be taxed to encourage enterprises to reduce their production of carbon dioxide, and taxes can be levied on non-renewable resources or resources which are difficult to renew (such as hardwood timber), which tend to be underpriced because people of the future cannot bid on present markets, to compensate for the loss of these to society.

The new environmentalism of the economists and policy scientists has been enormously influential. The idea of 'sustainable development' and the measures called for by economists have been embraced by business organizations and governments with enthusiasm. But in practice, mainstream proposals to deal with the environmental crisis have failed.[12] In particular, it has been found that utilizing the market through the issuing of tradeable pollution rights, tradeable rights to exploit resources, as well as charges for pollution and the exploitation of resources, has not achieved any significant reduction in pollution, diminution in the rate of exploitation of mineral reserves or reduction in the rate of destruction of resources.[13] Neither has regulation which sets allowable discharges or emissions had much effect in reducing global pollution.[14] The only legislation that has had real effect has been absolute bans on the exploitation of animal species or the use or production of particular types of material. Most improvements which have been made have been brought about by the pressure of direct action.

That such measures should have failed is a reflection on the limitations and defects of the market as a device for regulating economic, let alone social and political, activity. The argument of Nordhaus gives some indication of the nature of this blindness. It would follow from his argument about the insignificance of the greenhouse effect because of the negligible significance of agriculture to the economy that if breathable air were disappearing, this would be of no importance whatsoever, since breathable air affects 0 per cent of the economy. A further indication is the outlook of the World Bank's chief economist, Lawrence Summers, who argued that it is better policy to pollute areas where poor people live, because wages are lower and therefore the costs arising out of death and illness would be lower; and furthermore, that countries in Africa are underpolluted because they have clean air which is not being used to assimilate wastes.[15] Economists are blind because they take their abstract models of market exchanges for reality, leading them to assume that 'if money flows in an isolated circle, then so do some commodities; if money balances can grow forever at compound interest, then so can real GNP, and so can pigs and cars and haircuts'.[16] This is evident even in economists who are attempting to extend economic theory so that it takes into account environmental limitations. The future is taken into account, but future states are discounted, because this makes sense when thinking within the framework of monetary exchanges and evaluations. In short, the mainstream approach suffers from 'commodity fetishism'. It is Marx who grappled most profoundly with this issue.

MARXISM AND THE ENVIRONMENTAL CRISIS

From a Marxist perspective, environmental economics is attempting to solve environmental problems through the extension of the principles at the heart of the mode of production which is responsible for the global environmental crisis.[17] For Marx, the system which has come to dominate the world is capitalism, and it is the fetishism of commodities, that is, evaluating things in terms of their exchange or monetary value, precisely the way of thinking that environmental economists are extending even further, that is at the core of this system. It is seeing things as commodities which mystifies the relationship between nature and people and then prevents people understanding or controlling the system of which they are part. Through treating things as commodities, the natural conditions for human creativity become private property and are then treated as capital, while people's creative potential is reduced to labour power to be bought and sold on the market. Thinking in terms of money hides the power relations operating in society, the debasement of nature and people, the irrationality of a system where goods are produced not for use but to make a profit, the inevitable dynamism of an economic system in which firms, struggling for survival, must constantly improve their technology, extend their exploitation of nature and struggle for new markets, the growing instability of a society with unequal relations of power between component parts and no guarantee that consumption will equal production, and finally, the possibilities there might be for creating a better kind of society. It is only necessary to see what happens when capitalist forms of relationship penetrate and undermine traditional societies based on subsistence modes of production to see how environmentally destructive capitalism is. For example in New Guinea the dugong, now hunted in boats with outboard motors by people with unlimited wants who sell their catch to an insatiable market, is facing extinction. As Marx summed up the effect of capitalism:

> [J]ust as production founded on capital creates universal industriousness on one side – i.e. surplus labour, value-creating labour – so does it create on the other side a system of general exploitation of the natural and human qualities, while there appears nothing *higher in itself*, nothing legitimate for itself, outside the circle of social production and exchange. Thus capital creates the bourgeois society, and the universal appropriation of nature as well as of the social bond itself by the members of society. . . . For the first time, nature becomes purely an object for humankind, purely a matter of utility; ceases to be recognized as a power for itself; and the theoretical discovery of its autonomous laws appears merely as a ruse so as to subjugate it under human needs, whether as an object of consumption or as a means of production. In accord with this tendency, capital drives

beyond national barriers and prejudices as much as beyond nature worship, as well as all traditional, confined, complacent, encrusted satisfactions of present needs, and reproductions of old ways of life. It is destructive towards all this, and constantly revolutionizes it, tearing down all the barriers which hem in the development of the forces of production, and the exploitation and exchange of natural and mental forces.[18]

Marxism represents the Hegelian approach to the environmental crisis. Marxists are concerned to show that what is presented as a natural order by the ideologists of capitalism, essentially people dominated by Cartesian thinking, is a particular socio-cultural order which developed at a particular place at a particular time. For Marxists, Cartesian science is itself an historically conditioned product of this socio-cultural order.[19] While this socio-cultural order dominates the world at present, it is essentially irrational, and it has a tendency to undermine the conditions of its own existence. In doing so, it is paving the way for a more rational socio-cultural order, one in which people, acting in accordance with the categories which structure their social existence, will be able to realize rather than suppress the creative potential of humanity. While the Hegelianism in Marxist thought has predisposed Marxists to underrate the autonomous dynamics of nature, Marx's 'materialism' provides some counterbalance to his Hegelianism, and has facilitated the development of a strong environmentalist stream within the tradition of Marxism.[20]

While Marx and Engels occasionally considered environmental issues, the foundations for a systematic Marxist environmentalism were laid in Marx's lifetime when a Ukrainian socialist, Serhii Podolinski, attempted to reformulate Marx's theory of surplus value as appropriation of usable energy.[21] By focusing on energy, Podolinski revealed the extent of the exploitation of the peasantry, the exploitive relationship between different regions and the limits to economic development. Subsequently energism became a significant component of Marxism, particularly in Russia where it was developed by Bogdanov, the main target of Lenin's attack on Marxist revisionism in *Materialism and Empirio-Criticism*. Bogdanov's work is the ultimate source of, and a major representative of the tradition of environmentalist Marxism as opposed to Marxism-Leninism.

In reformulating Marxism through energetics, Bogdanov not only highlighted the limitations of and the need to conserve the natural environment,[22] but also criticized Marx's assumption that property relations are the sole basis of power relations, and rejected his analysis of socio-economic formations into bases and superstructures. For Bogdanov, what matters is not who owns the property but who organizes production, and so long as people do not organize their own productive activities, they will be oppressed. He argued that for this to be possible it would be necessary to create a new proletarian culture to replace the culture which reduced the working class to instruments of production. Such a culture would have to be such that people could control their own lives. This would require the development of a new, proletarian science, a science which would overcome the dualisms between mind and matter, idealism and materialism, that reflect the division of labour between organizers and workers under capitalism. He outlined the basics of this new science, a science of organization, in his three-volume work, *Tektology*,[23] which he described in his autobiography as 'a general study of the forms and laws of the organization of all elements of nature, practice and thought'.[24] This was an anticipation of, and arguably a superior version of, general systems theory, and included an early version of the theory of cybernetics.[25] After the October Revolution in 1917 Bogdanov set up a proletarian university and played a major part in the *Proletkul't* movement which he had inspired. This movement strove to create a new working-class culture as the condition for genuine socialism.[26] Although this movement was abolished by Lenin, along with the Worker's Opposition which had been partly inspired by *Proletkult* to establish industrial democracy, the Commissar for Education (or Enlightenment), Lunacharsky, was strongly influenced by Bogdanov, and encouraged efforts to create a new understanding of nature and humanity appropriate to a classless society.

The Commissariat of Education was also responsible for conservation, and in the 1920s Lunacharsky supported the development of a strong environmental movement and the development of the science of ecology. The most significant of the ecologists was Stanchinskii. Stanchinskii was the first person to trace the energy flows through ecosystems and to identify and give a mathematical formula for the energy transfers between 'trophic levels', showing how 'heterotrophs', those organisms which live by consuming 'autotrophs', the organisms which derive their energy directly from the sun, can only utilize a small proportion of the energy from the latter and can only be maintained with a fraction of their biomass. Stanchinskii argued that by studying the energy flows in a whole range of biocenoses (communities of organisms), humans would be able to calculate the productive capacities of these natural communities and would be able to structure their own economic activity in conformity with them. He saw his programme of research as an aid to achieving biotic protection of cultivated croplands and thereby overcoming the need to use harmful pesticides. Stanchinskii played a major part at the First All-Russian Congress for the Conservation of Nature held in September 1929, and argued that ecologists must play a major part in the formulation of the Five Year Plan, that conservation organizations must be able to review plan targets and monitor plan fulfilment. He argued that if civilization continues to disrupt the balance of natural communities it will eventually destroy itself. The Congress accepted his arguments and resolved:

The economic activity of man is always one form or another of the exploitation of natural resources. . . . The distinction and tempo of economic growth can be correctly determined *only* after the detailed study of the environment and the evaluation of its production capacities with the aim of its conservation, development and enrichment. This is what conservation is all about.[27]

The intellectual developments inspired by Bogdanov or supported by Bogdanov's disciples were all but eliminated in the Soviet Union (with the possible exception of his ideas on management).[28] However their insights are still important, and they have shown what can be achieved.

Concern for the environment by Western Marxists has been more sporadic. Opposition to instrumental rationality by the Frankfurt Institute philosophers was developed by Herbert Marcuse into a critique of the way the environment has been treated, but this was not developed in any depth.[29] The environment was taken up as an issue more vigorously in the 1970s by several Marxists, notably Richard England and Barry Bluestone in the USA and André Gorz in France.[30] The focus of these thinkers shifted to the imperatives of the market and how to overcome them. Richard England and Barry Bluestone, in what is still one of the best, if brief, Marxist analyses of the environmental crisis, argued the impossibility of solving the problem by the orthodox approach of 'internalizing externalities' through taxes on pollution.[31] Such an approach obscures the social conflict in the present system and in the tax reform, ignores the global dimension of the environmental crisis, ignores the political realities of a capitalist society and ignores several ecological realities of capitalist production and consumption that directly contribute to the ecological crisis.

The social conflict ignored is over who will suffer from environmental degradation and who will bear the cost of its protection. It is the poor who suffer most from pollution, in their workplaces, where they live and even where they holiday. They work in polluted environments, they are too poor to choose where they live and they cannot afford holidays which will get them away from it all. England and Bluestone predicted that taxes which ignore this reality will result in the poor bearing the burden of the cost for improvements in the environment of the affluent. These predictions have been borne out.[32] However it is the ignored global dimension of the environmental crisis which has come to be recognized as more significant. The effect of government regulation in affluent countries has been the resiting of polluting industries in the Third World. Pollution has been exported. However the biggest problem is that countries of the Third World have been virtually forced to destroy their environments for the benefit of the affluent of the First World. They have been exporting their minerals at very low prices, cutting down their rainforests and over-exploiting their land in order to survive in an economic struggle for development in a world system of unequal power relations. The situation is now far worse than when England and Bluestone wrote. Largely as a consequence of Third World debt, inequalities between nations are far greater, the exports of Third World countries have been devalued and environmental exploitation and destruction in the Third World expanded enormously.[33] Some improvements of environmental quality for the affluent of First World nations are insignificant when contrasted with the massive environmental destruction in the Third World.[34]

What is most important of all is that these social conflicts are not merely accidental side-effects of economic activity. They are the inevitable part of the expansion of a capitalist economy. A capitalist economy cannot be static. The basis of the whole economy is *material* growth. This means that in the long run, even if materials are processed efficiently, resources will be depleted and pollution will increase inexorably. As England and Bluestone put it,

> a private market economy is caught on a treadmill: to forestall mass unemployment, ever higher levels of consumption must be stimulated and ever higher levels of investment must be forthcoming. The environmental problem is that the presently required future increases in GNP will certainly result in the more rapid depletion of exhaustible resources and will tend to result in more pollution.[35]

This, in essence, is what James O'Connor, the editor of *Capitalism, Nature, Socialism*, has dubbed the second contradiction of capitalism.[36] Apart from this, the form which competition takes within capitalism generates more waste. It is not in the interest of firms to make durable products, but to promote products which will soon be obsolescent. Corporations then advertise to promote individual, rather than social, consumption. Through enormous expenditure on advertising what is created is an atomistic society of consumers forever striving for the latest product. One effect of this has been the rise of the private automobile at the expense of public transport, which from an environmental point of view, is far more efficient. Advertising has much expanded since 1973, and as was noted in Chapter 1, has resulted in a society of people who consume symbols rather than products. Consequently their demands are genuinely insatiable. It is this self-expanding system, now dominating the globe, associated with massive differences in power between individuals, governments, organizations and regions, which makes environmental rationality virtually impossible.

What Marxist environmentalism reveals is the virtual impossibility of solving environmental problems through the simple devices proposed by the environmental economists. But they also reveal the difficulties standing in the way of the state taking any more active role than manipulating the market. In the most powerful nations in the core zones of the world economy states are struggling from one crisis to the next, trying to control economies which are increasingly uncontrollable with very limited means to do so. As R.J. Johnston summed up the situation and its implications for the environment:

> [S]pecial interest groups tend to undermine resolute government, which uses short-term expediency to over-ride long-term commitments; political leaders prevaricate in the face of conflicting proposals and contradictory evidence; the authority of legislatures is eroded by the ability of special interest groups to evade regulation; citizens are weak when confronted with the power of the neocorporate state, and lack information necessary to counter that power; and pluralism is predicated upon compromise, but the fear of scarcity encourages confrontation and in such circumstances only the powerful are satisfied. In other words, the liberal-democratic state is largely oriented to the resolution of problems, but the potential environmental catastrophe facing the earth requires a solution that they cannot deliver.[37]

In the peripheries of the world economy effective political action is immeasurably more difficult. Most countries in these regions, regions containing most of the world's tropical rainforests, are struggling with massive foreign debts and declining terms of trade. They are manipulated politically and economically by more powerful nations and by transnational corporations, and their institutions are too weak and their populations are too uneducated and too socially fragmented to resist such manipulation. And this is an inevitable consequence of the different energy flows through core zone economies and transnational corporations on the one hand, and peripheral economies and their institutions on the other. The imperatives of economics and politics operative in the peripheries render sustainable development impossible. But so long as the peripheries of the global economy are powerless to deal with their problems, global environmental problems will remain unresolved. As Johnston argued, 'since the Third World . . . is but one component part of an integrated system of uneven development, if . . . [sustainable development] cannot be achieved there it cannot be achieved globally'.[38] Johnston concluded his study of the relationship between nature, the economy and the state by claiming that sustainability is not politically feasible while the capitalist mode of production prevails:

> [T]he creation of environmental problems is a product of the dominant mode of production in the world today, and the solution of those problems is difficult because the only institutions within which the

necessary collective action could be mobilised exist to promote the interests of that mode of production.[39]

Stephen Bunker, probably indirectly influenced by Bogdanov, has attempted to reformulate theories of the capitalist world-system, including theories of how states operate in this, through energetics, and in so doing has brought all the issues raised by ecological Marxists into clearer focus.[40] He argues that orthodox Marxist analyses of the reproduction of modes of production and of the relationship between global and regional economies must be revised to take account of the ecological interdependencies between extractive and resource-consuming economies, and to take account of the impacts of these relationships on natural ecosystems. By reformulating Marxist theory through energetics he has shown how the increased energy and material flows to productive societies have facilitated the substitution of human for non-human energies to increase their complexity and power, while the consequent reduced energy flows in peripheral societies have simplified them and reduced their power. Increased energy flows in the productive centres have made possible increases in scale, complexity and coordination of human activities, greater division of labour and the expansion of specialized fields of information. This has facilitated the development of increasingly complex systems of transport and communication and engendered the means for technological and administrative innovation, enabling these centres to change their technologies and thereby find substitutes for essential resources as these have been depleted. Conversely, extractive economies have lost energy and so become economically and socially simpler, less diversified and subject to the changes in market demand associated with new technologies produced by the centres. Under these circumstances, strategies tend to be adopted which maximize the short-term return to labour and capital, and which are little concerned with long-term social reproduction. Once the profit-maximizing logic of extraction for trade takes over, exploitation is concentrated on a limited number of resources at rates which disrupt the regeneration of these resources, the biotic community and associated geological and hydrological regimes. The development of state institutions in peripheral and semi-peripheral regions, being subject to manipulation by the productive centres of the world-economy, merely increases the rapidity of destructive exploitation of these regions. By exploiting such extractive economies, the industrial modes of production inevitably undermine the resource bases on which they depend; but they have evolved the social organizational and infrastructural capacity to change their own technologies and thereby to find substitutes for resources as they are depleted. However this process is finite as each new technology requires other resources from what is ultimately a limited stock.

The proposed Marxist solution to the global environmental crisis is a change in the mode of production which dominates the world from capitalism to socialism. But this raises the question, what is socialism? And is genuine socialism possible? One problem is that Marx himself seems to have conceived the future in terms of a mode of production which will be even more successful at dominating nature, giving rise to considerable debate among Marxists about whether and how Marx's ideas should be revised.[41] There is now almost universal consensus among Marxist environmentalists that socialism does not mean the centrally planned economy which existed in the Soviet Union, especially since the extent of environmental destruction caused by it was fully revealed after its collapse. However there is still no consensus on what socialism does mean. Rudolf Bahro, when he was still a Marxist, and André Gorz proposed alternative forms of socialism,[42] but they have not been received favourably, even by other Marxists.[43] At the most basic level, it means the extension of democracy to overcoming the alienation of people from nature, from each other, and from their own creative potential. But while for some this is consistent with the maintenance of a market, providing the means of production are publicly owned, others call for the dissolution of both the market and the state and the creation of self-sustaining communities, while others again argue that more powerful, though more democratic, states must be created.[44] Given Marxist environmentalist analyses of the present system of global capitalism, it follows that the establishment of a form of socialism able to deal with environmental problems will require some kind of delinking of regions, or at least the achievement of autonomy from the global economic system. So while it is accepted that genuine socialism demands decentralization of power in society and the development of industrial democracy, most Marxist environmentalists argue that it will also be necessary to develop strong states to achieve this delinking.[45]

Whatever institutions a socialist society is to be based upon, overcoming capitalism will require the creation and institutionalization of a new culture through which people will be able to define themselves and their potentialities in relationship to the potentialities of their own community, of humanity and of the rest of nature free from commodity fetishism. In the Hegelian sense, socialism will require the institutionalization of social and environmental rationality on a global scale so that people can be truly free.

POSTMODERN ENVIRONMENTALISM

While sympathetic to Marxist analyses of commodity fetishism and of the oppressive nature of capitalism, postmodern theorists are sceptical of the Marxist conception of humans, seeing it as continuing the technocratic orientation to nature of Western civilization and of capitalism. Post-modern environmentalists, that is, the 'deep ecologists' and associated movements (ecosophy, deep green and eco-feminism), are those who reject Euro-, anthropo- and andro-centricism, and the grand narratives of progress formulated in these terms.[46] Marx's criticisms of the categories dominating people's lives did not go far enough. As Jean Baudrillard argued:

> the system of political economy does not produce only the individual as labour power that is sold and exchanged: it produces the very conception of labour power as the fundamental human potential. More deeply than in the fiction of individuals freely selling their labour power in the market, the system is rooted in the identification of individuals with their labour power and with their acts of 'transforming nature according to human ends.'[47]

The rejection of this conception of humans is associated with a rejection of the conception of history as the progressive 'humanization' of nature and the destruction of all forms of life and modes of thinking standing in the way of this transformation.[48] Postmodernism is 'eco-centric'. It is associ-ated with respect for non-Western societies and cultures, for the previously suppressed ideas of minorities, for nature worship and Eastern religions and for non-human forms of life.[49]

While supporting new social movements, including the environmental movement, French poststructuralists have not been centrally concerned with the environment. However they have revived and contributed to the tradition of anti-Cartesian, anti-Hegelian, and more broadly, anti-Platonist thought begun by Nietzsche and Heidegger.[50] In particular they have supported Nietzsche's attack on the anti-naturalism of Western thought and Heidegger's attack on the technocratic orientation of Western civil-ization.[51] Heidegger is recognized by French philosophers as 'the first theoretician in the ecological struggle'.[52] And the ideas of the post-structuralists have been taken up by environmentalists in the USA to 'rethink resistance'.[53]

The importance of Nietzsche for the environmental movement has been pointed out by Max Hallman.[54] Nietzsche railed against Christianity for radically divorcing human beings from the natural world, and for radic-ally divorcing one aspect of human existence, the soul or spirit, from another aspect, the body or flesh, and for holding the latter in contempt. Nietzsche rejected the possibility of a transcendent world and criticized Western philosophy and Western religion for being other-worldly, and correlatively, rejected the dichotomy between humanity and nature, criticizing Western philosophy and religion for being anthropocentric. In *The Anti-Christ* Nietzsche argued that 'All the concepts of the Church are recognized for what they are: the most malicious false coinage there is for the purpose of *disvaluing* nature and natural values'.[55] Christian concepts are described as 'world-calumniating'.[56] This is associated with what Nietzsche referred to as 'an insane elevation of man above the world'.[57] In *The Will to Power* he suggested that

> Nature has been ill-judged to the extent to which one has brought into honour the anti-naturalness of a God. 'Natural' has come to mean the same as 'contemptible,' 'bad'. . . . With relentless logic one has arrived at the absolute demand to deny nature.[58]

Attacking anthropocentricism, Nietzsche wrote of the place of humanity in the cosmos:

> Man a little, eccentric species of animal, which – fortunately – has its day; all on earth a mere moment, an incident, an exception without consequences, something of no importance to the general character of the earth; the earth itself, like every star, a hiatus between two nothingnesses, an event without plan, reason, will, self-consciousness, the worst kind of necessity, *stupid necessity*.[59]

More generally, Nietzsche attacked the traditional metaphysical categories such as essence, thinghood, and selfhood which have underlain the exaltation of that which is, which endures through becoming, and which has been integrally related to the domineering orientation to nature and to the blindness to interdependence of humans and the rest of nature.[60] Rejecting the categories by which humans have devalued the world, Nietzsche argued:

> All the values by means of which we have tried so far to render the world estimable for ourselves and which then proved inapplicable and therefore devaluated the world – all these values are, psychologically considered, the results of certain perspectives of utility, designed to maintain and increase human constructs of domination – and they have been falsely *projected* into the essence of things. What we find here is still the *hyperbolic naïveté* of man: positing himself as the meaning and measure of the value of things.[61]

Finding out that the world may no longer be interpreted from this perspective therefore should be 'no longer any reason for devaluating the universe'.[62]

This 'perspectivism' was extended by Nietzsche to the whole universe. Nietzsche's new world conception, the world from *his* perspective, is a self-creating world of forces:

> The world exists; it is not something that becomes, it passes away, but it has never begun to become and never ceased from passing away – it maintains itself in both. . . . This world: a monster of energy,

without beginning, without end; a firm iron magnitude of force which does not grow bigger or smaller, that does not expend itself but only transforms itself . . . a sea of forces flowing and rushing together, eternally changing, eternally flooding back, with tremendous years of recurrence, with an ebb and flood of its forms . . . this, my *Dionysian* world of the eternally self-creating, the eternally self-destroying. . . . *This world is the will to power – and nothing besides!* And you yourselves are also this will to power – and nothing besides![63]

This is a perspective which acknowledges itself as a perspective of the will to power, but in doing so, acknowledges other perspectives:

Every centre of force adopts a perspective toward the entire remainder, i.e., its own particular valuation, mode of action, and mode of resistance. The 'apparent world,' therefore, is reduced to a specific mode of action on the world, emanating from a centre. Now there is no other mode of action whatever; and the 'world' is only a word for the totality of these actions.[64]

Consequently, Nietzsche argued: 'It is obvious that every creature different from us senses different qualities and consequently lives in a different world from that in which we live'.[65] This means that a 'thing' consists wholly of the diverse interpretations of it, that

A thing would be defined once all creatures had asked 'what is that?' and had answered their question. Supposing one single creature, with its own relationships and perspectives for all things, were missing, then the thing would not yet be 'defined'.[66]

As Max Hallman pointed out, this implies that 'with each loss of species there is a loss of one set of relationships and perspectives, and "reality" itself becomes poorer and less defined'.[67]

At the same time, however, Nietzsche celebrated the subjugation of the weak by the strong. His philosophy could be used to justify the total technological domination of nature by humans.[68] Heidegger argued that Nietzsche's notion of 'will to power' is still an expression of the tradition of Western metaphysics – and so is still too oriented towards domination of the other. For Heidegger, morality must be rooted in an *ethos*, an abode or dwelling place – the open region in which man dwells. He quoted with approval Heraclitus' phrase: 'Man dwells, insofar as he is man, in the nearness of god.'[69] Proper dwelling is nearness to Being, bearing witness to beings, letting things be. Heidegger was concerned to show where Western civilization went off the rails as the necessary, if not sufficient condition, of becoming again 'shepherds of Being'. Cartesian and Marxist thought were both condemned by Heidegger for their commitment to the domination of the world and for their failure to care for the Being of beings.

For Heidegger, all modern political systems, including Marxist political systems, are metaphysical and humanistic, and therefore part of the problem. They are the product of the long collusion between Greek metaphysics and Christian theology; they are dominated by onto-theology, and correspondingly, by science and a form of technology which only reveals the world as objects to be controlled. Consequently people organized by such political systems no longer dwell within their possibility:

> It is first the will which arranges itself everywhere in technology that devours the earth in the exhaustion and consumption and change of what is artificial. Technology drives the earth beyond the developed sphere of its possibility into such things which are no longer possibility and are thus the impossible.[70]

Correlative to the reduction of the world to objects, instruments at hand and to truth conceived of as certainty, modern philosophy posits a realm of values to deal with the issue of what is the ultimate point of controlling the world. If there are any challenges to the ways in which things are being done, to the goals being pursued, then this is seen as an issue of values. For instance environmentalists decrying not only the destruction of the environment for its effect on humans but because nature is seen to have a significance independent of human purposes call for a recognition of the intrinsic value of nature.[71] But the notion of value is rooted in Cartesian dualism. It is simply to call upon the subjective side of the subjective/objective divide to compensate for the 'devaluation' of the objective world by science. But then this subjectivizes all significance of the world. Consequently Heidegger argues that to ascribe value to anything is to debase it:

> [T]hrough the characterization of something as 'a value' what is so valued is robbed of its worth. That is to say, by the assessment of something as a value what is valued is admitted only as an object for man's estimation. . . . Every valuing, even where it values positively, is a subjectivizing. It does not let beings be.[72]

With unparalleled perspicacity, Heidegger has not only shown what it is about Western civilization which has driven people to be so environmentally destructive, but has shown why efforts to confront this crisis (by calling for the attribution of a higher value to nature) simply reinforce the forms of thinking responsible for environmental destruction. By revealing the problem we are at least provided with some direction for thinking about alternatives.

What have poststructuralists contributed to the insights of Nietzsche and Heidegger? To begin with, they have furthered the analyses revealing the drive to domination in Western thought, and thereby have helped to legitimate discourses, suppressed by the dominant discourses of science and by Marxism, which are not oriented towards the domination of the world and which accord more with a way of dwelling within the world which lets things be. They have also gone beyond language as such to investigate the institutional context of discourses and to show the way power operates in these. Finally, they have defended a new kind of political practice.

Derrida's work, supported in this by Lacan's psychology, is important for revealing how the domination of society by power groups and orientations to the world destructive of the environment are made to appear natural and inevitable. Derrida's project of deconstruction furthers Heidegger's critique of onto-theology and the domineering orientation to the world which it supports. But Derrida is also critical of Heidegger, rejecting in the spirit of Nietzsche, the anthropocentricism and ethnocentricism implicit in Heidegger's identification of the history of Being with the history of Western culture, and in treating Western culture and language as the house of Being – 'the last sleeping shudder of the superior man'.[73] Lacan is important for having revealed the way in which the symbolic order constitutes people as gendered subjects, in which the opposition between the masculine and the feminine is correlated with a sequence of oppositions. These oppositions impel, or at least constrain people to celebrate active domination as 'masculine' in opposition to 'feminine' passive receptivity. Lacan's analysis of this is supported by the research of Genevieve Lloyd, Brian Easlea and Carolyn Merchant, who have shown the extent to which people in Western civilization have been dominated by a privileged set of concepts identified with transcendence of the material world and equated with masculinity, defined in opposition to a suppressed set of concepts equated with femininity and the world of matter.[74]

At least as important in accounting for environmental destruction is the poststructuralist explanation of the consumption ethic – the ethic which, as Nicholas Xenos has shown, has created for the first time a state of universal scarcity in a world where human productive powers have never been greater.[75] Why cannot people be satisfied when their needs are satisfied? Because, as Lacan points out, they are driven by desire – gratification in and through the perspective of the 'other' upon themselves. There is desire to take the place of the 'other', desire to be what the other desires and desire for the object of the other's desire. Satisfiable need gets lost in the demand for love and admiration which can never be satisfied. This is exacerbated in Western culture by the special emphasis upon individuality and selfhood, which generates a special dynamism and drivenness. Attempting to gain success and happiness through such egotism amounts to a Death-drive. Correspondingly, for Baudrillard, Marx is not only, or even primarily defective in accepting the capitalist work-ethic. In wielding the concept of use-value, the principle of needs

91

against capital, Marx is under the spell of the capitalist consumption-ethic. Consequently, in modern societies 'a revolution has occurred in the capitalist world without our Marxists having wanted to comprehend it'.[76] Capitalist economies have moved 'from the form-commodity to the form-sign, from the abstraction of the exchange of material products under the law of general equivalence to the operationalization of all exchanges under the law of the code'.[77] We now live under a regime of controlled signs. We are faced with 'a structure of control and of power much more subtle and more totalitarian than that of exploitation'.[78] We are faced with 'the symbolic destruction of all social relations not so much by the ownership of the means of production but by *the control of the code*'.[79] It is this development, the possibility of which is explained by Lacanian psychology, which has entrapped people into an orgy of conspicuous consumption which can only end in the exhaustion of the earth's resources.

Poststructuralism not only exposes the structures which make environmental destruction appear inevitable and which constitute people as the agents of this destruction; it has been called upon to explain why environmentalists are failing in their struggle, and to show them how to be more effective. As Peter Quigley argued:

> Resistance movements, including the ecology movement, find themselves in disarray and in danger of becoming ineffective. . . . Because traditional and contemporary postures of ecological resistance share too many features with the power structure they wish to oppose, they could benefit from a thorough reconsideration in light of post-structural philosophy, which provides the basis for a sweeping resistance movement.[80]

According to Quigley, there is a tendency for resistance movements to continue positing some absolute, supposedly given as immediately present. Typical of environmentalists, Catherine Ingram suggests that 'we have forgotten a wisdom of the wild; we have forgotten our own spontaneity and intuitiveness'.[81] This is still logocentric, and affirms the deepest values of the structure it purports to oppose. It reinforces the idea that there is some absolute truth, and this gives some privileged group the authority to rule the rest of society. Such logocentricity is evident in some, although not all, eco-feminists.[82]

Logocentric thinking is also associated with efforts to subsume diversity under identity, to reduce the other to the same. Jim Cheney, in his postmodern critique of radical environmentalism, argues that there are strong authoritarian tendencies in environmentalist thought due to this refusal to acknowledge difference.[83] He argues against the claim that all knowers are essentially alike, and hence are able to resolve differences by appeal to objective standards of reason. Each person's history and place in the world is distinct, and their perspectives incommensurable with all others. The thesis of the sameness of all knowers can only be an ideological tool designed to coerce agreement, to socialize people to a particular conception of reality. There are potentially an infinite number of truths corresponding to the equally infinite number of different places that people inhabit in the world, and to claim that any position has priority over other positions is to be engaged in a rhetorical exercise in order to justify and enforce domination.[84] Cheney calls for respect for otherness, letting differences exist without any pressure to compromise so that each entity is given full latitude to develop the way that best expresses its own individual existence.

While Derrida has been concerned to deconstruct the privileging of certain discourses, Lacan has exposed the patterns of oppositions which lead to the celebration of domination, and Lacan and Baudrillard have revealed the insatiable forms of desire which lead to the celebration of wasteful consumption, Barthes and Lyotard have examined the kinds of narratives which have dominated Western civilization, and, in the case of Lyotard, how grand narratives of progress have devalued local narratives and local knowledge. The identification and recognition of the pervasiveness of the Western forms of narrative, revealing how subjects are constituted as gendered, how the goal of males is represented as the conquest of the world presaging a final but ever-deferred return to an impossible unity, and how females are represented as the passive (although insatiably demanding) bystanders or prizes for the winners in this struggle for conquest, provides the key to understanding how the conceptual oppositions revealed by Lloyd, Merchant and Easlea are assimilated and come to dominate people's lives. Revealing this has provided support for the efforts of eco-feminists and other environmentalists to revive the suppressed discourses of women and non-Europeans in opposition to partriarchal Western discourses (provided these are not in turn raised as absolutes).

Jim Cheney has taken up this critique of master discourses and grand narratives and has argued for their replacement by 'contextual discourse'.[85] Contextual discourse is not concerned with overall coherence, but is a mosaic which can serve as a tool for many purposes, including the articulation of human interaction with the land which ensures the health of the land and the community. On this basis Cheney has defended the contextualized language of traditional cultures such as Native Americans and Australian Aboriginals for bridging subject and object worlds, inner and outer. Following Alasdair MacIntyre's suggestion that to answer the question 'What am I to do?' it is necessary to answer the prior question 'Of what story or stories do I find myself a part?' Cheney has argued for bio-regional narratives as the basis for an environmental ethics:

> Narrative is the key then, but it is narrative grounded in geography rather than in a linear, essentializing narrative self. . . . What I

propose is that we extend these notions of context and narrative outward so as to include not just the human community, but also the land, one's community in a larger sense. Bioregions provide a way of grounding narrative without essentializing the idea of self. . . . What we want then is language that grows out of experience and articulates it, language intermediate between self and world, their *intersection*, carrying knowledge of both, knowledge charged with valuation and instruction. . . . The task then is to tell the best stories we can. The tales we tell of our, and our communities' 'storied residence' . . . are tales not of universal truth, but of local truth, bioregional truth.[86]

Cheney saw the development of such bio-regional narratives as also a solution to the fragmentation of the postmodern world:

[B]eyond the project of deconstruction is the goal of health and well-being, which is the primary reason for introducing the idea of bioregional narrative. . . . The fractured identities of postmodernism . . . can build health and well-being by means of a bioregional contextualization of self and community. The voices of health will be as various and multiple as the landscapes which give rise to them – landscapes which function as metaphors of self and community and figure into those mythical narratives which give voice to the emergence of self and community. The notion of socially constructed selves gives way to the idea of bioregionally constructed selves and communities. In this way, bioregionalism can 'ground' the construction of self and community without the essentialization and totalization typical of the various 'groundings' of patriarchal culture.[87]

The construction of such bio-regional narratives would not take us very far without some understanding of the workings of power, and particularly the workings of power in institutions and the relationship between power and knowledge. Foucault's work is important for precisely this reason, and although Foucault was not concerned with environmental problems, an understanding of how discursive formations are established and how they develop, of how power operates and how people are controlled, and of the role of 'knowledge' in this, is necessary for a proper appreciation of the forces at work in environmental destruction. Foucault's work deals with the kinds of institutions which interested the Marxist, Antonio Gramsci, but instead of assuming these to be the creations of the capitalist ruling class in its effort to 'organize consent', as Gramsci argued, Foucault maintained that the emergence of and transformations within discursive formations are autonomous and have been the condition for the development of capitalist society and for the power of the ruling class. If, as Foucault (and also Luhmann) has argued, knowledge is produced and sustained by discursive formations or social systems as part of their own process of reproduction, it becomes clear why it is so difficult to gain and validate the knowledge required to put environmental problems in the kind of perspective necessary to mobilize appropriate action. The work of Deleuze and Guattari, revealing the relationship between desire, power and interest and what leads people to struggle for power or to subordinate themselves to institutions of power, contributes further to Foucault's work on the relationship between knowledge, power and social control. If their ideas are valid, a different kind of political action is called for than envisaged by Marxists.

Even if we accept these analyses of the operation of power, there is still a problem of what action environmentalists can take. By rejecting any stand-point outside the system by which it could be judged, by condemning as the problem the strong subject capable of defining goals and mobilizing to achieve these, poststructuralists are only able to generate a fragmented opposition. However, Foucault, Deleuze and Guattari have defended such fragmented opposition.[88] In a recorded conversation published in 1972, Foucault and Deleuze considered the relationship between their work and political practice.[89] Foucault suggested that we have not yet fully comprehended the nature of power. Notions such as 'ruling class', 'to dominate', 'to rule', 'to govern', are far too fluid, and require analysis. Consequently, we are only beginning to find adequate forms of political struggle. What emerged from the conversation was that the old idea of intellectuals developing theory to be put into practice, or representing the interests of others, could no longer be considered acceptable. Theory must be regarded as practice, as an instrument or tool which must be useful or thrown away. Theories should be local and related to a limited field. It is these ideas which were developed by Deleuze and Guattari and received their fullest formulation in *A Thousand Plateaus* with the development of the concept of the rhizome. This concept not only provides an alternative to onto-theological thinking, but also provides a different way of thinking about politics. Although it is not fully spelt out and developed, Deleuze and Guattari are proposing a 'nomadic' politics based on local action against the massive 'sedentary' institutions which now dominate each nation and the world as a whole, action which will work against and finally overcome these institutions – as weeds gradually take over gardens.

This political philosophy provides support for the political orientation of the deep ecologists and other radical environmentalists. In grappling with political questions, Arne Naess, the philosopher who coined the term 'deep ecology', concluded:

> We need not agree upon any definite utopia, but should thrash our
> limited programmes of political priorities within the framework of

present political conflicts. . . . 'Everything hangs together.' This is still a good slogan. One consequence of the interrelatedness is that we all have the capacity to do something of relevance within a framework of our own interests and inclinations. *The ecopolitical frontier is immensely long* but we can only work effectively at one place at a time. It is more than long, it is multidimensional, and the pull of the pole of greenness can be felt in all our political positions and actions.[90]

Naess has promoted Ghandi's ideas of non-violent action as the best way of achieving results. However, other deep ecologists call for violent action. Such action, the sabotage of environmentally destructive enterprises, 'monkeywrenching', a strategy vigorously promoted by Dave Foreman of *Earth First!*,[91] also accords with the new kind of politics called for by Deleuze and Guattari.[92] The best example of postmodern politics in action is that of the Chipko movement of Northern India which has succeeded in putting a stop to logging and other environmentally destructive activities in the Garwhal Himalaya. This movement 'is the result of hundreds of decentralized and locally autonomous initiatives. Its leaders and activists are primarily village women, acting to protect their means of subsistence and their communities.'[93] The conclusion drawn by Vandana Shiva from her study of environmental problems and the struggles against them shows the accord between postmodern politics and environmentalism as it is actually practiced:

> Those who dare to think of solutions are precisely those who were declared incapable of thinking. Like the women in the Third World, they are clear that the man of the modern west is exposed today as a bundle of irrationalities, threatening the very survival of human-kind. When we find that those who claimed to carry the light have led us into darkness and those who were declared to be inhabiting the dark recesses of ignorance were actually enlightened, it is but rational to redefine categories and meanings. Recovering the femin-ine principle as respect for life in nature and society appears to be the only way forward, for men as well as women, in the North as well as the South.[94]

POSTSTRUCTURALIST, MARXIST AND MAINSTREAM ENVIRONMENTALISM

I have presented the different responses to the environmental crisis, from mainstream economics and policy-making, to Marxist and neo-Marxist analyses of exploitation, commodity fetishism and the global capitalist system, to Nietzschean, Heideggerian and poststructuralist critiques of the domineering orientation of the European civilization, as a dialectical progression. In this way I have evaluated them by presenting them as a sequence in which each later response is an effort to reveal and overcome the deficiencies of the earlier response or responses. But this presentation has been very sketchy. I have not attempted to explore all the achievements and defects of each set of ideas. To provide a fuller analysis of the achievements and limitations of the ideas involved I will now consider them and present them as a dialectical progression in reverse order.

The development of postmodern culture has revealed how oppressive the idea of progress driving Western civilization has been, and has revealed the tendency for those who oppose it to reduplicate the forms of thinking causing the oppression. However, while Nietzsche, Heidegger, the poststructuralists, and also the postmodernists who have appropriated their ideas, provide considerable insight into Western civilization's orientation towards domination, they leave it crucially unclear how people should respond to the present situation. These thinkers have represented people as constituted by language or by discursive formations. Heidegger saw the primary function of language as 'disclosing' the world, and people as merely fulfilling a destiny they have no part in creating. He wrote:

> No one can foresee the radical changes to come. But the technological advance will move faster and faster and can never be stopped. In all areas of his existence, man will be encircled ever more tightly by the forces of technology.[95]

Consequently he paid no attention to praxis, that is, to ethics and political philosophy addressing the issue of how to act, how to live and how to organize society.[96] The work of Derrida, Lacan and Lyotard is also of little help in this regard, despite the efforts of Derrida to demonstrate the political relevance of his work.[97] And the relativism argued for by those influenced by Derrida would fragment all oppositional political movements completely, and make any concerted response to the environmental crisis impossible.[98] Ultimately the effect of the social critiques of thinkers such as these is to disempower people.

Foucault adds little to this. All people, including those designated as powerful, are represented as constituted by the power relations which govern them anonymously, and his analysis of power is limited to discursive formations. By dissolving individuals into these formations and conceiving of rationality as itself a form of domination, he has blurred the distinctions between power, domination and resistance to domination. While arguing for local resistance, he has difficulty even justifying this. As Nicos Poulantzas argued:

> It has often been said that one can deduce from Foucault nothing more than guerrilla war and scattered acts of harassment of power; but in fact, no kind of resistance is possible if we follow Foucault's analyses. For if power is already there, if every power situation is

immanent in itself, *why should there ever be resistance? From where* would resistance come, and *how would it be even possible?*[99]

Deleuze and Guattari's concept of originating desire provides a possible answer to this question, but for this to be the basis for action it is necessary to distinguish 'good' desires from 'bad' desires. As committed Nietzscheans, Deleuze and Guattari promote desires based on affirmation rather than those based on negation or reaction, but in practice they define 'good' desires as simply those which negate the desires which augment the power of the state. The promotion of such desires in the United States over the last thirty years appears to have produced a fatter, less intelligent, more suicidal and more murderous population. The lifestyle of the ruling classes in Brazil illustrate the effect of the liberation of these desires. This is hardly a satisfactory basis for addressing the environmental crisis.

More importantly, while the analyses of how power operates in interpersonal relations and discursive formations is important, there is far more involved in the inexorable destruction of the environment than this kind of power. Capitalism has evolved into a differentiated system which now envelops the globe, and in this system, massive oppression and exploitation of vast regions of the world by the core zones of the global economy are inevitable. Individual states are part of a system of states situated within this differentiated economy, engaged in a struggle to augment their own power and to preserve or change the status of their region within the global system, to exploit other regions, to resist exploitation or to suppress local populations to facilitate exploitation by other regions. Poststructuralists fail to provide the framework necessary to analyse all aspects of power in particular societies, let alone the power relationships between the core and the peripheral zones of the worldeconomy, between productive and extractive economies and between states. While poststructuralist analyses of power in discourse and discursive formations can be utilized, to understand the dynamics of global environmental destruction and then to orient people for action it is necessary to put these analyses in perspective, to see them in relation to a broader concept of power which can serve to analyse the global system of capitalism.

The inability to provide the orientation necessary to respond to the environmental crisis as a whole points to another problem with poststructuralism. By abjuring any recourse to grand narratives or to any reference point beyond the immediate situation, poststructuralists are simply committed to the defence of local knowledge and local power against global knowledge and global power.[100] This celebration of local knowledge could just as easily serve to justify the extermination of Indians and the vigorous exploitation of natural resources by the local frontiersmen of the Amazon in defiance of state directives and public opinion in the affluent nations as to justify the Chipko movement in northern India. More fundamentally, by supporting the postmodernist dissolution of perspective, poststructuralists not only fail to reveal the interconnectedness of environmental problems and the global causes of the environmental crisis, but invalidate the efforts of those who are striving to reveal them. For poststructuralists, the notion of a 'global environmental crisis' can be deconstructed and shown to serve the power of those who are attempting to mobilize people to address it. And, with their opposition to extra-texts beyond the text and to texts which would sum up other texts, to grand narratives which would put all local narratives in perspective, poststructuralists leave environmentalists no way to defend their belief that there is a global crisis or to work out what kind of response is required to meet it. Poststructuralists come very close to the conservative sociology of Niklas Luhmann. They are bound by assumptions which make the idea of a global environmental crisis incomprehensible.

This inability to deal with the phenomenon of a global environmental crisis manifests the loss of contact with the world. While this might not have been the intention of poststructuralists, the way they have developed their scepticism about any simple relation between language (or texts) and 'reality' has engendered, or at least supported, a form of idealism in which intellectual life is increasingly centred on discussion of what other people have said, in which, as Baudrillard put it:

> Theoretical production, like material production, is ... losing its determination and is beginning to spin on its own, disconnectedly, *en abîme*, towards an unknown reality. Today we are already at that point: in the realm of undecidability, in the era of *floating theories*, like floating currencies. Every current theory, from whatever horizon it originates (including psychoanalysis), with whatever violence it arms itself, pretending to recover an immanence or fluidity without referent (Deleuze, Lyotard, etc.) – all are floating, and their only purpose is to signal one another.[101]

The continuing destruction of the global environment despite this incomprehension is a refutation of 'poststructuralist idealism'.

In their failure to orient people for action, their attack on rationality *per se* as a form of oppression, their effort to liberate suppressed desires, their rejection of perspective and finally, their loss of contact with any reality beyond language and texts, poststructuralists are expressing the spirit of postmodern culture, and the failures of the poststructuralists are revelations of the defects of this culture.[102] It is these defects which account for the career of the environmentalist cause in the affluent West. There is widespread support in the postmodern era for environmental concerns, and postmodern people, being sceptical of the notion of progress, are sympathetic to diversity, and respect cultures and groups throughout the world which are being crushed by 'progress'. Postmodernism is also associated with the development of and tolerance for what appear to be radically alternative ways of thinking and of understanding the world to those which have dominated Western civilization and which have been associated with aggression towards nature. Deep ecology, eco-feminism and the New Age movement can be regarded as examples of this, all contributing to the green movement, promoting a greater respect for nature and for the creation of a new social order free from such aggression. Yet hardly any of this support has translated into effective action, into changing the way people live and the way the economy is organized to make society less environmentally destructive. The postmodern politics championed by Arne Naess is not enough. In fact James Lovelock has suggested that the green movement, with its opposition to all industry and its contempt for science and technology, has been a potent force preventing the requisite environmental reform.[103] What has been generated by such environmental respect has been 'cosmetic environmentalism', displays of environmental concern without substance. Neither Nietzsche nor Heidegger nor the poststructuralists have anything to offer to overcome this situation.

So while it is unlikely that the environmental crisis can be properly defined, let alone overcome, without taking into account the insights of Nietzsche, Heidegger and the poststructuralists on the nature of Western culture and its Eurocentric, anthropocentric, domineering orientation towards the world, these insights will have to be absorbed into a comprehensive system of thought which is able to analyse and relate everything from the world ecosystem and the global system of capitalism and Western civilization to the lives of individuals struggling to come to terms with their situations in the world.[104] Rather than abasing itself before local popular culture this system must be able to reveal the defects in the cultural forms dominating people's lives, the contradictions and deficiencies in people's reflective thinking and embodied in their social practices, institutions and social and economic formations. It must then provide people with new ways of defining themselves and their relationships to each other and to nature to overcome these deficiencies, and reveal to them how they can act effectively. That is, while it is necessary to reject the Cartesian belief in the possibility of truly representing reality and to recognize such beliefs as part of an oppressive and destructive culture, it is necessary to affirm the quest for perspective and the commitment to rationality in the tradition of Hegelianism. What appears to be required then is a radicalized Marxism, a Marxism freed of all neo-Platonic tendencies to reduce particulars to means for the realization of Man's destiny to totally dominate the world, a Marxism which is not only able to focus attention on environmental destruction, and on the nature of cultural forms with some autonomy from the economy, but which is able to question the blindness to the significance of nature, and obversely, the celebration of agency, of human creativity and of history as universal progress on which not only capitalism, but the whole of European civilization has been based.

It could be argued that such a form of Marxism was already fore-shadowed in Marx's own writings and in the work of Bogdanov, although not fully developed. Marx was just as much committed to recognizing the primacy of becoming over being as Nietzsche. The fetishism of commodities was recognized by Marx as equivalent to the Platonic celebration of reified abstractions at the expense of the changing sensible world. At the same time he rejected the reification of history and the conception of history as the unfolding of Man's potential as vehemently as the poststructuralists who attributed this view to him. According to Marx, the effect of such reification of history and man is that 'the historical appears as something separated from ordinary life, as something extra-superterrestrial. With this the relation of man to nature is excluded from history and hence the antithesis of nature and history is created.'[105] What mattered to Marx were people struggling to come to terms with their particular circumstances, and this precluded any final, monolithic view of the development of humanity. Marx severely criticized those who presented such views, or who attributed such views to him. In a letter written in November 1877 and addressed but not sent to the editor of a Russian literary-political journal attacking a review of his work, Marx described how Ancient Rome had produced a situation very similar to that of late feudal Europe: peasants were expropriated from the means of production and subsistence in an economic formation consisting of large land ownership and large-scale capitalism. But instead of the dispossessed selling their labour-power they became an idle mob, and instead of a capitalist production system, a system developed based on slave labour. Marx concluded from this:

> Thus events of a striking analogy, because they took place in a different historical milieu, led to entirely different results. If one studies each of these developments by itself and then compares them with each other, one will easily find the key to each phenomenon, but one would never thereby attain a universal key to a general historical-philosophical theory, whose greatest advantage lies in its being beyond history.[106]

This attack on the idea of history as universal progress concurs with Marx's earlier attack in the *Theses on Feuerbach* on the contemplative materialism of Feuerbach where he argued that knowers and knowledge must be considered as part of the material world being understood, that the educators themselves must be educated, that consequently it is impossible to judge the validity of theories until they have been acted upon and made part of social reality: 'Man must prove the truth, i.e., the reality over the reality or non-reality of thinking which is isolated from practice is a purely *scholastic* question.'[107] On this view there can be no question of arriving at a stand-point from which some final, eternally valid knowledge of humanity and its destiny could be gained.

It is these insights of Marx which are supported by the work of Bogdanov, even if Bogdanov failed to consistently support these ideas. In an early work published in 1908, a utopian novel, *Red Star*, for the most part set on Mars where communism had already been achieved, Bogdanov questioned the inevitability of progress on Earth, the possibility of a final, perfect social order, and implicitly questioned the anthropocentricism of socialists. *Red Star* is the story of Leonid, a communist revolutionary who after the attempted revolution of 1905 is taken to Mars. There he is at first impressed by the harmony and fullness of life brought about by the communist revolution. However it soon appears that this harmony is superficial, that Mars is suffering an environmental crisis. The people of Mars have created a Colonial Group in their government and are preparing to create colonies on Earth or Venus, or both, to replenish Mars' resources, and are considering eradicating human life to enable them to exploit the Earth's resources. One Martian, Sterni, takes the position that Earthlings are so hopelessly malformed by their evolutionary past that even the Earth's socialist minority would never be able to work together amicably with their fellow socialists on Mars. To prevent a long guerrilla war of resistance, Sterni argues that the Earthlings should be wiped out in advance, painlessly, with death rays so that the riches of Earth can be used to build a more humane socialism on Mars. He argues: 'There is but one life in the Universe, and it will be enriched rather than impoverished if it is *our* socialism rather than the distant, semibarbaric Earthly variant that is allowed to develop.' Netti replies:

> 'There is but one Life in the Universe,' says Sterni. And yet what does he propose to us? That we exterminate an entire individual type of life, a type which we can never resurrect or replace.... [T]he Earthlings are not the same as we. They and their civilization are not simply lower and weaker than ours – they are *different*. If we eliminate them we will not replace them in the process of universal evolution but will merely fill in mechanically the vacuum we have created in the world of life forms.[108]

Similarly, the critical theorists of the Frankfurt School, in developing their version of Marxism to assimilate Freudian psychiatry and Nietzschean, Weberian and Heideggerian critiques of modernity, rejected the conception of history as the progressive and inevitable transformation of nature for human ends. Work by critical theorists is as much opposed to 'arboreal' political organization as Deleuze and Guattari, being radically opposed to Leninist and Stalinist forms of centralized control of political movements and justifying political action on multiple fronts to deal with different forms of oppression. However, while conceiving people as socially and culturally constituted, this form of Marxism does not dissolve individuals into their contexts, and it provides a place for reason in the struggle against domination. While Adorno analysed the weak, fragmented, narcissistic subjects engendered by late capitalism in terms similar to those of the poststructuralists, for him such subjects are degenerate. He suggested the possibility of people in favourable circumstances attaining some degree of rational autonomy. This idea has been developed much further by Habermas. For Habermas, communicative reason is quite different from and much broader than the instrumental form of reason which, through its 'colonization of the life-world', can be held responsible for much of the oppressiveness of modern civilization. With the development of 'ego-identity' in place of 'role-identity', personal identity is no longer determined by an unreflectively inherited cultural tradition, but is defined by procedures of critical examination and argumentation employed in the acquisition of cognitive and moral beliefs. Through such critical reflection it is possible for people to assess their cultural tradition, to reveal its contradictions and forms of oppression, and to establish new norms and values. What is needed is the preservation of public spheres free from coercion within which such critical reflection can take place.

While there are limitations in the ideas of Marx, Bogdanov and the Frankfurt Institute philosophers, it would appear that there is a common rejection of the neo-Platonism which, if consistently thought through, might enable their various insights to be united into a new form of Marxism. It is such a form of Marxism which seems to be emerging from the response of Marxists to the failure of the Soviet Union and to radical environmentalists. Ted Benton, Richard Levins and David Harvey in particular have been reviewing the ideas of radical, postmodern environmentalists, recovering to some extent the impetus and originality of the early Soviet conservationists.[109] Their work is important not only because it captures and assimilates to the broader social theory of Marxism many of the insights of postmodern environmentalists,[110] but because unlike the ideas of some of the deep ecologists, this form of Marxism does transcend the traditional binary distinction between humanity and nature. Human societies are seen as part of and within eco-systems, and the really important issue is not that nature is being subjugated, but that diverse forms of human life which are parts of complex, species-rich, stable and sustainable ecosystems are being destroyed by the form of life imposed by global capitalism, creating uniform, simplified, species-impoverished, highly unstable and in the long run, unsustainable ecosystems throughout the world.[111]

But where will this lead to? Can we pin our hopes for the future on colonization by instrumental reason? Or on the esoteric works of a few Marxists who can only be understood by a minuscule proportion of the world's educated population? Since Marxists, such as Bogdanov and those influenced by him, critical theorists from the Frankfurt Institute, Wallerstein and ecological Marxists have all been severely critical of Soviet communism, they can hardly be condemned for its failures. Nevertheless, the collapse of the Soviet Union and its allies and their unreserved embrace of capitalism severely weakens the claims of those who believed that there is a viable alternative to capitalism. How is it possible to justify 'delinking' from the world economy when the Soviet Union failed? What kind of society should we be trying to create? And how can we create such a new society? While radical Marxists have been much more concerned with these issues than poststructuralists, they appear to provide people with little guidance for overcoming the destructive imperatives of capitalism they have identified. Marxism appears to have become an ideology of radical academics, and as such, has become more of a comforter to people's consciences than a political force. The state of mind of Marxists, particularly since the collapse of Eastern European communism, is conveyed by the lament of Alvin Gouldner:

> The political uniqueness of our own era then is this; we have lived and still live through a desperate political and social malaise, while at the same time we have *outlived* the desperate revolutionary remedies that had once been thought to solve them.[112]

It would appear that barring some almost unimaginable catastrophe, the global market will remain with us until massive environmental destruction makes it impossible to function. Under these circumstances, and given the immediacy of the environmental crisis, it is clearly necessary to formulate critiques of the existing state of affairs and the thinking on which policies are based in terms which will facilitate the formulation of realistic alternatives.

While cultural critiques and cultural politics of both the Hegelian and Nietzschean varieties are intoxicating, they are ineffectual, merely sideshows. They have shown that Cartesian thought and the various forms of reductionist science which developed from this are the products of a particular culture, are a part of culture; but the achievements of Cartesian thought have been so immense, and the institutions based upon such thought are so powerful as a consequence, that no cultural critique of it by itself is likely to have any impact on its domination. Furthermore, it is wrong to condemn Cartesian thought as totally destructive. It is the scientists who have revealed the severity of the environmental crisis, and it is scientists who have been the most forceful spokespeople for the environment. Does not this indicate that what is needed to overcome the environmental crisis is more science and more power to those influenced by science? Perhaps what is needed is a fightback by scientists against the decadence of postmodern culture which is enabling the reduction of science to a mere instrument for the development of technology in the struggle for economic dominance between nations.

Science has come a long way since Descartes. It has extended Cartesian thinking from physics through chemistry to the life sciences. Through evolutionary theory, biochemistry and molecular biology, and more recently thermodynamics, information theory and cybernetics, it has largely accounted for the diversity of life on earth. It is now making considerable advances towards understanding humans. Utilizing information theory, cognitive psychology is making enormous strides in the study of perception and thinking. Socio-biology has provided support for this, and provided a way of thinking about culture. Cultural forms, called 'memes' by Richard Dawkins, are characterized as information-processing systems involved in a struggle for survival just as is every other entity in the universe. Through such theories, modern science is able to assimilate the most significant insights of Marx and the Marxists, of Nietzsche and of the poststructuralists. In fact it has already assimilated much, perhaps most importantly Bogdanov's cybernetics and his tektology, which has been transmogrified into systems theory. Nietzsche's will to power makes perfect sense in terms of present-day science as a characterization of the propensities of any entity which has managed to survive in the struggle for existence. The language forms examined by Nietzsche, Heidegger and Derrida can be explained in terms of the contribution they have made to the survival of the social systems of which they are part.[113] The discursive formations studied by Foucault are such social systems, and Foucault's analysis of their dynamics and internal transformations fits admirably into a Social Darwinist framework. And he has shown how the more benign forms of social control are more effective than brutal forms. The triumph of liberal democratic capitalism can be explained in terms of the efficiency of the feedback mechanisms which guide it, its suitability to its environment and its capacity to exploit to the best effect the resources at its disposal, or as Marx put it, through its capacity to develop the forces of production. Science itself is a successful product of the evolutionary struggle, as an entity successfully struggling for survival, and progress in science can be characterized as the outcome of a struggle between rival theories and concepts. So what we have in the modern world are the most efficient systems, systems which have proved themselves in the struggle of all against all. This does not mean there is any reason for complacency. Palaeontological and ecological research has revealed numerous instances of communities of organisms and species which have destroyed themselves by destroying the conditions of their existence. What is required to prevent humanity going the same way is to ensure that there is adequate feedback to the systems which dominate society.

Since the most important system in capitalism is the economy, at least where the environment is concerned, and since economics is the science through which this system is managed, it is only through reformulating economics that the limitations of the environment will be effectively addressed. What is required is the reformulation of economics so that it accords with the most advanced theories of natural science, or at least coexists with them.[114] As Georgescu-Roegen has pointed out, this is not the case – economists have ignored the second law of thermodynamics. At the same time economics can take into account the concerns raised by Marxists of the alienating effect of people being reduced to labour power. In managing the economy it is possible to give some value to the kind of employment in which people are fulfilled in their work. In fact there is no great problem in this, since it is clear from the success of Japanese management practices that companies which do not treat their employees as mere labour-power to be exploited are more successful than those wedded to earlier capitalist forms of thinking.[115] Finally, concerns about the effect of economic developments on the power relations between nations should also be taken into account. Again there is no major problem with this. The most economically successful nations in the modern world have long-term plans for development in which the conditions for long-term success, including power relations, are calculated and met. Environmental economics as it is being elaborated by economists such as Pearce and his colleagues, although at present defective in this regard, should eventually be able to incorporate such issues.

CONCLUSION

In presenting the major intellectual positions on the environment in opposition to each other I have not meant to imply that the final point, recent advances in mainstream thought which have drawn on and assimilated the insights of the major opposing positions, is adequate. On the contrary. What the double dialectic of this chapter should have revealed is that it is possible to construct narratives of dialectical advance in either direction, to interpret any of the major positions so that it can be seen as superior to its rivals. And what this shows is that none of these positions is adequate by itself. Each one has aspects which cannot be assimilated to the others, implying its superiority in some respects to its rivals. What is called for then is an alternative philosophy which transcends the limitations of all the philosophies considered so far while at the same time providing an appreciation of their achievements, a philosophy in terms of which a narrative can be constructed which puts in perspective each of the major positions, showing what they have achieved, why they have achieved what they have and why they could not advance further than they did, why they had to be blind to some aspects of the positions they were opposing.

Given my characterization of the major positions considered, it is possible to see what problems need to be overcome and to gain some idea of what shape this alternative must take. To begin with, Western civilization is faced with a basic rift between the way nature and the way culture are conceived. Those who approach the world through culture treat the science of nature as part of culture, while those involved in science attempt to conceive of humans as part of nature; but neither is able to do justice to the other. Underlying this opposition, those taking culture as their point of departure begin with a conception of human activity as essentially becoming in which 'being' is seen as a construct, while the science of nature takes as its starting point being, what is, and then attempts to account for change as a derivative aspect of being – as changing positions in space of immutable particles over time, or as deformations of fields. If this rift is to be healed, it will be necessary to develop a science which takes becoming as basic (or Being in Heidegger's sense) and conceives 'beings' as islands of stability within the flux of becoming. Only on this basis will science be able to provide an understanding of human culture, including science, in a way which does justice to the insights of thinkers belonging to the Vicovian tradition of thought.

But it is also necessary to heal the rift within the Vicovian tradition between the Hegelians and the Nietzscheans. In the light of Nietzschean critiques of Hegelian thought it is clearly necessary to abandon the kind of totalization aspired to by Hegel, a system which reduces particulars to nothing but parts of the grand totality, the Absolute and its destiny. But on the other hand it must be recognized that the Nietzschean absolutization of the particular is not only self-contradictory and dissolves into incoherence, as many 'Hegelian' commentators have noted, but is politically disastrous at a time when political failure could spell the end of humanity's continued existence. What is required is a recognition of the value of perspective without the assumption that the universe is a totally knowable, integrated totality.

Finally, the new philosophy must address the issues raised by Heidegger. I have presented Heidegger as on the side of Nietzsche against Hegel, but as attempting to radicalize Nietzsche's critique of the metaphysical foundations of Western civilization. Heidegger must be recognized as having done more than anyone else this century to get to the roots of the nihilism of the modern age. This is of central importance to environmentalists who, in confronting the forces of environmental destruction, are confronting the effects of nihilism in action. While Derrida's critique of Heidegger might be conceded to have some validity, and the lacunae in Heidegger's philosophy recognized, no philosophy unable to come to terms with Heidegger's insights can now be taken seriously.

4

POSTMODERN METAPHYSICS

Postmodern culture is characterized by a suspicion of coherence, and through the attacks upon it by Nietzsche, Heidegger and the post-structuralists, no intellectual endeavour has come under more suspicion than metaphysics. This suspicion has generated important insights into the root cause of the oppressive tendencies and environmental destructiveness of European civilization. Most importantly it has revealed how the postulation and celebration as the true reality of an eternal, rational order of being behind, and the cause of, the changing world of sense experience, that is, onto-theology, has engendered a conception of the world as an aggregate of things to be subjugated and controlled. Poststructuralists have also shown that traditional Marxism shares many of the assumptions of the dominant culture, and this has vitiated efforts by Marxists to overcome the oppressiveness of capitalism. However, the environmental crisis reveals just how misguided is the poststructuralists' 'magical assumption that the fragmentation of knowledge will somehow break the grip of the object of knowledge'.[1] Unless they pave the way for some alternative way of achieving a comprehensive understanding of the world, poststructuralist cultural critiques will merely dissolve the opposition to mainstream culture, leaving no alternative to the forms of thinking which have engendered the rise of Western civilization, its conquests and its domination of the rest of the world, and the outcome of all this, the destruction of the global environment. While Deleuze and Guattari's concept of the rhizome offers some promise of a new way of grasping problems, this needs to be far more developed before it can provide an effective orientation to the global environmental crisis. Alternatively, a revised form of Marxism, taking up themes in Marx's own writings, which was developed in the early years of the Russian revolution by Bogdanov and those influenced by him, but which was suppressed as the Soviet Union rose to challenge the hegemony of capitalism, could provide the answer. But to work out how to avoid those aspects in Marxism which enabled it to function as an oppressive ideology of an even more environmentally destructive economic order than capitalism, to work out what is salvageable from the works of Marx and the Marxists, requires some reference point which can put such issues in perspective. What is required is a 'postmodern metaphysics'.

Is it possible to justify metaphysics at all, and if so, is it possible to develop a metaphysics which is not Platonistic or onto-theological, which is not logocentric or guilty of 'the metaphysics of presence', and which gives primacy to becoming over being? Metaphysics is the science of what being is.[2] That it is even possible to talk about the nature of being is questioned by some postmodernists on the grounds that it is impossible to get beyond language to know reality itself. There is no 'extra-text'. The arguments for this echo arguments by earlier philosophers that it is impossible to get beyond the sense experience of consciousness, that all we can do is identify and record regularities in this experience. Consequently we cannot know there are other minds; we can only record regularities in the movements of perceived bodies. This form of solipsism was refuted by Hegel, and later by Wittgenstein and other analytical philosophers, who pointed out that all talk of individual conscious experience presupposes a language shared with other consciousnesses. But similar arguments could be elaborated to show that language itself would be unintelligible without the presupposition of a world beyond language within which language users function.[3] However while the existence of people who take linguistic idealism seriously is an important social phenomenon, suggesting a class of people who are so politically impotent and lead such impoverished lives that they have lost all sense of what action in the world is, the more important argument of Nietzsche and those influenced by him is that language, by its very nature, or at least languages deriving from the Aryan language, cannot but lead people to misunderstand reality because these languages privilege nouns. As Nietzsche argued: 'Linguistic means of expression are useless for expressing "becoming".'[4] Is it possible to have a metaphysics of a world of process?

Aristotle had already foreshadowed this possibility when he argued that if there are no beings which are both independent and immovable, then metaphysics would be about the general characteristics of natural beings, that is, changing entities.[5] Charles Sanders Peirce, the philosopher whose fallibilism and whose theory of 'endless semiosis' strongly influenced Derrida, defended and practised metaphysics in this sense.[6] The turn by Deleuze towards the philosophy of Bergson also suggests the possibility of developing metaphysics free of the incoherencies identified by the anti-metaphysicians, a possibility which is increasingly being explored as a postmodern alternative to poststructuralism. Philosophers and philosophically-oriented scientists are calling for a postmodern science based on a process view of the world, the tradition of thought inspired by Bergson and Whitehead, both to justify a new attitude towards nature and to justify the conception of humanity which has evolved from the Vicovian tradition of anti-Cartesian thought.[7] What they are arguing for is a conception of nature which allows humans to be conceived of as essentially cultural beings, while still seeing them, or us, as part of and within nature. This is what Ilya Prigogine called 'the new alliance'.

French poststructuralists have recognized radical changes within science which undermine its domineering orientation. In *The Postmodern Condition* Lyotard argued that science had abandoned its quest for a deterministic picture of the world:

> Postmodern science – by concerning itself with such things as undecidables, the limits of precise control, conflicts characterized by incomplete information, *'fracta,'* catastrophes, and pragmatic paradoxes – is theorizing its own evolution as discontinuous, catastrophic, nonrectifiable, and paradoxical.[8]

This clearly destroys efforts to justify science in terms of maximizing performance; but Lyotard argues that postmodern science cannot be justified by any grand narrative, that each new idea can only be justified by a little narrative (*petit récit*) immanent to the game of science. This misrepresents the way in which postmodern science developed in the first place, and second, how it is defended against efforts to reduce the world to objects to be controlled. Most of the major figures in the development of postmodern science have been inspired by philosophical concerns, and they have defended their ideas in terms of their philosophical positions, that is, in terms of a grand narrative portraying science as it was previously practised as something to be transcended if the problems of present civilization are to be overcome. Many of those who participated in the development of quantum theory were Germans, who, after the First World War, reacted against the mechanistic thinking deriving from the West.[9] C.H. Waddington, whose work in epigenesis from 1930 onwards revolutionized biology and inspired the development by René Thom of catastrophe theory in mathematics, explicitly acknowledged Whitehead as his mentor, and defended the concepts developed on this basis as necessary to come to grips with the environmental crisis.[10] Ilya Prigogine, who ascribed the basic direction of his research to Bergson, argued in 1984:

> we are in a period of scientific revolution – one in which the very position and meaning of the scientific approach are undergoing reappraisal – a period not unlike the birth of the scientific approach in ancient Greece or of its renaissance in the time of Galileo.[11]

He hailed this revolution as necessary to create 'new relations between man and nature and between man and man'[12] to deal with problems engendered by the demographic explosion. These are the sentiments of most of those engaged in what Lyotard called postmodern science, from those developing what Paul Davies has called the 'New Physics' to those developing radically new approaches in biology and the human sciences. As David Ray Griffin pointed out in his introduction to the anthology *The Reenchantment of Science: Postmodern Proposals*, 'physics no longer disenchants our stories; physics itself provides us with a new story which can become a common, unifying story underneath our more particular stories'.[13]

In this chapter I will show that this philosophy is not subject to the criticisms of metaphysics made by Nietzsche, Heidegger and post-structuralists such as Derrida, that it is an effort to elaborate fully the conception of physical existence they have assumed, and that it can incorporate their concerns while providing an alternative basis for the natural and the human sciences.

EPISTEMOLOGY AND METAPHYSICS

To defend metaphysics is to defend a claim to knowledge, and this presupposes a theory of knowledge, an epistemology. Like metaphysics, epistemology has come under suspicion for privileging some discourses over others and thereby legitimating oppressive power relations. Postmodern culture tends towards relativism. But relativism is merely the obverse of objectivism and dogmatism. Both deny any value to dialogue; if no point of view is better than any other, differences are not worth arguing about, while if we already have the truth, or at least a method for gaining and accumulating certain knowledge, there is no need to consider alternative ideas. In practice, relativism and dogmatism complement each other as relativists silence dialogue, allowing dogmatists to impose their conception of the world on others. But is there an alternative to relativism and dogmatism? If it could be shown that while there are no absolute foundations on which knowledge can be built, yet it is still possible to judge between competing knowledge claims, such an alternative would be demonstrated. It is just such a position which in recent decades has emerged as the most defensible theory of knowledge within the philosophy of science.[14]

The logical positivists had struggled to show that knowledge, particularly scientific knowledge, has absolute foundations in observation and logic. Their opponents pointed out that observations are at least partly relative to the theories they are supposed to validate or falsify, and it has become evident that there is no one logic but a multiplicity of logics, not entirely compatible with each other, between which it is necessary to choose. Theories, that is, ways of understanding or gaining insight into the world, far from being derived from sense experience and logic, appear to be more basic than sense data and logic. Theories are ways of experiencing the world, conceptual frameworks in terms of which the world is interpreted and made sense of, and the use of mathematics must be seen as the refinement of theoretical concepts. Concepts, both non-mathematical and mathematical, even the concepts of logic, have been shown to have sense and to cohere with each other because they are articulations of image schemata and metaphors. Vico's defence of metaphor and Nietzsche's insight that what are taken as truths are metaphors which have lost their embossing have been justified by research on science and its history. Understanding through image schemata and metaphors is far more than the ability to affirm the validity of propositions or to deduce some propositions from others. Understanding is how we experience our world as a comprehensible reality; it is our mode of being in the world. But it is not only as embodied agents that individuals understand the world, but as cultural beings. We perceive the world in response to what has been experienced and understood in the past, and with a view to what can be communicated in the future. As Mark Johnson has argued, understanding 'is the way we are meaningfully situated in our world through our bodily interactions, our cultural institutions, our linguistic tradition, and our historical context'.[15] Being 'meaningfully situated in our world' involves being able to appreciate the world against past struggles to understand it, and being oriented for action and for the further development of understanding. Theories are not simply to be accepted or rejected. They are research programmes to extend understanding into new areas and are new orientations to live by.

While the breakdown of logical positivism, along with the demonstrated relativity of observations, logic and theories to each other, seemed to dissolve the claims of science to be able to ascertain truth about the world or to provide any justification for preferring one way of understanding the world over another, relativism can be avoided by acknowledging the importance of narratives about science. Supporting Vico's claim for the priority of rhetoric over logic and mathematical abstraction, Alasdair MacIntyre has shown how the acceptance of radically new theories is dependent upon the capacity of their defenders to construct narratives about their ideas. Since major advances in knowledge transcend old assumptions and create new ways of arguing, changing the standards of relevance and proof, they cannot be evaluated in terms of existing criteria. The superiority of the new theories is only revealed by the comprehension they facilitate of the achievements and limitations of the theories transcended. As MacIntyre pointed out:

> Wherein lies the superiority of Galileo to his predecessors? The answer is that he, for the first time, enables the work of all his predecessors to be evaluated by a common set of standards. The contributions of Plato, Aristotle, the scholars at Merton College, Oxford and Padua, the work of Copernicus himself at last all fall into place. Or to put matters in another and equivalent way: the history

of late medieval science can finally be cast into a coherent narrative. . . . What the scientific genius, such as Galileo, achieves in his transitions, then, is not only a new way of understanding nature, but also and inseparably a new way of understanding the old sciences' way of understanding. . . . It is from the stand-point of the new science that the continuities of narrative history are reestablished.[16]

While MacIntyre provides a defence of Vico's views (which on the surface is similar to the defence of narrative in science offered by Lyotard),[17] his claims for narratives are a challenge to poststructuralist theories of meaning. MacIntyre implies that it is necessary, and shows how it is possible, to construct narratives which are not merely new narratives or discourses but which subsume other narratives, reorganize them and interpret them in new ways. Not only does he imply the possibility of this, but his analysis of the role of narratives in evaluating knowledge claims shows that the struggle to create new narratives which make sense of previously irreconcilable narratives and discourses is central to the way people orient themselves to the world and to each other, and to how traditions of inquiry are constituted. It is a central feature of communication and a condition of it. Implicit in this analysis is the recognition that the struggle to create grand narratives, narratives which enable all other discourses and practices to be understood, is an imperative, whether or not they are achieved or are even possible.[18] Furthermore, while the struggle to create grand narratives is recognized as an imperative, it is also acknowledged that there can be no final closure, that it is always possible to make some creative advance in understanding which breaks with all preconceptions.

On MacIntyre's view, narratives are not merely chains of signifiers. They are formulated in terms of ways of understanding the world. This means that grand narratives, as totalizing constructions, must be told from the perspective of a totalizing perspective, a metaphysical theory. While the logical positivists were concerned to validate the claims to knowledge of science against metaphysics, the view of science which emerged from the destruction of logical positivism gives a central place to metaphysics. Metaphysics as the theory of being provides the grand theories, the grand metaphors and the grand research programmes in terms of which all particular theories are situated and legitimated. All scientists presuppose some metaphysical framework in their research. As the physicist David Bohm summed up the conclusions of a conference on theoretical biology:

I think the most important aspect of the interchange is the emergence of a common realization that metaphysics is fundamental to every branch of science. Metaphysics is . . . something that pervades every field, that conditions each person's thinking in varied and subtle ways, of which we are not conscious. Metaphysics is a set of

assumptions about the general order and structures of existence. . . .
It seems clear that everybody has got some kind of metaphysics,
even if he thinks he hasn't got any. . . . [W]hat is needed is the
conscious criticism of one's own metaphysics, leading to changes
where appropriate and, ultimately, to the continual creation of new
and different kinds. In this way, metaphysics ceases to be the master
of a human being and becomes his servant, helping to give an ever
changing and evolving order to his overall thinking.[19]

Aristotle provided a metaphysical theory which served as a grand
research programme, a programme which was pursued vigorously in the
late Middle Ages. The seventeenth-century revolution in science was a
metaphysical revolution, a replacement of Aristotle's metaphysical framework by a new metaphysical theory developed by reformulating Platonism
though the elaboration of the machine metaphor.[20] While in the late Middle
Ages particular theories were formulated in terms of participation in or
actualization of forms, after the seventeenth century most scientific theories
were formulated as analyses of complex entities into constituents and the
laws of motion of matter, and after Darwin, supplementing this with the
notion of evolution brought about by different rates of survival of different
kinds of entities. There have since been challenges to the Cartesian/
Newtonian metaphysics by field theories and theories which place energy
as the primary being of which everything else is a manifestation (the most
fully developed version of which was that of Bogdanov). However it has
only been with the elaboration of the insights of Bergson and Whitehead
that mechanistic materialism has been able to be challenged in all branches
of science.

PHILOSOPHY OF PROCESS AND ONTO-THEOLOGY

The idea that science utilizes metaphors and is based on metaphysics is
nothing new to Heideggerians. Heidegger, following Nietzsche, recognized this and was critical of science accordingly. Science, along with
metaphysics, is part of the forgetting of Being. But if science were to be
based on a philosophy privileging process, would it still involve the
forgetting of Being? Heidegger assumed that the natural sciences are
irrevocably oriented towards the domination of the world, and argued that
the claims to truth of science must be delimited, that such 'knowledge'
must be subordinated to thinking about Being. But it is arguable that
through process philosophy, science itself is regaining awareness of Being
as presencing of the present, that this philosophy is a post-onto-theo-
logical metaphysics, and science, insofar as it has been based on process
philosophy, is ceasing to an instrument of world subjugation.

Philosophers of process are as opposed to Cartesian thought as

Heidegger. Their philosophy is the product of an attempt to overcome the dualism between mind and body, subject and object. Humans are conceived of as being within the world, as participants in the world's becoming. Through Bergson's defence of 'intuition' and Whitehead's defence of continuous experience over system and language, process philosophy can be seen as attempting to return us to an appreciation of the being of the world as presencing in much the same way as was Heidegger. And like Heidegger, these philosophers stress the temporality of Being, and are suspicious of the primacy given to vision in the way the world is now understood. Bergson argued that it is to control the world that it is understood in spatial terms deriving from vision and is thereby conceived of as composed of a multiplicity of separate objects.

To overcome such thinking Bergson suggested that we move from visual analogies to auditory analogies, that we understand the world as analogous to music. This offers us a quite different conception of the world, one in which Nietzsche's problem of representing becoming is overcome. As Bergson pointed out:

> Let us listen to a melody, allowing ourselves to be lulled by it: do we not have the clear perception of a movement which is not attached to a mobile, of a change without anything changing? This change is enough, it is the thing itself. And even if it takes time, it is still indivisible; if the melody stopped sooner it would no longer be the same sonorous whole, it would be another, equally indivisible. . . . If we do not dwell on . . . spatial images, pure change remains, sufficient unto itself, in no way divided, in no way attached to a 'thing' which changes.[21]

This analogy has since been taken up and developed systematically by Milic Capek and Victor Zuckerkandl.[22]

Whitehead attempted to develop Bergson's ideas in a more systematic way, to produce a coherent metaphysical system which, while rejecting the Cartesian reduction of physical existence to a mathematical order, could reveal how mathematics can be applied successfully to understanding the world. Consistent with the conception of the world as creative becoming, Whitehead rejected the idea that metaphysics grasps some immutable reality behind appearances. For Whitehead, speculative philosophy is fallible. Introducing his major work of systematization he wrote:

> When we survey the history of thought, and likewise the history of practice, we find that one idea after another is tried out, its limitations defined, and its core of truth elicited. . . . At the very least, men do what they can in the way of systematization, and in the event achieve something. The proper test is not that of finality, but of progress. . . . Philosophy is the welding of imagination and common sense into a

restraint upon specialists, and also into an enlargement of their imaginations. By providing the generic notions philosophy should make it easier to conceive the infinite variety of specific instances which rest unrealized in the womb of nature.[23]

The generic notions offered by Whitehead are designed to make sense of the world as a process of becoming.

Understanding the world in this way was associated with the rejection of the tendency to conceive of the world as a collection of predictable things which can be controlled. Whitehead was as much opposed to this world orientation and the assumptions on which it has been based as Heidegger. In *Modes of Thought* he argued:

> Science can find no individual enjoyment in nature: Science can find no aim in nature: Science can find no creativity in nature; it finds mere rules of succession. These negations are true of natural science. They are inherent in its methodology.[24]

For Whitehead, the problem of science is that abstractions have been taken for concrete reality. It is this which he characterized as the 'fallacy of misplaced concreteness'. It is through a process of constructive abstraction that science arrived at simply-located bits of material on the one hand, and minds on the other. There are two problems with this. The first is taking abstractions as reality and thereby ignoring the contexts from which science of necessity had abstracted. The second is remaining wedded to a particular set of abstractions, being blinded to the possibility of developing an alternative set. As Whitehead argued:

> You cannot think without abstractions; accordingly, it is of the utmost importance to be vigilant in critically revising your *modes* of abstraction. It is here that philosophy finds its niche as essential to the healthy progress of society. It is the critic of abstractions. A civilization which cannot burst through its current abstractions is doomed to sterility after a very limited period of progress.[25]

Here Whitehead displayed as much sensitivity to concrete experience of the world as Heidegger and as much sensitivity to the impossibility of giving final meaning to words as Derrida. This is not to say that Whitehead anticipated all the subtleties of Heidegger's analysis of Dasein and the Being of beings, or of the complexities of linguistic constructions revealed by Derrida's deconstructions, but it does mean that Whitehead was aware of the tendencies in Western thought condemned by Heidegger and Derrida, and avoided these tendencies. But instead of resting content with dissolving philosophy into poetry or undermining congealed abstractions portrayed as absolutes, Whitehead set out to construct a more adequate set of abstractions – while rejecting even the possibility of arriving at absolute truth through these abstractions. Describing the aim of metaphysics, he argued:

> Philosophers can never hope finally to formulate these metaphysical
> first principles. Weakness of insight and deficiencies of language
> stand in the way inexorably. Words and phrases must be stretched
> towards a generality foreign to their ordinary usage; and however
> such elements of language be stabilized as technicalities, they remain
> metaphors mutely appealing for an imaginative leap.[26]

In the tradition of Western metaphysics, Whitehead offered a 'category
of the ultimate' which he characterized as '"creativity," "one," "many"'.[27]
Is this yet another example of onto-theology? Has Whitehead offered
another version of primary being as an underlying and constantly present
'ground' which produces all particular things? After all, 'creativity' is for
Whitehead the ultimate source of unending actual entities and the concept
though which such actual entities must be understood. However, Whitehead
was concerned to conceive of beings as self-creating, not as created
by some ground. In *Process and Reality* he characterized the ultimate as that
'which is actual in virtue of its accidents. It is only then capable of
characterization through its accidental embodiments, and apart from these
accidents is devoid of actuality.' Whitehead contrasted this way of
conceiving of the ultimate with monistic schemes in which 'the ultimate
is illegitimately allowed a final, "eminent" reality, beyond that ascribed
to any of its accidents', noting that his own philosophy is closer to some
strains of Indian or Chinese thought than to western Asiatic or European
thought: 'One side makes process ultimate; the other side makes fact
ultimate.'[28] In *Adventure of Ideas* he elaborated and further clarified this:
'[T]he word Creativity expresses the notion that each event is a process
issuing in novelty. Also if guarded in phrases of Immanent Creativity, or
Self-Creativity, it avoids the implication of a transcendent Creator.'[29]
While the universe is a unity it is also a multiplicity in which different
kinds of beings must be understood to some extent in their own terms.

So instead of arguing for a new form of dualism between Being and
beings, Whitehead attempted to reconceive what 'beings' or 'things' are.
To begin with, he rejected the notion of space as something existing at a
durationless instant, and along with it, the doctrine of simple location: the
assumption that entities have a clearly specifiable spatio-temporal position. He argued that 'the immediate fact for awareness is the whole
occurrence of nature. It is nature as an event present for sense-awareness,
and essentially passing.'[30] The representation of entities as existing at an
instant, necessary for mathematical calculations and measurements in
scientific theory, was shown to be derived from 'events' by a process of
'extensive abstraction'. Further reflection on the nature of physical existence led Whitehead to conceive of events as 'processes of unifying', a

conception which inspired the whole elaborate scheme of *Process and Reality*. Here, the world of 'things' was conceived of as the world of potentialities: '"potentiality for process" is the meaning of the more general term "entity" or "thing"'.[31] Thus 'things' have a derivative place in the world in relation to processes – among which are humans. It is processes which 'objectify' the world as part of their own becoming. The 'eternal objects' of mathematics are pure potentiality, and are applicable to the world of things or to what is objectified, that is, to the becoming of potentialities for other processes: 'mathematics is concerned with certain forms of process issuing into forms which are components for further process'.[32] It is we who abstract mathematical objects to reveal the potentialities of the world for our own becoming, and mathematical objects have a reality as part of our becoming.

Through this scheme Whitehead reinterpreted developments in modern physics. He argued that modern physics has abandoned the doctrine of 'simple location'. An entity, whether a star, a planet, an electron or quanta of energy, 'is what it does, and what it does is this divergent stream of influence'. There is a focal region, but this cannot be separated from the external stream, and '[i]t obstinately refuses to be conceived of as an instantaneous fact'.[33] Characterizing the structure of the epoch of the universe in which we find ourselves, he argued:

> this structure exhibits successive layers of types of order, each layer introducing some additional type of order within some limited region which shares in the more general type of order of some larger environment. Also this larger environment in its turn is a specialized region within the general epoch of creation as we know it. Each one of these regions, with its dominant set of ordering relations, can either be considered from the point of view of the mutual relations of its parts to each other, or it can be considered from the point of view of its impact, as a unity, upon the experience of an external percipient. There is yet a third mode of consideration which combines the other two. The percipient may be an occasion within the region, and may yet grasp the region as one, including the percipient itself as a member of it.[34]

To conceive of the world in this way is to abandon onto-theology.

RECENT DEVELOPMENTS IN THE PHILOSOPHY OF PROCESS

True to the spirit of its progenitors, those influenced by Bergson and Whitehead have not followed them slavishly. They have continued to develop and refine their ideas, to transcend their incoherencies and to reformulate them to provide a more powerful challenge to mechanistic thinking. On the basis of work by Ivor Leclerc, Milic Capek, Edward Pols and others it is now possible to offer a simplified categorial scheme which can serve as the basis for science, and ultimately, as the foundation for a postmodern culture. In outlining a categorial scheme for process philosophy it is necessary to assume as the basic coordinating metaphor for understanding the world the auditory metaphor suggested by Bergson. The main problem with Whitehead's categorial scheme has been its complexity. As a number of sympathetic scientists have noted, if categories are to be of heuristic value to science, they must be kept fairly simple. What I will offer here is such a simplified categorial scheme based on the work of modern process philosophers.[35]

Whitehead classified his categories into four kinds: the categories of the ultimate, of existence, of explanation and of obligations. While accepting the first three of these, I wish to replace 'categories of obligations' by 'categories of ultimate potentiality', and to offer a simplified characterization of the categories so classified. The categories of the ultimate – into which all that exists can be analysed – I suggest should be 'activity', 'order' and 'potentiality' (rather than 'creativity', 'one' and 'many'). These are presupposed by the other categories to be defined. As such they are the most difficult categories to define, and to do so it will be necessary to refer back continually to the underlying auditory analogy. The categories of existence – which I propose should be 'process', 'structure' and 'event' – characterize what exists in the world. The categories of explanation – various kinds of causation – pertain to the explanation of all that has existed, does exist and could exist, while the categories of ultimate potentiality – space-time – are the most fundamental concepts of potential relationships between actual and potential existents.

'Activity' (corresponding to 'creativity' in Whitehead's philosophy – 'the ultimate behind all forms, inexplicable by forms and conditioned by its creatures') I wish to equate with the 'energy' of modern science, while giving this concept a new meaning – or at least a more definite meaning since the notion of energy has never had a clear meaning.[36] In terms of the auditory analogy, the very being of sound is activity, and no unchanging substratum of activity need be supposed. It is in this sense that 'activity' must be understood, and identifying this with 'energy' transforms this concept. 'Activity' can be understood as an identification or conflation of the Milesian (and Heraclitean) concept of *kinesis* and Aristotle's notion of *hyle*.

Order is perhaps the most difficult category to define. Whenever anyone thinks about anything they are assuming order – its quantity (whether one or many), its quality, its endurance, etc., its composition and context and the spatio-temporal order in which it is located. I think order is best defined as 'facilitating constraint'. In thinking of sound and the different types of constraining which occur with the becoming of a piece of music, the ordering of activity can be seen as any constraining or modulation of the sound which differentiates it into identifiably similar aspects, or which constrains such differentiated aspects into similarly different aspects.[37] Through the constraining of sound individual notes emerge, which can be ordered into melodies and so on. The way such a conception of order provides a basis for analysis can be seen by considering what is involved in the generation of extension. Locomotion as change of position can be seen as a particular type of ordering whereby potential relations for independence and interaction are changed, and extension can then be understood as the order generated through such changing of potentialities. In such terms a line can be understood as a similar difference in point positions. The generation of a circle can be understood as similar differences between similar differences in the point positions, and a spiral, with three dimensions, as simultaneously three separate similar differences of point positions. In each case, the order makes possible further ordering to generate new types of order.

Potentiality can be understood as the possibilities – including the powers tending to realize these – for ordering and being ordered which are produced and which can be realized or undermined in the becoming of the world. Referring back to the auditory analogy, it is the 'oriented tension' in a piece of music which constrains without determining its becoming. Potentiality corresponds to the Greek notion of *dynamis* – a power only inherent in something without being manifest – the concept which was virtually eliminated in the deterministic mechanical conception of the world and by field theory.

The category of process is meant to characterize primary being, *ousia* – that which exists in the full sense rather than through analysis or derivatively. A process can be defined as an ordering activity which is to some extent (although never entirely) an immanent cause of its own being, a self-ordering activity in which activity constrains itself and reproduces these constraints. So, to be in the primary sense is to be a process (although it is also possible for there to be a background of unordered activity unknowable in itself, but knowable as the condition for the emergence and continued existence of processes – e.g. the vacuum in quantum field theory), and everything else must be understood as a part of or as an aspect of some process or processes, or in terms of the relationship between processes. As such this notion of process is designed to replace the post-Renaissance category of self-subsistent matter or body conceived of as essentially inert, along with the associated categories of space, time and motion which have also been conceived of as primary beings within the mechanical view of the world. A process is that which in Aristotle's terminology has in it its own source of movement, or in Whitehead's terminology, that 'which constitutes its own becoming'.[38] What is involved in any relationship between processes is always additional constraining of activity so that processes relating to other processes are different from processes not relating to these processes. Emergence and hierarchical ordering can then be seen as self-ordering activities coming to be or being involved in further ordering, that is, being subject to further constraints, as parts of higher-level processes which are the ordering activity creating and reproducing these, and other, constraints. Under these circumstances the constituent processes of the supervening process are changed so that they act to constitute the emergent activity and thereby to produce and reproduce these constraints.[39] It is also possible for supervening processes to emerge which are the ordering of the emergence of a sequence of new hierarchical levels of ordering.

Ordered potentialities produced and maintained by processes are structures. Most of what people identify in the world as things or objects or bodies are what I am calling structures. As ordered potentialities, structures can be understood only in terms of being maintained and produced by processes. They are only potentialities in relation to the becoming of processes which can realize these potentialities. It is through identifying such potentialities and their relationships that processes of becoming can be analysed. 'Structure' corresponds to what Whitehead designated as the 'potentiality for "objectification" in the becoming of other actual entities' of an actual entity, where '"objectification" refers to the particular mode in which the potentiality of one actual entity is realized in another actual entity'.[40] In terms of process philosophy a tree must be regarded as a process of becoming which is durational. What we normally identify as a tree at a particular time is a structure, the potentialities produced and maintained by this process of becoming – the potential to maintain shape, to resist penetration, to reflect light, etc. – which are realized as such in the process of becoming of other processes, and also by the tree itself as a necessary part of its own becoming.

Along with processes and structures there are also events, such as the coming into being or destruction of processes, 'decisions' to take one path of development rather than another, significant changes within or differentiated activities of processes and contingent interactions between processes. Events must always be understood in relation to processes, and it is not possible completely to analyse processes into events.

As a category of explanation, the notion of cause has a long and complex history. The term derives from the Latin *causa* which was a translation of the Greek *aition* or *aitia*. This term referred to the voluntary action of an agent for which he or she could be held responsible. It was originally applied in legal contexts but was generalized to refer to any action designed to bring about an event or state of affairs. This was then applied by analogy to nature, first to events produced by people designed to get nature to do things for them (for instance, lighting a fire to cook food), and then as a simple explanatory principle as when lightning is seen as the cause of fire. It was this notion of causation which was developed systematically by Aristotle, who analysed it into four aspects: the material cause, the efficient cause, the formal cause and the final cause; the material cause being the matter involved in the process, the efficient cause the exercise of power, the formal cause the form aimed at by this action and the final cause the reason for aiming at this form. In describing biological growth efficient, formal and final causation tended to be conflated.

However, with the birth of modern science there was a radical break with Aristotelian concepts. It is widely assumed that final causes were excluded from scientific explanation. However, the Pythagorean Platonism of the major proponents of the 'new philosophy' in the seventeenth century excluded not only final causes but also efficient causes. The notion that power was exercised in causation was replaced by the notion that inert matter moves according to formal principles or laws. The failure to grasp this change in thinking led to a conflation by many of formal and efficient causation. Thus, cause was defined by Hobbes as:

> the aggregate of all the accidents both of the agents how many so ever they be, and of the patient, put together; which when they are all supposed to be present, it cannot be understood but that the effect is produced at the same instant.[41]

But this would imply that each cause and effect, and therefore all causes and effects, must occur instantaneously. There can only be one instant. The incoherence of treating the exercise of power or natural necessity as a logical necessity in this way paved the way for David Hume to argue that the world consists of atomic events without any relation between them but that they follow each other in a regular way. The laws of nature are then conceived of as simply the means for making predictions from one event to another.

With the world conceived of as a multiplicity of semi-autonomous self-producing processes, causation can best be seen to consist of, first, immanent causation (that is, self-creation) consisting of supervening causation whereby constituent processes are constrained and efficient causation or action on the rest of the world, and second, conditional causation (the production of the conditions of any process's existence). On the emergence of a process conditional causation differentiates into environmental causation, the environmental conditions of a process and material causation, the maintenance of the constituents of the process (although these are not always entirely separable). Causation cannot be understood as simply the production by an agent of an effect, since the effect must be seen as itself an active response of or appropriation by a process, or as the destruction or coming into being of a semi-autonomous process with its own form of immanent causation which relates itself to the conditions of its emergence. Causally related individuals are not

122

externally related to each other but are part of the being of each other. The notions of immanent and conditional causation are complementary, with each instance of causation being characterizable as either an immanent or a conditional cause depending on which individual they are being defined in terms of. Causation as understood from the perspective of process philosophy must always be understood as durational. As Edward Pols argued:

> The power is exerted in and through a time-unit, and it cannot therefore be isolated as an exercise of power unless we take the whole time-unit into consideration. Any present moment of that time-unit is like a Bergsonian durée, carrying with it its past as qualifying it, and carrying it with it as a means to its own completion.[42]

While such causation is potentially divisible in that it is possible to divide it, it is actually indivisible in the sense that in a shorter period than this duration the exercise of power does not exist.[43] This also is fully intelligible if referred back to the analogy of a piece of music which ceases to be that piece when it is divided; and this leads to another point. Different causal activities require different durations. This is extremely important in hierarchical relations where, as in a melody where the ordering of notes must be of a longer duration than the individual notes, the immanent causation of higher-level processes must have longer durations than the processes ordered by them.

With these categories of activity, order, potentiality, process, structure, event and cause defined, it is now possible to reject the conception of space and time as the self-subsistent, continuous receptacles of all other entities in the universe and to define space-time in relational terms. That is, space-time can be conceived of as emerging or becoming through the constraining of causal interactions within the world. This idea is difficult to comprehend when conceived of in terms of visual analogies but follows automatically once the world is conceived of in terms of auditory analogies.[44] Listening to music, the differentiation of sound produces from the indefinite a directionality and extension. In this, becoming is basic and extension derivative. The past is that which has been formed, while the future is open and yet to be established. And rather than space being an order of places external to each other, this is an order from which extended places emerge from a dynamic, flowing continuum as sub-processes differentiate themselves and achieve some degree of autonomy. Space-time is then an order of potentialities which becomes or emerges with the ordering of activity by a supervening process to produce sub-processes with the potential for independence and interaction. It is the order of potentialities for coexistence and interaction between these sub-processes, and is continually produced and reproduced with the becoming of processes. There is no reason to assume that space-time as an order of potentialities must be of any particular dimension, and three-dimensionality must be seen as a particular constraining of activity.

Conceiving of space-time in this way opens the possibility of there evolving a number of space-time orders. Since all processes, and the space-time orders they produce, are locatable within the space-time of the universe as a whole, it is necessary to acknowledge this as the most basic space-time. However it would be a mistake to disregard the reality of the sub-orders of space-time which have emerged and continue to emerge. The potentials for interaction between various levels of sub-processes cannot be adequately understood within a space-time order in which distances are characterized in terms of light years. It is necessary to acknowledge that this space-time has been articulated in a number of ways, and to pay due regard to this articulation. Thus while galaxies must be seen as coexisting and interacting within cosmic space-time, the nature and coexistence of stars can only be fully understood in terms of galactic space-time, geological processes in geological space-time, life processes in ecological space-time, organic processes in life space-time, perception and action in subjective or lived space-time, social life in terms of a complex of interpersonal space-times, and so on.[45]

THE PHILOSOPHY OF PROCESS AND POSTMODERN SCIENCE

While there is still no final unified vision emerging from postmodern science, or rather, unified understanding, since it is clear that it is no longer possible to conceive of the world as picturable, it is clear that what is emerging is a theory of the world as a creative process of becoming, a world which is irreducibly complex and a world of which it must be recognized that we, as beings struggling to understand the world, are part. That is, it is a conception of the world either inspired by process philosophy, or at least in accordance with it. There are now a large number of works describing the new science, and there is little point in giving a detailed exposition of the whole range of advances being made. However, to show how the categorial scheme described above is applicable to understanding the world and to show how humanity and its place in the cosmos must be reconceived to accord with the philosophy of process, I will offer a brief account of the major scientific theories. There are three major branches of physics, each of which can be interpreted in terms of process philosophy and is being elaborated accordingly: the special and the general theories of relativity, quantum theory and thermodynamics.

The theories of relativity are essentially theories dealing with macro-domains of reality. The special theory is formulated in relation to inertial systems, while the general theory is formulated to take into account accelerating systems also. While there are arguments to the contrary, relativity theory is essentially a rejection of the Newtonian view of space and time as the containers of moving matter, and its replacement by a world conceived of as becoming, in which space-time or time-space is relative to a particular reference system as an emergent order of potentialities for independence and interaction between processes.[46] For any reference system the past is that which can be known about and which can have an effect on the reference system, while the future is that which can be causally affected by the reference system. It is no longer possible to define the present as a simultaneous juxtaposition of points, and this virtually destroys the traditional notion of space as a timeless order spread out under events. As the ultimate order of potentialities, space-time is measured in terms of light-years, the minimum time from the perspective of any particular reference system within this order for different processes or events to be known about or causally influenced from this reference system.

In this scheme, mass is no longer the property of matter, but is a product of motion or activity. Mass can be understood as the sum of both inward and outward activity. Motion or outward activity increases mass in a straightforward way which is easily calculated from Einstein's equations. But the rest mass can also be seen as due to the velocity of movement; of inward activity. For instance, a major component of the rest mass of an atom is contributed by the velocity of the electrons. This leaves only the problem of the rest mass of such elementary constituents which can be neither points nor rigid objects. If rest mass is defined as inward activity then it follows that where there is no rest mass, there is no inward activity and all activity is outward. This is true of all forms of radiation which travel at the velocity of light, c, in all frames of reference, and so can never be considered at rest. This suggests that where there is a velocity of less than c, this is due to an inward reflecting of activity cancelling out the velocity of outward activity, and the creation of elementary particles or entities can be thought of as relatively invariant patterns of inward activity with no substratum apart from this activity.

Quantum theory, the basis for understanding the microdomains of reality, also requires the abandonment of a number of basic assumptions of classical physics. First, the observational situation has to be treated as a whole, and no independent 'reality' can be abstracted from it. Second, the quantum of action is indivisible. Transitions between stationary states are discrete, with systems moving from one state to another without passing through intermediary states. Third, matter has a wave–particle duality, behaving in some cases more like a wave, in others more like a particle, but always in certain ways like both together. Fourth, it is impossible to predict in detail what will happen in each individual observation, implying some degree of indeterminacy in the world.

One of the most important efforts to make sense of these notions is the attempt by David Bohm and his colleagues to develop a non-localizable hidden variable theory.[47] Non-localizable hidden-variable theory has been explicitly formulated in terms of a philosophy of process. It is an attempt to elaborate a theory of the quantum domain which accepts the role of the scientist in the world and the indivisibility of the experimental situation, but takes these features to be characteristics of the world which must be explained. In this theory, the quantum-mechanical wave-function becomes an actual field, but with unusual properties. The particles and waves acknowledged in present quantum theory are seen as manifestations, 'relevated' by particular experimental arrangements, of the more basic non-local order of the quantum field. This provides a coherent conception of the quantum domain in which what are generally taken to be 'things' are seen as emergent processes within the becoming of the universe. As Bohm described his theory:

> What we are suggesting . . . is that all matter is to be understood as a relatively autonomous and constant set of forms built on and carried by the universal and indivisible flux. . . . Such material forms have a certain subsistence, in the sense that under appropriate conditions they can continue with a certain limited possibility for stable existence. However they are not to be regarded as substance, which would be completely stable, permanent and not dependent on something deeper for their continued existence.[48]

The universal flux, the 'holomovement' as it is elsewhere described by Bohm, is an undivided whole, not in the sense that it is indivisible, but in the sense that division has no meaning in relation to it. Difficulties associated with interpreting and developing this theory can be seen to derive from the assumption that only a few kinds of order are intelligible: continuous motion of objects through space, and continuous wave motion through a force-field. To conceive of the holomovement it is necessary to conceive of a kind of order which is prior to localization in any particular place. This is what David Bohm has been trying to do using the hologram as an analogy.[49] Holograms are such that if a photographic plate is illuminated by a laser beam, the eye will see from a range of possible viewing points a three-dimensional structure, as though looking through a window. But the order in the photographic plate is not localized. If only a small part of the plate is illuminated the viewer will still see the whole structure, but with less sharply defined detail and with fewer possible points of view, as though looking through a smaller window. There is an order 'implicated' non-locally in the whole plate. To add a temporal dimension to this conception of order, Bohm and his colleague have utilized an auditory analogy.[50]

While thermodynamics is relevant to all reality, from the macro- to the microdomains, it is most immediately relevant to understanding reality between these domains. In recent years immense strides have been made in the realm of non-equilibrium thermodynamics. The main interest of scientists working on this subject has centred on the study of the generation of new order in thermodynamically far from equilibrium systems: the dissipative structures which either increase or slow down the rate of dissipation of negative entropy.[51] Non-linear thermodynamics deals with the emergence of types of ordering through the amplification of fluctuations which, once established, have a dynamics of their own beyond the conditions of their emergence. Typical examples of this are the turbulence which develops in a laminar flow of fluid (as for instance when a tap is turned on until turbulence develops in the flow of water) and the cellular convection patterns which develop when a liquid is being heated at one end and cooled at the other. Each of these increases the rate of creation of entropy. But such dissipative 'structures' (in terms of my categorial framework 'processes') can also slow down the rate of dissipation of entropy. Dissipative structures have also been revealed in chemical reactions which exchange energy and matter with the environment and are auto- or cross-catalytic. In these there can be a multiplicity of types of order: temporal organization as in a limit cycle, stationary inhomogeneous structures, spatio-temporal organization as in a wave form and localized structures. In all these cases a large number of molecules manifest a coherent order over a large region and period of time. Unlike equilibrium structures which are uniquely determined by their environmental parameters, dissipative structures are involved in cycles of activities in which, if the system is large enough, they establish their own boundaries and undergo state transitions autonomously.

While the work of Prigogine and his colleagues has been concerned with the emergence of order from disorder, this has been complemented by studies of how determinate systems generate indeterminacies, a field which has become widely known through the development of chaos theory.[52] Chaos theory enables systems which were once only describable through statistics to be conceptualized by a form of mathematics which reveals why initially deterministic systems are not entirely predictable. When the notions of dissipative structure and chaos are combined, a picture emerges of a world consisting of both indeterminate and determinate processes, with neither being more basic than the other. Any appearance of determinate order must be seen as emerging from an indeterminate order (or disorder) at one level while generating unpredictable behaviour at another level.

Combined with the breakdown of the reductionist project and with the developments of relativity theories and quantum mechanics, these developments in thermodynamics have inaugurated a new era in science concerned with the emergence of new levels of order and the relationship between microscopic and macroscopic order.[53] Such notions provide a bridge between the science of the animate and the inanimate world. Life forms can be conceived of as complexes of dissipative structures emerging from indeterminate physical and chemical processes and generating in turn indeterminate biological processes. While entropy initially appeared to be an anthropocentric concept, defined only in terms of potentiality for human purposes, the concept of dissipative structures, themselves defined in terms of the transformation of negative entropy into entropy, enables negative entropy and entropy to be defined in terms of potentiality for dissipative structures, of which humans can then be seen as one kind. Humans, cognizing, analysing, experimenting on and engaging with or utilizing negative entropy, must be seen as themselves ordering activity within nature in relation to which potentialities and the processes which generate and maintain them must be defined. This finally invalidates all efforts to reduce thermodynamics to mechanics. As Prigogine and Stengers wrote, 'irreversible processes have an immense constructive importance: life would not be possible without them'.[54]

POSTMODERN BIOLOGY

Radical opposition to mechanistic thinking is much more widespread in the physical sciences than in the biological sciences. This has led to the odd situation described by David Bohm where:

> just when physics is moving away from mechanism, biology and psychology are moving closer to it. If this trend continues it may well be that scientists will be regarding living and intelligent beings as mechanical, while they suppose that inanimate matter is too complex and subtle to fit into the limited categories of mechanism.[55]

Yet even in biology there is a strong stream of anti-mechanistic thinking.

Mechanistic thinking in biology is so widespread because of the success of evolutionary or population biology in accounting for the diversity of life forms in terms of an excess production of individuals struggling for survival, and the success of molecular biology in accounting for heredity and the production of the chemicals which make up organisms. The most recent extension of mechanistic thinking is socio-biology in which efforts are being made to account for social life through population biology. However despite the vigour with which mechanistic thinking is being developed in biology, it is becoming increasingly evident that the gaps in mechanistic explanations of life are immense. There are four main areas where post-mechanistic thinking is making an impact. First, there is epigenesis, the area of biology dealing with the differentiation of cells and the generation of forms. Second, there is the area of biology dealing with self-regulation, where developments in thermodynamics are being utilized to reveal complex forms of hierarchical controls operating in the maintenance and functioning of organisms. Third, there is ecology, where ways of conceiving of the relationships between organisms and between eco-systems and their environments are being forged which transcend both mechanistic approaches – where eco-systems are conceived of as being nothing but aggregates of individuals occupying a given region – and organismic accounts, which reduce individuals to manifestations of the whole. Fourth, through the work of ethologists, the irreducible reality of awareness and thinking in organisms has come to be acknowledged, and in some cases at least partly accounted for in terms which transcend mechanistic thinking.

While such epigenesis is not yet fully understood, a number of facets have been revealed. Most importantly, it has been shown how the development of the organism is canalized along different paths. These have been described by Waddington as 'chreods' (time-paths) and self-stabilization along these paths as 'homeorhesis', corresponding to the notion of homeostasis as self-stabilization at a point. For instance, the development of a piece of tissue is canalized to form a limb, and then canalized to form a fore-limb or hind-limb. If, before the canalization to hind-limb tissue, tissue from the hind-limb is grafted onto the fore-limb region, the disturbance will be buffered out and the tissue will develop into part of a normal fore-limb. If this transplantation is made after canalization to hind-limb tissue, it will develop as hind-limb tissue, but in accordance with its position in the fore-limb. For instance if tissue from the thigh of a bird is transplanted to its wingtip, it will develop into toes and claws. This raises the question of how morphogenetic fields operate, how individual cells gain the positional information which enables them to develop in the appropriate manner and how individual cells are able to respond to this positional information. There is no reason to think that there is only one means for achieving this, but there is evidence that a major role is played by fluctuations and oscillations. This could explain the differentiation into fore-limb and hind-limb tissue which cannot be entirely explained in terms of gene activation, since the behaviour of transplanted tissue rules out the existence of genes for the fore-limb or for the hind-limb.[56]

Both while organisms are developing and after they have reached maturity they are engaged in a perpetual process of self-maintenance and self-realization directed by internally defined criteria of stability and organization. They are involved in self-creation or, as Maturana and Varela described it, 'autopoiesis'.[57] Self-creation in the organism has two fundamental dimensions. While it involves a struggle by the organism to maintain itself as a distinct unit, it must differentiate itself in order to meet requirements which cannot be met in the same place or simultaneously. For instance, in a single cell, chromosome replication must involve temporal differentiation, and since ribosomes cannot occupy the same place as DNA, a nuclear zone is required involving a spatial differentiation. This means that the stability of self-creation cannot be the classical type in which a system is stable in relation to a point, but must be a dynamic stability in which there is a spatio-temporal differentiation. The central feature of this form of organization is that it involves hierarchical levels of constraints of a particular kind. For instance, in the cycle of events by which organisms reproduce themselves, there must be a supervening order to coordinate the temporal differentiation by providing phase information for the relative timing of such events as DNA replication and cell division. Such hierarchical ordering can be achieved on the basis of oscillations generated by states of far from thermodynamic equilibrium. Such oscillations allow for both hierarchical ordering and ordering through entrainment, as with the epigenetic ordering of morphogenetic fields described above. The central feature of hierarchical ordering is that 'levels of control must be distinguished by different time constants' (that is, the relaxation times or times required for the variables to reach a steady state after a 'small' disturbance).[58] If two systems have very different relaxation times, the variables of the faster system can be regarded as always being in a steady state relative to the time required for significant changes to occur in the slower system, while the variables of the slow system will enter into the equations of motion of the fast system as parameters of the environment rather than as variables. In this way the genetic system can be seen as constraining the epigenetic system, and the epigenetic system the metabolic system.[59] A.S. Iberall has shown entrained oscillations to be ubiquitous in organisms.[60] They include the bio-electric nervous cycle, the endocrine systems, the heat balance system, water cycles and so on. The time scales of these were shown by Iberall to vary greatly but to be such as to be able to be entrained in chains so that each oscillation comes to form a coherent part of a whole system. Research in this area has made rapid advances in recent years associated with the advances in non-linear thermodynamics, virtually transforming biology.[61]

The history of ecology in the West is largely the history of early organismic analogies being displaced by reductionist approaches in which the distribution of organisms is accounted for purely in terms of the physical environment.[62] Both these approaches have been severely criticized by Richard Levins and Richard Lewontin, who argue for a conception of the eco-system which 'views the whole as a contingent structure in reciprocal interaction with its own parts and with the greater whole of which it is a part. Whole and part do not completely determine each other.' The ecological community is 'an intermediate entity, the locus of species interactions, between the local species population and the biogeographic region'.[63] Five general properties are assigned to ecological communities. To begin with, the community is a whole in interaction with the lower- and higher-level wholes, while not being completely determined by them.

Second, some of the properties at the community level are definable for that level and are interesting objects of study in their own right. Third, the properties of communities and the properties of constituent populations are linked by many-to-one and one-to-many transformations. This means that there are many possible ways in which the integrity of the whole can be maintained, and many ways in which the parts can adapt to the conditions created by the dynamics of the whole. Fourth, law and constraint are interchangeable. While in physics the boundary conditions within which lawful action is manifest are generally ignored as irrelevant, in ecology the boundary conditions are just as much the object of interest as the lawful behaviour. Fifth, species interact, either directly, as in the predator–prey relation, symbiosis or aggression, or indirectly, through alteration of the common environment.

It is a simple matter to extend this analysis to include the world eco-system as a whole, the 'biosphere' as first Eduard Suiss, then Vladimir Vernadsky called it, or 'Gaia' as James Lovelock and Lynn Margulis more recently have called it.[64] If there is anything distinctive about the biosphere as an eco-system, it is the extent to which interaction is based on alteration of the common environment. Suiss, Vernadsky and Lovelock have been pre-eminently concerned with geological, chemical and atmospheric trans-formations of nature by life processes. The biosphere is taken to include all those geological, atmospheric and biological processes and cycles through which organisms maintain and transform the conditions for life on Earth.

The initial direction of ethology was given to it by Jacob von Uexküll who analysed the constitution by animals of their worlds, focusing on how the perception world and the action world of organisms are related through function circles (for food, for enemies and so on) to constitute first their surrounding worlds, and then, through the coordination and relating of perception and action in different function circles, to inner worlds. By studying the function circles of each organism he revealed the distinctive worlds of different organisms, showing how 'there are as many surround-ing worlds as animals'.[65] The effect of von Uexküll's influence has been to focus attention on the nature of action and perception. Through this focus, ethologists have examined and come to understand the vast variety of life-worlds of organisms, and the diverse means by which these are con-stituted. They have defined awareness and thought in terms of such constitution, and in this way they have revealed the various stages which have led to the complex, social, open-textured worlds constituted by humans.[66]

How then is such cognitive development related to physiological development? The central nervous system is an essential means for regulating interaction and exchanges with the environment in multi-celled organisms and is the precondition for the emergence of consciousness; but

131

consciousness is more than the central nervous system. It is the emergent ordering which actually constrains the functioning of the nervous system. Roger Sperry argued that consciousness can be understood as an emergent feature of the brain. However, while Sperry's analysis of the functioning of the brain provides a good account of emergent properties, he provides no justification for believing that these emergent properties could be equated with conscious awareness. Conscious awareness can only be made sense of in terms of the organism in interaction with its environment. The emergent properties of the brain are better understood in relationship to the total organism defining its environment as a world and then acting within and on this world. This is essentially the view argued for by Gerald Edelman.[67]

HUMANITY'S PLACE IN THE COSMOS

To accord with process philosophy, humanity must be understood as an emergent process or complex of processes within nature, as part of the biosphere, the complex of dissipative structures which has emerged in the thermodynamically far from equilibrium situation maintained on earth by the sun. Like all living entities, humans are processes which define their environments as their world, a world in which they are then sensuously engaged – attracted and repulsed by it, taking it in, incorporating it and excreting it, transforming it and being transformed by it. This characterizes both human individuals and human societies. As Richard Adams wrote:

> societies operate as dissipative structures; they are continuities of form that are constituted by the very flow of energy that is expended (i.e. converted) in the process of acting out the behaviours and doing the work (from both human and non-human sources) that is carried out in the context of social relationships.[68]

However, while humanity is a form of life, not all life is humanity. So what is distinctive about humanity?

Humans cannot be distinguished from other animals by their using tools or by their having a culture which changes from generation to generation. Ethologists have shown that animals have such characteristics also.[69] The evolution of humanity has involved the simultaneous emergence of a complex of interdependent processes and structures. Conceiving of humanity as emergent for the most part provides support for Hegel's conception of humans, although in such a way that the criticisms of the 'Nietzscheans' against the Hegelian assumption of a teleologically ordered cosmos are met. Like the poststructuralists, Hegel rejected Kant's notion of the pre-formed ego, the 'I' represented as a pure unity relating to itself. However, he did not dismiss it as a grammatical fiction, portraying it instead as something which develops from immediate sensitivity to self-

awareness, to self-consciousness gained through a reciprocity of perspectives in interpersonal relationships and then to universality through
participation in ethical and cultural life. Personal identity is not a starting
point, but an achievement. Rejecting the mechanistic reduction of reason
and spirit to mechanical instruments of the appetites, Hegel described this
final formative process of spirit as consisting of three interdependent
dialectical patterns: symbolic representation which operates through the
medium of language; recognition which operates through moral relations;
and the labour process which operates through the tool.[70] In his works
Hegel described the dialectical patterns in which this self-definition is
achieved, and attempted to show how together they constitute the
dynamics of history, conceiving of this as the world spirit coming to
consciousness of itself.

It is this notion of history as the world spirit coming to consciousness
of itself – in Germany – which Nietzsche, Heidegger and the poststructuralists have effectively attacked. However, accepting their arguments does not entail that these dialectical patterns must be dismissed
as the will to power turned against itself, as the 'forgetting of Being' or
as mere illusions. They can be understood as emergent phenomena, and
their development recognized as achievements of humans, as their self-
creation. As dialectical patterns they cannot be understood simply in terms
of individuals, nor as emergent processes transcending individuals, but
must be understood as processes through which individuals emerge to
become semi-autonomous participants in the on-going creative becoming
of these patterns, which at the same time transcend these individuals.
Individuals are struggling for goals which are neither final ends nor
simply potentialities for achieving final ends, but are simultaneously both
ends desired and potentialities for participating in further such desired
ends. The potentialities produced are potentialities both of the dialectical
patterns themselves and of individuals participating in them, and the
becoming of the patterns and of the individuals who emerge in this
becoming is endless. Associated with this, dialectical patterns have no
definite boundaries, either temporal or spatial. Although there is considerable spatial differentiation of social activity insulating people from
each other, all dialectical activity relates itself, even if only through
exclusion, to all potential participants. Finally, dialectical activity carries
with it the possibility of critical reflection and transcendence. To be
participating in these dialectical patterns is to be at least provisionally
committing oneself to certain evaluative stances within these patterns, and
to be at least tacitly aware that such stances are incompatible with other
possible stances and that one's own stance is therefore questionable. So as
Hegel saw, the dialectic of representation carries with it the tendency for
people to transcend limited, one-sided forms of thinking and replace them
with forms of thinking which come nearer to grasping the whole in its

complex diversity; the dialectic of recognition tends to reciprocity, carrying with it a tendency to generate social relations which extend recognition and respect to greater proportions of the population; and the dialectic of labour tends to generate more effective technologies and organizations. The provisional justification of any position within any of these dialectical patterns requires the construction of an historical narrative able to reveal its superiority over rival positions. Humans must constantly construct and reconstruct historical narratives to orient themselves and evaluate actual and possible social and cultural transformations. The breakdown of narrative construction, as is occurring with postmodernity, must inevitably be associated with the fragmentation of communities and with the decline of the societies afflicted.

Each of the three dialectical patterns identified by Hegel has been used by different thinkers as the sole basis for explaining cultural evolution. Structuralists and poststructuralists have reduced all human formation to the dialectic of representation, symbolic interactionists inspired by George Herbert Mead have reduced it to the dialectic of recognition and Marxists have reduced it to the dialectic of labour. This reflects the inadequacy of prevailing theories of causation. However, by using the categories of a philosophy of process, particularly the categories of conditional and immanent causation, it becomes possible to acknowledge the inseparability of each of these dialectical patterns, while still acknowledging that each of them has its own dynamics which must be understood in its own terms.

Such categories also allow for further complexity in the process of human self-formation; for the emergence of multiple processes transcending the imperatives of these dialectical patterns while being dependent upon them. As Georg Simmel argued:

> Whenever life progresses beyond the animal level of culture, an internal contradiction appears. . . . We speak of culture whenever life produces certain forms in which it expresses and realizes itself. . . . But although these forms arise out of the life process, because of their unique constellation they do not share the restless rhythm of life, its ascent and descent, its constant renewal, its incessant divisions and reunifications. . . . They acquire fixed identities, a logic and lawfulness of their own; this new rigidity inevitably places them at a distance from the spiritual dynamic which created them and which makes them independent. . . . This characteristic of cultural processes was first noted in economic change.[71]

Simmel's research programme involved identifying and analysing the nature, generation and reproduction of these forms (structures). Marx's analysis of socio-economic formations, Robert Michels' analysis of the iron law of oligarchy in political parties, Bakhtin's analysis of genres, Michel

Foucault's identification of discursive formations: the asylum, the clinic, the prison and so on, Bourdieu's examination of cultural fields, the work of Wallerstein and his colleagues in describing the development of the world-system of capitalism with its dynamics concentrating economic and political power and differentiating the world economy into cores, semi-peripheries and peripheries, and the accounts of Flannery, Rapaport and Bunker of the tendency of dominant social systems to 'hypercoherence', to increase control, to use up more and more available energy, until a stage is reached where they have so much power that they can survive while contributing little or nothing to the systems on which they are dependent – until they destroy these systems, the conditions of their own existence[72] – these can all be interpreted as studies of emergent social processes in accordance with this research programme.

The conception of society in which a number of semi-autonomous processes are recognized leads to the problem of understanding the relationship between these diverse processes, which in turn has led to the study of different temporalities and spatialities associated with these processes.[73] Most notable in this regard have been the historians of the *Annales* school, who have emphasized the distinction between, as Braudel described it,

> the conspicuous history which holds our attention by its continued and dramatic changes – and that other, submerged history, almost silent and always discrete, virtually unsuspected either by its observers or its participants, which is little touched by the obstinate erosion of time.[74]

Developing this idea further, Braudel argued that a multiplicity of temporalities should be recognized, and the relationships between them investigated:

> History accepts and discovers multidimensional explanations, reaching as it were, vertically from one temporal plane to another. And on every plane there are also horizontal relations and connections. . . . Certain structures live on for so long that they become stable elements for an indefinite number of generations: they encumber history, they impede and thus control its flow. Others crumble away faster. But all operate simultaneously as a support and an obstacle.[75]

Elsewhere he recognized a multiplicity of spatial orders interrelated with these temporal orders.[76]

Thus a society must be understood more as an eco-system of processes (and the structures maintained by them). Such processes incorporate ways of conceiving of the world in terms of which people define themselves and act purposefully, frequently develop according to dynamics which transcend and constrain the dialectical processes, and at the same time are processes within nature and must be understood in relation to geographical and ecological conditions of humanity. These processes are often in conflict with each other, and such conflict can eventually lead to the destruction of one process by another which is dependent upon it for its very existence. The concepts of conditional and immanent causation provide a means to understand and clarify such a multiplicity of relationships of partial dependence and autonomy, and often partial conflict, between the different human processes and between these and other natural processes. These concepts can also be used to make intelligible and to analyse what a spatio-temporal order is (an order of potentialities for coordinated interaction such that this facilitates and is constrained to maintain these potentialities), how different processes generate different spatio-temporal orders and the significance of this for understanding the interrelationships between processes.

With the abandonment of the notion of history as a teleological unfolding of an inner essence, whether of the world spirit or of humanity, a different conception of the place of the individual in the world is required than that implied by Hegelian or Hegelian Marxist thought. This does not require the dissolution of the subject as an illusion, or as simply a manifestation of language and the product of the discipline of discursive formations, as the poststructuralists, following Nietzsche, have argued. Individuals can be seen as emergent processes from, and within, nature, culture and society, and as participants in the process of becoming of the world with some degree of autonomy from the conditions of their emergence. This autonomy amounts to providing further constraints upon oneself than those imposed by entry into the symbolic order or those imposed by discipline, but it is this which is freedom, the freedom to create oneself as a person of integrity.

It is here that process philosophy supports some of the arguments of the existentialists, although with important modifications. The existentialist critique of Hegel began with Schelling's later philosophy and was further articulated by Kierkegaard, who had attended Schelling's lectures. Kierkegaard was troubled by how in Hegel's system 'the existing subjectivity tends more and more to evaporate'.[77] Rejecting Hegel's faith that the finitude of existence could be transcended by taking the perspective of the Absolute, that philosophy could escape 'from the weary strife of passions that agitate the surface of society into the calm region of contemplation'[78] Kierkegaard argued:

The principle that the existing subjective thinker is constantly occupied in striving, does not mean that he has, in the finite sense, a goal toward which he strives, and that he would be finished when he had reached this goal. No, he strives infinitely, is constantly in the process of becoming.[79]

Kierkegaard did not make the mistake of taking the subjective thinker as an absolute reference point, a Cartesian cogito. In *Sickness Unto Death* he argued:

> The self is a relation which relates itself to its own self, or it is that in the relation that the relation relates itself to its own self; the self is not the relation but that the relating relates itself to its own self. . . . So regarded, man is not yet a self.[80]

In this way, Lacan's and Derrida's objections to the subject taken as an absolute were anticipated. However, Kierkegaard still abstracted the individual from all physical, biological, social and cultural contexts.

In terms of a philosophy of process, the individual as a process of becoming must be understood as an emergent process within the world. It justifies a conception of humans as essentially creative, characterized not so much by their ability to produce a culture but by their ability to transcend old cultural forms. Through participation by the sensitive organism in the dialectical processes of becoming and the various semi-autonomous processes of society, the organism is individuated as a subject, and this individuation consists in the emergence of the capacity, inherent in the nature of the different dialectical processes, to reflect on the conditions of its existence, to take responsibility for its conception of the world, to choose which others to regard as significant and to strive to live life accordingly, modifying or transforming relationships of power in the process. That is, the individual has the potential (cultivated in some societies, suppressed in others) to develop a mind.[81] The mind is not a substance. It is something achieved. To make up one's mind is to interpret one's situation, to commit oneself to projects accordingly, and to have gained sufficient self-mastery to persist against obstacles in the effort to realize these projects. To have a mind of one's own is to have developed one's understanding, to have established one's convictions about the nature of the world and oneself and what projects are worth striving to realize, and to be able to formulate effective projects of action in accordance with these convictions and to be prepared to act accordingly. Freedom as the potential for self-determination is a function both of the development of mind and the nature of the individual's situation, and there is no guarantee that it will be achieved. Children are born in chains, and the challenge of life is liberation; but this liberation is always socially, biologically and physically situated.

The nature of this situated creativity has been illuminated in a way which accords with a philosophy of process by Paul Ricoeur's analysis of narrative. For Ricoeur, life itself is lived as an inchoate narrative. Second, action is configured by being represented according to specific rules of emplotment. Innovations are made by inventing plots by means of which 'goals, causes, and chance are brought together within the temporal unity of whole and complete action'.[82] A complete action can consist of a number of other actions, and it can be the action of an individual – from some particular achievement to having lived a whole life, or of a group or community, such as winning a war, founding a nation or establishing or destroying a civilization. The third aspect is the reception and actualization of such representations, and the refiguring by people of their lives. People are confronted with and drawn into the quasi-world, distancing them from their own life-worlds, revealing and challenging their taken-for-granted horizons of expectations. They are provided with room to manoeuvre, to think about the way they live and to live according to the new narrative structure.

5

TOWARDS A NEW WORLD ORDER

While postmodern culture has contributed to the dissolution of all opposition to the latest and most rampant force for environmental destruction – global capitalism dominated by transnational corporations and financial institutions, and controlled by a new international bourgeoisie – it has exposed some of the most basic cultural structures on which Western European civilization in general and modernity in particular have been based. This has provided the conditions for a radical critique of Western civilization. However, despite the insights which have been gained, and despite some effort to develop a new political philosophy, those engaged in this critique, the poststructuralists, have not provided the means to come to terms with the situation confronting us. What is required is a new postmodernism which not only negates the cultural forms of modernity, but which can replace these forms. In the previous chapter it was argued that the development of postmodern science based on process philosophy, a philosophy which supports poststructuralist or postmodernist attacks on the reification of abstract entities, could provide the foundation for such a cultural movement.

But it is not enough to defend a new cosmology in opposition to the cosmology which has underpinned modernity. It is necessary to articulate this in such a way that it can effectively challenge the hegemonic culture, so that it can orient people in practice, in their daily lives, to create an environmentally sustainable civilization. To do this it will be necessary to construct a new grand narrative, a grand narrative formulated in terms of the cosmology based on a philosophy of process.

TOWARDS A NEW GRAND NARRATIVE

One of the consequences of the postmodern loss of faith in grand narratives, and all narratives to some extent, is to have revealed the importance of narratives for the constitution of subjects, social organizations and societies.[1] It has shown how we only know what to do when we know what story or stories we find ourselves a part of. If this is the

139

case, then to know what to do about the environmental crisis requires the creation of stories which individuals can take up and participate in, which will reveal to them why there are the problems there are and how they arose, how they can be resolved and what role individuals can play in resolving them. The bio-regional narratives called for by Cheney are important in this regard; but given the way the world-economy functions, more is required. What is clearly lacking are stories of sufficient power and complexity to orient people for effective action to overcome environmental problems, to relate the multiplicity of social and cultural forms implicated in or affected by environmental destruction, to reveal what possibilities there are for transforming these and to reveal to people what roles they can play in this project. Environmental problems are global problems and their causes are global; it will be impossible for stories to effectively orient individuals for effective action to overcome these problems unless the stories pertaining to people's individual lives and to local problems can be integrated with broader narratives, and ultimately with a grand narrative revealing the relationship between the lives of individuals and the dynamics of the global political and economic order.

In order for such stories to 'work', to inspire people to take them seriously, to define their lives in terms of them and to live accordingly, such stories must be able to confront and interpret the stories by which people are at present defining themselves and choosing how to live in an environmentally destructive way. It is also important to reveal the way power operates, and show why those individuals who are concerned about the global environmental crisis are unable effectively to relate their own lives to such problems. The new grand narrative must enable people to understand the relationship between the stories through which they define themselves as individuals and the stories by which groups constitute themselves and define their goals, ranging from families, local communities, organizations and discursive formations, to nations, international organizations and humanity as a whole. Quite apart from the need to relate individuals to the dynamics of the world economy, a new grand narrative is required to comprehend and reveal the inadequacies of the grand narratives which have dominated societies in the past, and which are still operative in the present.

While it can be acknowledged that all previous grand narratives were oppressive, this can be avoided. Past grand narratives were essentially 'monological', narratives in which all participants were subordinated to the rule of one, non-reflexive perspective. However Mikhail Bakhtin has identified a second kind of narrative, a polyphonic, dialogical narrative in which a multiplicity of perspectives are represented, where through dialogue the narrative reflects on its own development and, as Julia Kristeva put it, 'constructs itself through a process of destructive genesis'.[2] A polyphonic grand narrative in the form of a dialogic discourse could take into account the diversity of cultures and the multiplicity of local stories by which humanity has formed and is forming itself, and allow that any totalizing perspective utilized to give coherence to the narrative must only be accepted provisionally, that it has rivals and that it is always possible that in the future some better alternative might be developed.

What gives coherence to narratives is the interpretations of the world on which they are based. Even the simplest stories assume one or more relatively coherent ways of interpreting the world, of defining the possible relationships between people and between humans and nature. The evaluations of what futures are possible and what futures are most worth realizing are tied up with such ways of interpreting the world. Grand narratives have always embodied a cosmology, a conception of the nature of humanity and the place of humanity in the cosmos. The grand narratives which have dominated European civilization, which have conceived of history as progress towards some final catastrophe which will inaugurate an ideal future state, or as the education of humankind and the advance of reason, or as the liberation of humanity from bondage or as the domination of nature through technology, embody the cosmology formed through the synthesis in Ancient Rome of neo-Platonic philosophy and Hebraic religious thought. The grand narratives dominating modernity embody the transmutations of this cosmology which was effected in the seventeenth, eighteenth and nineteenth centuries with the rise of modern science. The orthodox formulation of Marxism is a grand narrative which embodies a radicalized version of the cosmology of Christian neo-Platonism – and is only a modification of the dominant grand narrative of progressive domination of nature. It is by virtue of the cosmologies of neo-Platonic Christianity and mechanistic materialism and the basic assumptions about the nature of existence on which these are based that it has been possible to construct the complex order of narratives which have constituted European civilization. While it is these interpretations which must be challenged, this is only possible through the construction of a new complex of narratives, integrated into a grand narrative founded on an alternative cosmology.

As an alternative cosmology, a philosophy of process gives a place to beings who partially create themselves by constructing narratives, and provides a way of interpreting the world on the basis of which new, polyphonic, environmentally sensitive narratives can be constructed. The two dimensions of the problem are solved together. Science based on mechanistic materialism lent itself to being identified with technology and its development. Its central problem was that while serving as an instrument for dominating the world, it made agency inconceivable, and finally reduced people themselves to things to be controlled. While it has permeated social life through the narratives of technological advance which have been formulated in terms of it, it has made it impossible to account for the way people are able to create themselves as human beings through constructing narratives. Conceiving of the world as a process of creative becoming consisting of a multiplicity of different types of processes in various complex relations, each making its own unique contribution to the becoming of the world, which must be understood at least to some extent as an immanent cause of its own becoming, can allow that humans create themselves through culture, and in particular, through being enacted by, reformulating and then enacting stories about themselves and their place in the world. It can allow for people having intentions formulated in relation to the stories by which they define themselves, and through realizing these intentions, coming to embody within the world, in the relationships between people, in the relationships between individuals and society and in the relationships between humans and nature, the interpretations of the world on which these stories are based. With its rejection of reductionism, it lends itself to being formulated into a dialogical rather than a monological grand narrative, and thereby enables the achievements of all communities, societies and civilizations of the world to be appreciated.

Once the world is conceived of as a creative process of becoming, the notion that the meaning of anything is given by the end which it helps to realize, the notion which as Nietzsche pointed out is the ultimate source of the nihilism of European civilization, can be abandoned. Each individual process or sub-process within the universe is like a melody singing itself within a symphony. While it must be evaluated in terms of its contribution to the whole symphony (which in the case of the cosmos is never complete), a symphony cannot be evaluated in terms of its final outcome, its end. The whole duration of a symphony matters, and each melody within the symphony, each note within the melody, are significant in themselves as parts of this duration. People understanding the world and themselves in such terms should be able to appreciate processes ranging from atoms, molecules, clusters of galaxies, galaxies, stars, planets, global eco-systems and species, to individual organisms, societies and cultures, as having an intrinsic significance as contributions to the unfinished becoming of the world. They should be able to appreciate the significance of their own lives and each decision and action as contributions to the world as a whole as well as to the cultures, societies and eco-systems of which they are part. But they should also be able to appreciate the intrinsic significance of their own lives as such, and that part of the significance of cultures, societies and eco-systems and the world as a whole is as conditional causes of their own becoming, for having made it possible for them to live an intrinsically significant life.

Formulating stories about the lives of people and the history of societies in these terms will enable people to be understood in the context of and as part of nature, as destructive or constructive contributions to the eco-systems which sustain the conditions of their existence. However, such narratives must have a more complex form than the narratives which have dominated European civilization in the past – and must abandon the Oedipal form of narrative which legitimates present suffering as the unavoidable path to some final reunification of the world. Since the world is conceived of as consisting of a multiplicity of processes and sub-processes, each partially autonomous yet inseparable from a multiplicity of other processes which are the conditional causes of its existence, it is impossible to accept a linear narrative in which all but the history of the main subject is treated as a passive background of the drama. For any individual, whether this be a person, an institution, a movement, a class, a nation, a civilization or humanity as a whole, what is required is a multi-dimensional narrative at least acknowledging thousands of different temporal and spatial orders, both within the becoming of humanity and within the rest of nature. Such a narrative should then highlight the way the becoming of any individual is promoting or stultifying other processes.

Conceiving of narratives in this way would avoid the tendency noted by poststructuralists of reducing people differentiated from the prot-agonists of a story to the 'Other'. For instance, it would avoid the tendency of history to focus on the rise of Western civilization and to deny a story to societies subjugated by it, those whom Eric Wolfe described as the 'people without history',[3] to characterize 'women' and Orientals not in terms of their unique histories, but only in opposition to or as a counterpart to the history made by males of European descent.[4] This does not mean that a history of humanity should not grant a central place to the rise and world domination of Western civilization; but rather than conceiving of this as progress, it should be understood as analogous to the situation in China in the third century BC. The Ch'in, founded on the mechanistic philosophy of Legalism, had by their ruthless aggressiveness ended the period of the warring states by unifying China under an extremely oppressive social order. Western civilization has through its ruthless aggressiveness united the world into one economic system. In ancient China the Ch'in were overthrown and replaced by a much more benign rule inspired by the philosophies of Confucianism and Taoism. What is required of a new grand narrative is an account of how we arrived at the present global environmental crisis, and a characterization of the challenge now confronting humanity as the replacement of the oppressive and destructive civilization which has united the world by a new global civilization based on a more adequate world-orientation in which nature, the oppressed, non-Europeans and women throughout the world are accorded due recognition.[5]

Lyotard argued that even if a new grand narrative were formulated, there is no reason to assume that people will accept it. To begin with, this is certain to be the case. Postmodern culture is so fragmented and fragmenting that to get a new grand narrative taken seriously is far more difficult than was the case when people at least accepted the need for some grand narrative. People defining themselves and orienting their lives through a new grand narrative will be like the Christians in the last years of the Roman Empire described by St Augustine, strangers in the societies in which they must live their everyday lives. But like these Christians, those adhering to the new narrative must become the seeds which will crystallize a new post-European civilization.[6] Given the immediate threat to the global environment, it is not enough for those adopting the new narrative to withdraw into monasteries to wait for the collapse and total disintegration of the present order, as Alasdair MacIntyre suggested in *After Virtue*.[7] It will be necessary to begin to build this new civilization while the old civilization, despite its nihilism and the fragmentation of its culture, is still vigorous and powerful; more powerful than any civilization which has ever existed. For a new grand narrative to be efficacious under these circumstances it must be articulated so as to be able to inform political action. But this raises the question of what kind of political action can be efficacious in a postmodern world? – a world in which discursive formations are proliferating and augmenting their own power at the expense of individuals and in which the global economy now transcends the reach of even the most powerful states? My contention is that it will be necessary to develop an environmentalist form of nationalism to subordinate the discursive formations which are dominating people's lives, to counter the power of global capitalism, and to move large numbers of people to action. That is, it will be necessary to reconstruct narratives about regions which will enable all members of this region to identify themselves as participant agents committed to conserving and preserving the environment of their region. Then to articulate this, to provide the basis for decision-making, it will be necessary to develop a science of humanity which can analyse the complex power relations between social, political and economic processes and provide an alternative to the mainstream social sciences, particularly economic theories, as a basis for formulating policies and programmes of action.

NATIONALISM

Postmodern culture has been profoundly anti-nationalistic. The theoretical opposition to nationalism, utilizing poststructuralist philosophy, has come from 'subaltern historians', that is, historians of the Indian subaltern classes.[8] The consequences of this are now with us. Anti-nationalism has enabled the New Right to break down efforts to control national economies, and because of the success of the New Right in the 1980s, the world is now facing the most severe depression since the 1930s. As in the depression of the 1930s, the extreme right has been granted almost exclusive rights to the banner of nationalism. This has facilitated the rise of racist, fascist political parties throughout the world. The only alternative offered to this racism and to the ethnic violence associated with the breakup of the communist countries of Eastern Europe and the Balkans has been a vapid internationalism.

While environmental problems require a global orientation, and while the development of institutions to represent and foster such an orientation is an essential part of the environmentalist struggle, in a world in which even most national governments in the economic centres have failed effectively to confront their own environmental problems it is hardly likely that actions taken by international organizations will have much success unless backed by strong local organizations. The struggle against global environmental problems is only likely to succeed through the development of strong nation-states committed to subordinating the operations of the market to politically defined ends – notably the conservation and preservation of the environment, and which can effectively represent local environmental concerns within broader regional and international organizations. To be successful, environmentalists will have to struggle for representation of the environment in both national and regional politics, and then use the environment as a focus to mobilize people to liberate themselves from the destructive imperatives of the world economy. What is required is an environmentalist nationalism which can harness the legitimate anger against global capitalism to carry out the massive transformations necessary to create an environmentally sustainable civilization.

At the same time, the promotion of nationalism is required to recreate the sense of community and personal identity, to overcome the fragmentation of postmodern culture which is undermining any concerted opposition to existing trends. In the modern world, radical political movements, including Marxist movements, have only ever been successful where they have been more or less explicitly fused with local cultural traditions as nationalist movements, and nationalism has been central to the struggles of every other country which has been at all successful in overcoming its subjugation by the world-market. As Dudley Seers argued in *The Political Economy of Nationalism*, only by cultivating nationalist sentiments will it possible to mobilize people to bear the costs of the struggle for regional control over economic life, to generate concern by people for justice for their compatriots, to inspire them to develop forms of life which conserve resources and to develop institutions powerful enough to tackle broader environmental problems.[9] Only through nationalistic struggles has the hold of the consumer-oriented culture of the economic cores been broken, forms of relationships between people transcending commodity fetishism been developed, the organizational basis and the cultural conditions for confronting the long-term problems associated with the environment created and the possibility of transcending capitalism altogether revealed.

The point is that except for professional intellectuals, pure cosmopolitanism is too rarefied an orientation in the struggle for justice. Most people need to feel that they will be recognized and taken into account at a more immediate level before they will define their own lives in terms of the struggle for justice.

Nationalism must continue to be fostered in the Third World. Environmental limitations have exposed the illusion that present hardships in the Third World are just stages on the way to affluence and that it is possible for everyone in the world to live the lifestyles of people in the affluent North. They have revealed the cost to peripheral nations integrating into the world-economy to be the loss of their reserves and the destruction of their resources. Those people who have overcome their poverty have been those who have relied on their own efforts. As Denis Goulet argued on the basis of a study of strategies for development in Guinea-Bissau: 'Paradoxically, the lesson of greatest importance is that the best model of development is the one that any society forges for itself on the anvil of its own specific conditions.'[10] So, as James Lamb argued:

> Development should be a *struggle* to create criteria, goals, and means for self-liberation from misery, inequity, and dependency in all forms. Crucially, it should be the process a people choose, which heals them from historical trauma, and enables them to achieve a newness on their own terms.[11]

This has been the secret of the success of Kerala in India and Zimbabwe in Africa.[12] For the sake of humanity Third World people should recognize this, and struggle through local, national and regional organizations to preserve their environments from exploitation by the economic core regions. Given the location of most environmental destruction in the Third World, this struggle for liberation should be recognized as the most important struggle for the preservation of the world environment.

The primary goal of environmentalists in the affluent core economies should be the termination or radical reduction of the economic links between their countries and Third World economies, an end to the exploitation of Third World reserves and resources, an end to the importation of agricultural products and timber and an end to interference in governments or support for oppressive governments in the Third World. What is needed is action by states and other political organizations to break up the power of transnational corporations and international finance, and most importantly, to reduce the voracious appetite for materials by the core zones. As Stephen Bunker argued: 'Ultimately the need is to slow the flow of energy to the world centre.'[13] But this struggle should not be thought of in purely altruistic terms. It should be seen as part of and linked to the struggle to stop the bankrupting of farmers and the deindustrialization and associated unemployment and subsequent impover-

146

ishment of people in these core zones.[14] For all regions of the world, to avoid exploitation, to escape the vicissitudes and pressures of the international capitalist system and to gain democratic control over their economies, to turn the advantages of improved technology to bettering the conditions of life, as far as is possible regions should aim at economic self-sufficiency.[15] As John Maynard Keynes argued in 1933: 'Ideas, knowledge, science, hospitality, travel – these are the things which should of their nature be international. But let goods be homespun whenever it is reasonably and conveniently possible, and above all, let finance be primarily national.'[16] With recent developments in technology, such localization of production is now more possible for most goods than ever. The task ahead of people in the economic core zones and semi-peripheries is to escape their enslavement from the dynamics of the international capitalist order, to create steady-state economies for their own benefit, for the benefit of people in the Third World, for the benefit of all future generations and for the benefit of all other forms of life. The most potent ideological weapon in the struggle for such economic and political autonomy is nationalism.

NATIONS AS NARRATIVELY CONSTITUTED IMAGINARY COMMUNITIES

It would appear then that the liberation of life will be achieved through the development of a reformulated nationalism or it will not be achieved at all. But in the past nationalism has been linked with imperialism, wars of aggression and the persecution of minorities. So just what is nationalism? How does it mobilize people? And are its destructive tendencies inevitable? Nationalism is essentially 'a territorial ideology',[17] while modern states are territorial political institutions. Nations are both cultural and political phenomena. As Benedict Anderson has argued, the nation is 'an imagined political community' which is created through being imagined.[18] The type of imagination which made nationalism possible was created by the rise of the novel and the newspaper, allowing for an 'anonymous' community with members conducting their affairs simultaneously, yet independently and without awareness of what other members are doing. In the modern world, nationalism, affirming the community of people in a region despite the fact that only a very small proportion of these people know each other personally, provides people with an identity as part of this community. It relates both to the traditions of the people in a region, and to the future, the common destiny of these people. In short, nationalism situates people as part of an unfinished story of the people of a region.

Nationalism serves to coordinate people's actions and lives, to mobilize them for action, and to legitimate the institutions of the state – at least insofar as the state represents the nation. It serves the state by strengthening the institutional relationships between the state and civil society, by furthering the internal unification of culturally and economically diverse regions into a more homogeneous state territory, determining the geographical boundaries of the state and dividing one political community from another accordingly. Conversely, by affirming the existence of a community, nationalism legitimates demands that the state itself be just and that it put to rights injustices perpetrated against its members, that is, that the state properly represent all members of the nation. As John Breuilly argued on the basis of his exhaustive examination of the history of nationalism: 'an effective nationalism develops where it makes political sense for an opposition to the government to claim to represent the nation against the present state'.[19]

Nationalism has taken a variety of forms.[20] To begin with, nationalism emerged in Spain, England and France as the merchant classes of these societies struggled for political representation in the new absolutist states which had emerged from the late feudal kingdoms. While this nationalism developed through the cultural unity engendered by the development of new print-languages, culture was not an issue in its development, and the nations involved were assumed to correspond to the territorial boundaries of the state. Such nationalism was identified with the democratization of government. The growth in power of England and France was a stimulus for the development of two other forms of European nationalism – the separationist nationalism of the Irish, of Belgium and Norway, and the unificationist nationalism of Italy, Germany and Poland. In each of these cases the promotion of national cultures was central and preceded the emergence of national states. Outside Europe, nationalism first developed among European colonies in the struggles for independence, then a 'reform' nationalism developed in countries threatened by European imperialism, notably in Japan, Turkey and China. Towards the end of the nineteenth century and culminating in the Second World War, European nationalism was extended to include the working class in the community of the nation, but at the same time, at least among the major powers, it became more authoritarian and expansionist. It came to be associated with a rejection of the right of every nation to political self-determination and independence and the assertion of the privileged position of one's own nation – the 'chosen nation'.[21] However, there were other European states in which a new reform nationalism developed to mobilize people against the vicissitudes of the world capitalist economy without this chauvinist quality. Such reform nationalism, associated with the development of the social or liberal corporate states, became increasingly influential among small European nations after the Second World War.[22] There also emerged at this time a post-colonialist nationalism in the Third World, in some cases serving to unify inherited political divisions, in others to separate regions from inherited state structures or to combine regions across state boundaries. Finally, a new set of nationalist movements have emerged within Europe striving for independence from old states, for instance in Scotland, Flanders, Croatia and Estonia.

While the fostering of nationalism has led to greater justice and vast improvements in the quality of life of those who are united by it, it is undeniable that nationalism is associated with tendencies to deny justice to racial minorities and outsiders. Morishima wrote of the Japanese:

> there are two quite different yardsticks governing the behaviour of the Japanese, one applied to those within one's own circle, and another applied to those outside it. In this sense neither have the Japanese been logical, nor have they shown any sensibility towards the precepts of universal justice.[23]

This seems to be typical of nationalist societies, and such double standards have been responsible for some of the most devastating wars and persecutions the world has known. It is these destructive tendencies of nationalism which have been used to justify the claim of cosmopolitan intellectuals that nationalism is essentially pathological. But are double standards and their consequences inevitable? Benedict Anderson has argued that they are not. He reminds us that far from being a concomitant of nationalism, racism is a throwback to notions of class. As he put it:

> The fact of the matter is that nationalism thinks in terms of historical destinies, while racism dreams of eternal contaminations, transmitted from the origins of time through an endless sequence of loathsome copulations: outside history. . . . The dreams of racism actually have their origin in ideologies of class, rather than in those of nation: above all in claims to divinity among rulers and to 'blue' or 'white' blood and 'breeding' among aristocracies.[24]

The ideology of nationalism is more consistent with quest for universal justice. One case which illustrates this relationship is the nationalism promoted in the 1930s in Sweden.

Up until the 1930s, Sweden was dominated by the export-oriented fraction of the bourgeoisie. This group was defeated during the Great Depression when the workers, in alliance with farmers' interest groups and manufacturers producing for the home market, gained power. This alliance recast Swedish political culture through the concept of 'peoples' home' (*folkshemspolitik*). Gören Therborn described the role of this concept:

> The Peoples' Home had an implicit connotation of 'family' – rather than 'house' – of family community and equality with 'no favourites or stepchildren'. It connoted common concern and caring for each other and had its focus on society rather than on the state and particular institutions.[25]

This universalism transcended the notion of individuals' social rights, and replaced it with a *Weltanschauung* of national solidarity. In accordance with this, Alva Myrdal presented the case for social security not as a question of social insurance, but as a question 'of social policy, as a productive social policy – as common investment by the nation in its future welfare – with its accentuation of family policy and of preventative measures'.[26]

It is notable that the Swedes defined their ideals in terms of a conception of people as essentially creative social beings rather than as consumers. The Social Democratic Party did not formulate the goal of equality in utilitarian terms, but as equal freedom for people to shape their future, 'to develop their inherent talents and fully express themselves in society'.[27] This enabled them to create the most egalitarian society of the modern world.[28] Correspondingly, the Swedes more consistently and successfully addressed environmental problems than virtually any other nation (although most of their environmental problems had causes outside Sweden), and despite their cold climate, they used only one half as much energy per head of population as people in the USA.[29]

Such reform nationalism has been emulated by a number of countries since the Second World War in their efforts to mobilize against the vicissitudes of the international economy.[30] And it would seem that it is a suitable model for at least small core or semi-peripheral nations. However, Partha Chatterjee has condemned nationalism in the colonial world as a foreign doctrine that has facilitated the emergence of Western-oriented élites.[31] To avoid such tendencies, a new kind of nationalism is required. It is necessary to develop a multi-levelled nationalism, one in which extended nationalisms are developed to unite weaker states against the states of the economic core zones and the global economy, so relieving the pressure to exploit sub-regions, while simultaneously sub-nationalisms are developed in sub-regions of states to gain or regain local control over their administration.

In relation to major regions of the world, the role of the black African block in opposing South Africa, the Islamic block in opposing international imperialism, the European Economic Community in moving against the domination of the world politico-economic order by the USA, and the Latin American block in supporting Argentina during the Falklands/Malvinas war, suggest the increasing role that an extended form of nationalism might play in the resistance to domination and exploitation and in the promotion of justice within these regions. This is likely to be important in the near future for South America, since it is only by following the sort of advice given by Jacobo Schatan – to collectively refuse to recognize that part of its debt deriving from the rise in interest rates and the decline in the prices of its resources – that the present debt crisis will ever be resolved.[32] This will require unity on the part of all Latin America against US bankers and their representatives in the US government if it is to be successful.

At a local level, the sense of community promoted within the 3,000 communes, 192 districts and 22 cantons of Switzerland illustrates the role local or sub-nationalism can play. Through a commercial code which allows companies to choose their shareholders, set limits to the number of shares held by any one shareholder and to refuse to register shares,[33] the Swiss have been able to prevent the takeover of their companies by outsiders and to ensure that shareholders are in a weak position relative to 'stakeholders' – bondholders, employees, customers, suppliers and members of the local community.[34] This has enabled cantons as moral communities to take responsibility for their members in a way which has virtually eliminated poverty and unemployment, and prevented the enforced migration of people to the major cities. Switzerland is virtually free of the large regional divisions in prosperity which afflict most capitalist countries, particularly Great Britain, the USA and Italy. Associated with this subordination of the economy to the community, there is minimal private conspicuous consumption (at least compared to the United States) which, along with the greater decentralization of the population, has resulted in a rate of consumption of energy per head of population one third of that within the USA, despite their higher standard of living.

NATIONALISM AND COSMOLOGY: POSTMODERN NATIONALISM

The question is then, how can a form of nationalism be promoted which mobilizes people to preserve and conserve their environments and to accord with the struggle for international justice, rather than to expand their economies, and without the tendency towards racism, ethnic violence and militarism? As we have seen, the development of nationalism first requires a struggle for the cultural independence and the development of a sense of cultural identity in the regions in which people live. For this reason Dudley Seers argued for the development of national cultures. To this end he called for education in the traditional arts subjects, arguing that 'the centre-piece of education is history, the history of the nation *in relation to its continent and the world*, ranging right up to the present'. And he argued for the importance of 'making people familiar with their nation's cultural heritage – myths, fables, songs, dances, carvings and sculpture, buildings, etc. – which expresses national experience and can help inhibit the growth of cultural dependence'.[35] These are important. But such an education by itself is too passive. There is no reason to suppose that the culture of any region will be adequate in its existing form for what is required of it. What is required of education is the induction of people into

151

an on-going dialogue so that they can become critical participants in the formulation of the story of the nation of which they are part and define their own lives in terms of participation in this story;[36] and to achieve this it is necessary to see cultural development and nationalism in terms of a theory of culture, a cosmology and a general philosophy.

The philosophy of process provides this perspective. The culture of a region can be seen as part of the process of a people's self-creation, part of their on-going struggle (with varying degrees of success) to orient themselves, practically and theoretically, in relation to nature, to each other, to their society and to outsiders; to recognize and appreciate nature's, their own and each other's significance and potentialities, and to work towards realizing these potentialities. At the same time each culture can be seen as a contribution to life and to the culture of humanity, as part of humanity's and the world's self-creation. All such self-creation is genuine creation, not entirely determined by past and present conditions, and yet is dependent on its environmental and material conditions, including the cultures of others in the past and in the present. By highlighting the point that only through some cultural diversity is it possible for unique situations to be appreciated, different possibilities explored and the limitations of each culture revealed, this conception of culture enables the unique significance of one's local culture and all its sub-cultures (and the members of one's society bearing and developing this culture) to be better appreciated, while at the same time providing a critical perspective on this and all other cultures, allowing individuals to assimilate aspects of other cultures to their own culture. By seeing this cultural development in terms of the new cosmology, this struggle for national independence can be seen as a struggle within nature, as part of the world's struggling to become conscious of itself in all its diversity and to reveal and realize its potentialities. The study of the local environment is part of the development of culture, and by fostering a recognition of the relationship of society to its environment in the past, present and future, nationalism can be fused with the commitment to conserving and preserving the integrity of this environment.

Nationalism can then be redefined as the commitment by a regional community, through the stories by which it defines itself, to justice within the region, where justice is understood as the appropriate recognition and acknowledgement of all beings – individuals, communities, animals and eco-systems, in thought and action. It is the commitment to preserving and developing the potentialities of beings – natural, cultural, social and individual – for survival, for a full life and for contributing to society, to humanity, to local and world culture and to life itself. Above all, as the ultimate condition of all potentialities, nationalism must involve a commitment to preserving and conserving the local environment, its fertility, the genetic diversity of its fauna and flora, the integrity of the eco-systems

152

which maintain these and its mineral reserves; and to preserving and developing built-up environments which provide the conditions for the maintenance and development of local culture, society and its individual members.

By providing a way of thinking about one's place in the world which neither atomizes the world nor dissolves each part into the totality, the new cosmology makes it possible to formulate a multi-levelled nationalism, to acknowledge the significance and partial autonomy of the community of one's local region while seeing this as participating in a national community which itself has a partial autonomy, which is in turn participating in a broader regional community with some partial autonomy (such as South America or Western Europe), which again is participating in a world community which is more than the sum of all the particular communities which compose it. Individuals can then be simultaneously nationalistic in relation to their local region, to their country and to a major region of the world, while at the same time being committed to international justice and to the subordination of national interests to the interests of humanity and to non-human life where appropriate. The question then is one of justice, of appropriately acknowledging the uniqueness and significance of each level of the communities of which people are part.

Nations can then be evaluated according to their generativity or decadence, according to whether or not their members are willing and able to realize their highest ends or are 'falling away' from these ends; that is, whether they are participating creatively rather than destructively in the becoming of the world, whether they are producing rather than undermining the conditions for the becoming of other people, other societies and other life forms. The prime duty of governments must then be seen as striving to preserve and develop the potentialities of the society – its members, its organizations and its environment – to participate creatively in the becoming of the world, and any government which is not striving for this must be regarded as corrupt. Environmental nationalism must then be seen as the struggle to maintain, to transform or to create power structures, from the local to the international level, which appropriately recognize the people of a region, their future generations, non-human forms of life and the general environment, which effectively articulate the needs, concerns, potentialities and aspirations of these people, whatever their race or ethnic origins, and which at least strive for the conditions for generativity.

POLICY FORMATION AND POLITICAL ECONOMY AND THE SOCIAL SCIENCES

Even when people are mobilized by a commitment to justice they are unlikely to have much impact unless they can formulate clear social,

153

political and economic policies and programmes. One of the most important requirements for translating nationalist sentiments into effective action
to create a new, environmentally sustainable social order is the means
systematically to formulate such policies and programmes. At present,
government policies and programmes are overwhelmingly formulated on
the basis of neo-classical economic theory, in which the economy is treated
as a closed system, driven by greed, tending towards equilibrium, and in
which nature is treated as nothing but a passive resource. Evaluation is
generally based on some version of cost-benefit analysis. Cost-benefit
analyses, extending the logic of commodity fetishism, assume that the
world can be understood as a collection of actual or possible states of
affairs and events which can be evaluated by measuring people's preferences. Such analyses cannot take into account the complex interdependencies of the world, and replace democratic procedures by a managerial
approach in which decisions are taken on the basis of quantification
procedures. But a simple alternative strategy and policy-making procedure exists which assumes a dynamic, active world, which accords with
the conception of people as creating themselves through constructing
narratives within which they can situate themselves, and which tends to
democratize decision-making rather than concentrating it in the hands of
'experts'. This is 'retrospective path analysis' which has been developed
by Cliff Hooker.

Retrospective path analysis is essentially a means for constructing
narratives to live by. It consists in, first, the selection of macroeconomic
goals by considering a variety of end-points forty to fifty years in the
future, and then second, examining various paths to the desired future
state. This procedure departs from the normal approach in calculating a
course of action retrospectively from some future date, specifying 'those
key transitions in social structure and functioning generally which, taken
in proper sequence, will lead from the present to the desired future social
condition'.[37] Such an approach focuses attention on the conditions necessary for achieving the desired future states, on the tendencies inimical to
the realization of such ends and on the crucial social decisions at the branch-
points of different possible paths of development. Recognizing the limits
of knowledge, such decisions must take into account how much room for
manoeuvre they give to different actors during the process of reaching
desired ends, and they must be constantly open to re-examination and
reformulation. Furthermore, since the ends must ultimately include the
way people think, relate to each other and the world, these must be
incorporated into the path analysis. This means that retrospective path
analysis does not attempt to reduce people involved in realizing ends into
predictable instruments. It opens up for discussion the question of what
sort of future we want, which can include questions of what sort of people
we wish to become, what sort of relationships should exist between people

and what kind of narratives people should define themselves in terms of. It can contribute to transforming people's attitudes to a process world-orientation, from seeing themselves as beings standing outside the world trying to control it to experiencing themselves as processes of becoming actively participating in the becoming of the world.

Formulating policy in this way requires the development of a social science which subordinates abstract analyses to narrative, which can analyse existing economic processes, cultural forms, power relations and social dynamics, and reveal what paths to the future are possible. While cost-benefit analyses implicitly assume a crude positivistic theory of science in which knowledge amounts to the ability to predict the probabilities of the occurrence of different future states and events, retrospective path analysis requires of social science that it identifies and comprehends the dynamics of and interrelationships between a multiplicity of semi-autonomous processes. It requires a social science which does not objectify social reality, which does not blind people to its becoming and to the reality of their own participation within this becoming. The philosophy of process provides a conceptual framework for such a social science, at the same time overcoming the divisions between the natural and the social sciences, between the sciences and history and between theory and practice. By conceiving of the goal of science as the development of understanding, and by providing a unified conceptual framework for analysing the relationships between the dynamics of the physical world, the biological world and the complex of processes which make up the social world, and which at the same time can situate conceptually and analyse the structures of the life-worlds of people, the philosophy of process promises to provide a thermodynamically and ecologically based socio-political economics which can relate problems into an integrated perspective. Through such a social science, people – conceived of as situated but partly self-creative processes of becoming within the processes of becoming of the world, as participating in this becoming with each thought and action – could be provided with the means to extend and deepen their understanding of themselves and their potentialities as embodied subjects participating in the becoming of the world.

All social science is evaluative, with evaluation being grounded in the conception of humans and their place in nature on which this science is built. What is required of social science is that this be acknowledged, that the conception of humanity underlying specific research be open to revision or to replacement, rather than, as with the assumptions about humanity of prevailing social science, being presupposed. This would reincorporate questions of evaluation into the realm of rational discourse. With the process conception of humanity as the reference point for evaluation, social science would first of all evaluate societies in terms of their contribution to the stability and resilience of the world's eco-systems and their sustainability, and in terms of the quality of the life-worlds generated by them. These life-worlds and the social relations, institutions and social dynamics based on them would be judged in terms of the adequacy of the conceptualizations of the world embodied and reproduced by them, that is, in terms of whether they facilitated or stultified the dialectical patterns of representation, recognition and labour through which people are striving to orient themselves in the world, develop their identities and gain control over their destinies.

Social science should be more than just analysis and evaluation of the social world. Social science should also provide an orientation for action. The development of such a social science should be seen as part of culture and subordinate to history, that is, as part of the process of humanity's self-formation. By trying to illuminate the present in the light of the past, it should aim to contribute to the construction of the future, to enable people better to comprehend the different tendencies within the world, the extent to which their own ends are being frustrated or facilitated by these and what part they could play in furthering or inhibiting these tendencies. It should aim to facilitate deeper understanding of the world so that its significance and the significance of different possible projects can be judged, and thereby to orient people to live better lives. This requires more than just exposing the failings of the existing order. One only refutes what one replaces. And as Rom Harré pointed out: 'people create themselves and their patterns of interaction by virtue of the psychological and social theories to which they subscribe.'[38] Social science should be providing people with new ways to conceive themselves, their society and the world to make possible new relationships between people and between humanity and nature to replace the forms of life being revealed as defective.

To some extent environmental economics, Marxist and institutionalist political economy and various schools of anti-mechanistic thought in sociology and psychology are providing such theories; but these developments need to be seen as only stages towards a more radical reformulation of the human sciences and a more radical transformation of society. A social science based on philosophy of process would confront the commodity fetishism of capitalism. However, rather than simply oppose the reification of abstractions, it is necessary to replace the categories of economic theory, the 'forms of existence' of capitalist societies.[39] 'Labour-power' would be replaced as the dominant concept defining work relationships by a concept which acknowledges the full needs and potentialities of people as creative social agents and the dynamics and intrinsic value of other forms of life. Podolinski's energy theory of value and the associated reformulation of the concept of 'surplus value' would replace the neo-classical concept of exchange value, and Cobb and Daly's 'index of sustainable economic welfare', taking into account all that contributes to or undermines a good life, and how potentialities for achieving the good life in the future are affected by economic activity,[40] would replace the notion of 'gross national product' in order to situate the money economy within the environment and to focus on the real contribution of economic activity to the conditions of life – both human and non-human.

However, it is not only particular concepts which need to be transformed, but along with this, the 'images' of societies. There will always be an image of society dominating any community, and this will always function to some extent as an ideal. One of the most important tasks at present is to replace the analogy of the machine which underlies prevailing economic thought and which provides the dominant image of society with an auditory analogy, to create an ideal which does not reduce the present to a means for realizing the future, which does not promote the destruction of life and spontaneity, which assumes that human life is participation in the becoming of nature and culture. At the same time it is important to promote some variant of Wallerstein's notion of world-system, since quite apart from its role in revealing the causes and extent of economic exploitation, political oppression and environmental destruction, such a notion contributes to the construction of a world community by creating an image of it. To achieve all this, social science needs to transcend the disciplinary boundaries which at present dominate the study of humanity. These disciplinary boundaries are so at odds with the complex interdependencies within social reality that the general population are being blinded by prevailing social science rather than informed by it. As James O'Connor argued:

> as social theory becomes more specialized, the economy, society, and polity become more unified. . . . Hence, never before has it become so essential to invent, however crudely and provisionally, a method which combines historical interpretation, ideology critique, political economy, economic sociology, and political sociology.[41]

At most, two broad disciplinary boundaries might be regarded as acceptable within the human sciences: psychology and a radically redefined economics, although even these should be related through philosophical anthropology and should be in constant interaction; and all studies of humanity should be historical, while all history should be theoretically informed. Psychology should conceive of its object of study, the individual subject, as being essentially biological, social and cultural as well as personal, and therefore incapable of being totally abstracted from the study of the dynamics of societies,[42] while economics, or rather political economy, dealing with the processes and structures associated with and emerging from people's transformations of their physical, biological, socio-cultural environments, reformulated in terms of the philosophy of process and encompassing geography, sociology, politics, law and cultural studies,[43] should assume a conception of humans and then continually

157

revise this in the light of advances in psychology. These sciences should strive to understand people, from individuals to humanity, as a whole, in the broader perspective of the world eco-system, as a complex of dissipative structures ultimately maintained by the condition of far from thermodynamic equilibrium produced by the sun in which all power is ultimately control over the transformations of usable energy.[44]

Such a science of humanity would not be able to provide a transparent representation of the social world, since it is impossible to reduce social reality to a single plane of becoming. As Foucault argued (reflecting the influence of Braudel, and ultimately, of Bergson):

> It's not a matter of locating everything on one level, that of the event, but of realising that there are actually a whole order of levels of different types of events differing in amplitude, chronological breadth, and capacity to produce effects. The problem is at once to distinguish among events, to differentiate the networks and levels to which they belong, and to reconstitute the lines along which they are connected and engender one another.[45]

This means that it is impossible to formulate a social theory that enables the dynamics of society to be totally predicted. Rather, social inquiry and social theory should acknowledge the irreducible complexity of social reality, and that at most, only trends can be identified. But this does not mean that abstract models implying predictability of the kind used in economics cannot be of use to the social sciences. What is required of social scientists is that when focusing on any particular aspect of this complex reality, they always acknowledge the level of abstraction involved in its study; that they make use of abstractions, including abstract models, but never mistake these abstractions for reality, that they never commit the 'fallacy of misplaced concreteness'. Nor should social scientists presuppose a privileged perspective within this process of becoming of humanity. In place of prevailing economic thought which tacitly presupposes the perspective of governments and businesses in the economic centres of the world, the new social science should aim to provide the means for people to define and orient themselves to the world from their own particular situations, whether they be businessmen, workers, peasants or unemployed, males or females in any part of the world, representatives of governments in core, semi-peripheral or peripheral regions of the world, representatives of international or local organizations, or whatever. Social scientists should see themselves as servants of the general public, as only contributing anything of value to the world if they can provide insights which can be appropriated by all members of society.

Through analysis of the various tendencies within the existing societies, social scientists should also be directed to mobilizing people to replace prevailing concepts and images by revealing the commonality of interests between those who are oppressed by the present system, by presenting images of the future worth striving for, and by giving some idea of the paths which people, individually and collectively, could take to help realize this future. As Marx argued, the validity of social theories can only be judged by whether people take them up and define the world accordingly, and then by whether the promise of these theories, the potentialities they purport to reveal, are realized in action: 'Man must prove the truth, i.e., the reality and power, the this worldliness of his thinking in practice.'[46] To prove the truth of this social science goals must be formulated in terms of it. Social science based on the new cosmology could give a place to people as agents forming policies and programmes of action, while at the same time it could provide the means for situating policy analyses of any group or organization within the broader socio-economic and cultural dynamics of particular societies and of humanity as a whole. It could also facilitate the consideration, and balancing of different claims to justice, of acting upon such policies. It would facilitate and require of policy-making that it not only deal with people in interaction with their physical and biological world, but that it situate economic processes of nations or regions in relation to the political and socio-cultural dynamics of societies, and situate these dynamics in turn in relation to the economic, political and socio-cultural dynamics of the whole of humanity. Having situated policy formation, such a social science could then provide a means for formulating policy and strategy analyses for the broader socio-cultural dynamics of particular societies and of humanity as a whole, so that each organizational actor and his or her modes of thought, policies and strategies could be seen and considered in the context of these broader dynamics.

Provided with such a means for interpreting the world, retrospective path analysis could be developed beyond macroeconomics to deal with multiple levels of decision-making by diverse groups and organizations. It would be possible to consider what sort of future we want for the whole of humanity, and to project goals several hundred years in the future, and then to consider shorter-term goals of different nations, of economic and political sectors in these nations, of particular political movements and of local pressure groups in terms of their contribution to realizing these longer-term goals. In this way, people would have the means to work out a complex of narratives, embodying an image of the future ranging from the short term to the long term, from local communities to the whole of humanity. In terms of these they could then situate their own lives and activities in relation to the communities and organizations they belong to, in relation to different nations and regions, in relation to humanity as a whole and in relation to the dynamics of nature. It is such a form of policy formulation which is required to confront the present environmental and cultural crises in all their complexity.

To become an effective political force environmental movements need to articulate the problems and aspirations of people in the short term with intermediate and long-term problems and aspirations, the problems and projects of local areas with regional and world problems and projects, the immediate problems and goals of individuals with national problems and goals and with the problems and goals of humanity. First, using retrospective path analysis it is necessary to work out what form of world-society and civilization could provide the best conditions for people to live in while preserving the environment. This can be posited as something to be aimed at several hundred years in the future, and the paths which must be taken from our present situation to realize that goal can then be examined. In the light of this general project, it should then be possible to consider each region in the world and for each nation to consider in more detail what paths they need to take if humanity is to achieve a sustainable world-order. In this way it should be possible to formulate regional and national goals for a hundred years or so into the future, and then to consider how different locations, institutions and organizations can be developed to realize these goals. These goals could be developed as part of nationalistic struggles to provide the conditions within each country for people to contribute as much as their abilities will allow to their nation, to humanity and to life itself. It is then necessary to examine the immediate problems of societies and of individuals from within this general framework to relate these to the broader problems of civilization and the world eco-system. It is particularly necessary to identify forms of oppression which are preventing the realization of such national goals and the long-term goals of humanity so that struggles against this oppression can be integrated with nationalism, humanism and the struggle to preserve the world eco-system. As each more local and immediate goal and path is worked out, this should then enable broader and longer-term goals and their associated paths to be revised. Developing an image of the future in this way should involve a constant shifting of focus between the general and the specific and between the short term and the long term. Ultimately it should enable individuals to construct narratives which can relate their own lives to a new grand narrative, the global struggle for an environmentally sustainable civilization.

POLICIES FOR THE PRESENT

Environmentalism has become a growth industry, and like many other growth industries which have sprung up since the early 1970s, it has, absorbed people's time and money without producing much effect. If academic work on the environment is ever to become more than the mass production of high-sounding platitudes, it needs to be related to people's immediate situations. It seems only fitting then that I should end this work, which is essentially an effort to explain the nature of a culture which makes so much of the environment, treatment of animals, poverty, gender relationships, exploitation of the Third World, and yet generates so little action, with some consideration of what people should do immediately. However, it follows from what I have been arguing that it is impossible to prescribe for everyone what should be done. To this extent, postmodern political philosophy is right. What is required is a 'politics of the rhizome' in which everyone, every community, every nation and every major region comes to terms with the uniqueness of their situation and acts accordingly – and realizes that it is only by vast numbers of people, of groups and organizations acting in accordance with the possibilities of their situations that the environmental crisis will be solved. The actions required of different regions and different nations will differ according to their situations within the global economy – according to whether they are cores, semi-peripheries or peripheries of this economy. What is required of Eastern Europeans in the wake of the collapse of communism is different from what is required of Western Europeans, and what is required of Japanese is different from what is required of Brazilians.

Despite this, it is still necessary to identify forces at work affecting all individuals, all nations and all regions, and to see diverse actions as contributions to the broader project of overcoming these forces and creating an environmentally sustainable civilization. A knowledge of the dynamics of the global system of capitalism is required by everyone. Such knowledge should alert East Europeans to the likely costs of their integration into the economic operations of the global economy, and alert those in the Third World of the impossibility of ever participating in the benefits of capitalism. However it is the situation of people in the affluent nations which I wish to address; and in particular the situation of environmentalist members of the middle class: the salariat, self-employed professionals, artists and writers, and the new fraction of the petite bourgeoisie, the service class.

It is clear from the very limited influence of environmental movements in times of maximum public support, that is, in boom times, and the rapid decline of support for environmental issues in times of recession, that nothing much will be achieved unless environmental concerns are integrated into a broad strategy for dealing with the loss of state control over national economies. Environmentalists should respond to the existing economic crisis with a struggle for political hegemony over all those groups who are being adversely affected by the globalization of the market – farmers, workers, the salariat and the new petite bourgeoisie. As family farms go broke and blue-collar workers decline as a proportion of the workforce, it is the middle class which will decide the future of these societies. Members of the middle class are now losing their niches within society, heralding the end of their honeymoon with the new international bourgeoisie. The services offered by them are less valued by those with money to pay, and they are beginning to face the same economic insecurity and social devaluation long accorded to members of the proletariat, who for a while also claimed special skills. Unless members of this class overcome the fragmentation of their culture and mobilize themselves into an effective political movement to wrest control of the economy from the new international bourgeoisie, they will continue their downward slide and will sink into permanent semi-employment, insecurity and impoverishment.

To prevent this, the cosmetic environmentalism of this class must now be forged with nationalism into a new ideological force able to inform political praxis. This means refomulating and rejuvenating the narratives defining nationhood. Nationalism should be identified with the struggle for democratic control over the financial institutions, transnational manufacturing and agribusiness companies which are at present destabilizing the world-economy, breaking down democratic institutions and creating economic and political pressures forcing people to wreck their environments to stay alive. Similarly, in order to provide the conditions for the development of institutions able to plan for the long-term future and with the power to subordinate the functioning of the market to long-term national and international interests and goals, nationalism should be identified with the struggle to erect economic barriers to break up the world economy and to control the flow of capital. In their struggle for this power environmentalists should redefine the very meaning of economics from the promotion of money-making to managing, preserving and developing the national household, with the environment – the foundation of this household – at the centre of concern. They must formulate their goal as the creation of full employment through the redirection of economic life towards preserving and improving the environment, and their long-term aim as improving the quality of life through the reduction of material throughputs in these economies by eliminating wastage, simplifying life and radically reducing the power and incomes of the wealthy.

Correspondingly, environmentalists should spearhead the attack on the policies and the institutional changes effected by the champions of greed as a nationalist struggle against global capitalism and its quislings. In the immediate future they need to formulate policies to reduce the power of shareholders in companies relative to stakeholders as the first stage towards the decentralization and democratization of industry. Most importantly, to undermine the concentrations of power in society, to free people from the tyranny of the market, to put an end to conspicuous consumption and to allow some people to devote their lives to the long-incomes – that is, with 100 per cent marginal taxation beyond a certain level.

In this struggle, it is necessary to create and maintain an image of and a sense of belonging to a just community committed to realizing people's potentialities, a community with which people can identify, can commit themselves to and can look to for support. In opposition to the ruling hegemonic ideology, it is necessary to develop an image of nations as 'people's homes', committed to recognizing the significance of all its members, its future generations and also the organisms and eco-systems of its environment. To support such images, it is necessary to cultivate a reorientation in thinking, not only from the mechanistic world-orientation of those who at present dominate society, but also from the woolly-minded relativism and consumerism of postmodern culture to a process world-orientation, both in thought and in practice. Environmentalists should attack not only the ideological despotism of economists and pedants, but should also strive to counteract the nihilistic decadence which is now undermining civilization. In the process they must strive to create an image of the future not as the triumph of any particular movement, class or nation, but as the triumph of life. It is around this image of the future that they must elaborate a new grand narrative.

NOTES

INTRODUCTION

1 Arthur Kroker and David Cook, *The Postmodern Scene: Excremental Culture and Hyper-Aesthetics*, 2nd edn, New York, St Martin's Press, 1988, p.27.
2 Thomas A. Sancton, 'Planet of the year', *Time*, 2 January 1989, p.14.
3 Karl Marx, *A Contribution to the Critique of Political Economy*, Moscow, Progress Publishers, 1970, p.211.

1 WHAT IS POSTMODERNITY?

1 *The Independent*, 24 December 1987; cited by Mike Featherstone, in 'In pursuit of the postmodern', *Theory, Culture and Society*, vol.5, nos.2–3, June, 1988, p.195.
2 Jean-François Lyotard, *The Postmodern Condition: A Report on Knowledge*, tr. Geoff Bennington and Brian Massumi, Minneapolis, University of Minnesota Press, 1984 (first published 1979), p.xxvi.
3 Robert Nisbet, *History of the Idea of Progress*, New York, Basic Books, 1980, p.317.
4 Friedrich Nietzsche, *The Will to Power*, ed. Walter Kaufmann, tr. Walter Kaufmann and R.J. Hollingdale, New York, Vintage, 1968, §666, p.351.
5 Richard Newbold Adams, *The Eighth Day*, Austin, University of Texas Press, 1988, p.234.
6 Roland Robertson, 'Mapping the global condition', in *Global Culture: Nationalism, Globalization and Modernity*, ed. Mike Featherstone, London, Sage, 1990; 'Social theory, cultural relativity and the problem of globality', in *Culture, Globalization and the World-System: Contemporary Conditions for the Representation of Identity*, ed. Anthony D. King, Houndmills, Macmillan, 1991; and *Globalization*, London, Sage, 1992.
7 On this, see David Harvey, 'Time-space compression and the postmodern condition', *The Condition of Postmodernity*, Oxford, Blackwell, 1989, Ch.17. On changing management, see Stewart R. Clegg, *Modern Organizations: Organizational Studies in the Postmodern World*, London, Sage, 1990.
8 Stephen Hymer, 'Internationalization of capital and international politics: a radical approach', in Edward J. Nell, *Growth, Profits, and Property: Essays in the Revival of Political Economy*, Cambridge, Cambridge University Press, 1980, pp.189–203. This paper is a blend of two papers, one written in 1972 and the other in 1974, shortly before the author's death. The developments identified

164

by Hyman were analysed and described in more detail by Richard J. Barnet and Ronalde E. Müller, *Global Reach*, New York, Simon & Schuster, 1974, and more recently by a number of political economists in *International Capitalism and Industrial Restructuring*, ed. Richard Peet, Boston, Allen & Unwin, 1987, and Robert B. Reich, *The Work of Nations*, New York, Vintage, 1991.

9 Claus Offe, *Disorganized Capitalism*, Cambridge, Polity Press, 1985, and Scott Lash and John Urry, *The End of Organized Capitalism*, Cambridge, Polity Press, 1987.

10 Jonathan Friedman, 'Narcissism, roots and postmodernity', in *Modernity and Identity*, ed. Scott Lash and Jonathan Friedman, Oxford, Blackwell, 1992, pp.331–66, p.334.

11 See for instance George W. Stocking, Jr, 'The dark-skinned savage, the image of primitive man in evolutionary anthropology', in *Race, Culture, and Evolution*, Chicago, University of Chicago Press, 1982.

12 On this, see R. Hofstadter, *Social Darwinism in American Thought*, New York, Braziller, 1959.

13 On this, see Stuart Hall, 'The local and the global: globalization and ethnicity' and 'Old and new identities, old and new ethnicities', in *Culture, Globalization and the World-System*, ed. King.

14 The loss of self-assurance of the French is superbly described by Robert Young, in *White Mythologies: Writing History and the West*, London, Routledge, 1990.

15 The rise of symbolic analysts as a sub-class in alliance with the international bourgeoisie has been described by Robert B. Reich, *The Wealth of Nations*, New York, Vintage, 1991.

16 The term used by Benedict Anderson to characterize nationalism. See Benedict Anderson, *Imagined Communities: Reflections on the Origin and Spread of Nationalism*, London, Verso, 1983.

17 On these groups, see Friedman, 'Narcissism, roots and postmodernity'.

18 On the issues this has raised, see *Nation and Narration*, ed. Homi K. Bhabha, London and New York, Routledge, 1990.

19 On the changing relations between classes in modern capitalist societies, see Richard Peet, 'The geography of class struggle and the relocation of United States manufacturing industry', in *International Capitalism and Industrial Restructuring*, ed. Richard Peet, Boston, Allen & Unwin, 1987.

20 On this, see Jim Moore, 'Socializing Darwinism', in *Science as Politics*, ed. Les Levidow, London, Free Association Books, 1986, and the essays in Robert Young, *Darwin's Metaphor*, Cambridge, Cambridge University Press, 1985.

21 Alvin W. Gouldner, *The Future of Intellectuals and the Rise of the New Class*, New York, Seabury, 1979, p.68.

22 See for instance Anthony Giddens, *The Consequences of Modernity*, Cambridge, Polity Press, esp. pp.45ff.

23 Alex Carey, in 'The ideological management industry', in *Communications and the Media in Australia*, ed. Ted Wheelwright and Ken Buckley, Sydney, Allen & Unwin, 1987, describes this, mainly in relation to Australia, but also looking at other countries.

24 The ideology of the new bourgeoisie is essentially the ideology of the New Right. I have traced the roots of their ideology, and shown its environmental destructiveness in *Nihilism Incorporated: European Civilization and Environmental Destruction*, Bungendore, Eco-Logical Press, 1993.

25 See Z. Brzezinski, *Between Two Ages: America's Role in the Technotronic Era*, Harmondsworth, Penguin, 1976. Brzezinski argued that we are entering the 'technotronic' (technological + electronic) age in which humans will be

remoulded by the new technologies and sciences associated with information processing.

26 On the dominant ideas of recent economic thought, see Lester C. Thurow, *Dangerous Currents: The State of Economics*, Oxford, Oxford University Press, 1983.

27 This development within Australia has been described by Michael Pusey, *Economic Rationalism in Canberra*, Cambridge, Cambridge University Press, 1991.

28 Francis Fukuyama, *The End of History and the Last Man*, Harmondsworth, Penguin, 1992.

29 On the operations of the new class of financiers, see Adrian Hamilton, *The Financial Revolution*, Harmondsworth, Penguin, 1986.

30 The deleterious effects of corporate takeovers have been examined in *Corporate Takeovers: Causes and Consequences*, ed. Alan Auerbach, Chicago, University of Chicago Press, 1988, and David Ravenscroft and F.M. Scherer, *Mergers, Sell-Offs and Economic Efficiency*, New York, Brookings Institute, 1988. On the general effects of this on the US economy, see S. Melman, *Profits Without Production*, New York, Knopf, 1983. On an international level their activities have had disastrous effects. See Susan George, *A Fate Worse than Debt*, Harmondsworth, Penguin, 1988, and *The Debt Boomerang*, London, Pluto Press, 1992.

31 On this see Susan George, *How the Other Half Dies*, Harmondsworth, Penguin, 1977, and *Ill Fares the Land*, Harmondsworth, Penguin, 1990 (first published 1984); Jon Bennett, *The Hunger Machine*, Cambridge, Polity Press, 1987; and Michael W. Fox, *Agricide*, New York, Schocken Books, 1986.

32 Cited by Robert L. Heilbroner, *An Inquiry into The Human Prospect*, New York, W.W. Norton, 1975, p.170.

33 For an analysis of the economic success of Asian societies, see Nigel Harris, *The End of the Third World*, Harmondsworth, Penguin, 1986.

34 This has been cogently argued by David Carr, *Time, Narrative, and History*, Bloomington, Indiana University Press, 1986.

35 On the control of the media by the new bourgeoisie and its effects, see Jeremy Tunstall and Michael Palmer, *Media Moguls*, London, Routledge, 1991, and Armand Mattelart, *Transnationals and the Third World: The Struggle for Culture*, South Headley, Mass., Bergin & Garvey, 1983.

36 Daniel Bell, 'The cultural contradictions of capitalism', in *The Cultural Contradictions of Capitalism*, New York, Basic Books, 1976, pp.33–84, and 'Beyond modernism, beyond self', in *Sociological Journeys*, London, Heinemann, 1980, pp.275–302.

37 Lionel Trilling, *Beyond Culture*, Harmondsworth, Penguin, 1967, p.12.

38 That they would do so was to some extent anticipated by Baudelaire who argued that 'since the complete absence of the right and the true in art amounts to a lack of art, the entire man perishes'. Cited by Michael Hamburger, in *The Truth of Poetry*, London, Methuen, 1982 (first published 1969), p.5.

39 Bell, 'Beyond modernism, beyond self', p.288.

40 Hannah Arendt, 'Society and Culture', in *Culture for the Millions?*, ed. Norman Jacobs, Princeton, Van Nostrand, 1961, pp.43–53. Cited by Bell in *The Cultural Contradictions of Capitalism*, p.45.

41 For a summary of Ong's research, see his *Orality and Literacy: The Technologizing of the Word*, London, Methuen, 1982.

42 Mark Poster, *The Mode of Information*, Cambridge, Polity Press, 1990, p.46.

43 Neil Postman, *Amusing Ourselves to Death*, London, Methuen, 1987, p.72.

44 This is essentially the thesis of Alex Callinicos in *Against Postmodernism: A Marxist Critique*, Cambridge, Polity Press, 1989.

45 The relationship between this class and postmodernism has been argued by Lash and Urry in *The End of Organized Capitalism*, pp.292ff.

46 As Lash and Urry have argued, ibid., pp.296ff.

47 On this see Bernice Martin, *A Sociology of Contemporary Cultural Change*, Oxford, Blackwell, 1981.

48 Pierre Bourdieu, *Distinction: A Social Critique of the Judgement of Taste*, tr. Richard Nice, Cambridge, Mass., Harvard University Press, 1984 (first published 1979), p.370.

49 John H. Marx, 'The ideological construction of post-modern identity models in contemporary cultural movements', in *Identity and Authority: Exploration in the Theory of Society*, ed. Roland Robertson and Bukhart Holzner, Oxford, Blackwell, 1980, pp.145–89, p.162.

50 On this, see Bill Ryan, *Making Capital from Culture: The Corporate Form of Capitalist Production*, Berlin, Walter de Gruyter, 1992.

51 Ernest Gellner, 'Crisis in the humanities and the mainstream of philosophy', in *Crisis in the Humanities*, ed. J.H. Plumb, Harmondsworth, Penguin, 1964, pp.45–81, pp.71–3.

52 Alasdair MacIntyre, 'Philosophy: past conflict and future direction', *Proceedings and Addresses of the American Philosophical Association*, Supplement to vol.61, #1, September 1987, pp.81–7, pp.81–5.

53 On this, and the state of modern philosophy generally, see Kenneth Baynes *et. al.*, *After Philosophy: End or Transformation?* Cambridge, Mass., MIT Press, 1987.

54 Richard Rorty, *Philosophy and the Mirror of Nature*, Princeton, Princeton University Press, 1979.

55 See for instance Terry Eagleton, 'Introduction: what is literature?', in *Literary Theory: An Introduction*, Oxford, Blackwell, 1983.

56 In Britain, this movement was led by the X Club, consisting of Huxley, Tyndall and Spencer among others. On the X Club, see Ruth Barton, *The X Club: Science, Religion, and Social Change in Victorian England*, Ph.D. dissertation, University of Pennsylvania, 1976.

57 See Paul Feyerabend, *Science in a Free Society*, London, Verso, 1982. Feyerabend quotes Bakunin in *Farewell to Reason*, London, Verso, 1987, p.22n.

58 E.D. Hirsch, Jr, *Cultural Literacy*, Australian edn, Moorebank, NSW, Schwartz Publishing, 1989, p.vi.

59 David Dickson, *The New Politics of Science*, Chicago, University of Chicago Press, 1988, p.46.

60 Lyotard, *The Postmodern Condition*, p.45.

61 It is not only universities in Anglophone nations which have fallen from grace. French and German universities are similarly afflicted. On this see the articles in *Telos*, no.81, Fall 1989.

62 Paul Feyerabend, 'How to defend society against science', in *Scientific Revolutions*, ed. Ian Hacking, Oxford, Oxford University Press, 1981, pp.156–67, p.165.

63 This has been pointed out by Russell Jacoby in *The Last Intellectuals: American Intellectuals in the Age of Academe*, New York, Basic Books, 1987.

64 Jim Collins, *Uncommon Cultures: Popular Culture and Post-Modernism*, New York and London, Routledge, 1989, p.xiii.

65 Andreas Huyssen, 'Mapping the Postmodern', in *After the Great Divide: Modernism, Mass Culture and Postmodernism*, Houndmills, Macmillan, 1988, pp.178–221, p.217.

66 This is how Charles Jencks characterizes postmodern architecture; see *The Language of Post-Modern Architecture*, New York, Academy Editions, 1982.

67 This way of characterizing postmodernism comes from N. Katherine Hayles, 'Chaos and culture: postmodernism(s) and the denaturing of experience', in *Chaos Bound*, Ithaca, Cornell University Press, 1990, Ch.10. The fullest study of postmodern culture revealing these features is Fredric Jameson's, *Postmodernism: or, The Cultural Logic of Late Capitalism*, Durham, Duke University Press, 1991. The first chapter of this is a slightly elaborated version of his famous paper, 'Postmodernism, or the cultural logic of late capitalism', *New Left Review*, 146, July–August, 1984.

68 Jean Baudrillard, 'Simulacra and simulations' in *Selected Essays*, ed. Mark Poster, Cambridge, Polity Press, Ch.7.

69 This phenomenon was identified and brilliantly analysed by Walter Benjamin in 'The storyteller: reflections on the works of Nicolai Leskov', in *Illuminations*, ed. Hannah Arendt, tr. Harry Zohn, New York, Shocken Books, 1969.

70 N. Katherine Hayles, *Chaos Bound: Orderly Disorder in Contemporary Literature and Science*, Ithaca, Cornell University Press, 1990, p.272.

71 The relationship between the changing organization of space and time in late capitalism and postmodern culture is brilliantly analysed by David Harvey in *The Condition of Postmodernity: An Inquiry into the Origins of Cultural Change*, Oxford, Blackwell, 1989, Parts III and IV.

72 Jameson, *Postmodernism*, p.44.

73 The role of narrative in the construction of the modern identity has been revealed by Franco Moretti in *The Way of the World: The Bildungsroman in European Culture*, London, Verso, 1987.

74 Christopher Lasch, *The Minimal Self*, London, Picador, 1985, p.15.

75 Jameson, *Postmodernism*, p.27.

76 Ibid., p.25.

77 On this see Scott Lash, 'Discourse or figure? Postmodernism as a "regime of signification"', *Theory, Culture and Society*, vol.5, nos 2–3, June 1988, pp.311–36. This has been reprinted in Scott Lash, *Sociology of Postmodernism*, London, Routledge, 1990.

78 Pierre Bourdieu, 'On symbolic power', in *Language and Symbolic Power*, Cambridge, Mass., Harvard University Press, 1991, pp.163–70, p.166.

79 Pierre Bourdieu, *Distinction: A Social Critique of the Judgement of Taste*, tr. Richard Nice, Cambridge, Mass., Harvard University Press, 1984 (first published 1979), pp.370–1.

80 Ibid., p.371.

81 See Stuart Ewen, *All Consuming Images: The Politics of Style in Contemporary Culture*, New York, Basic Books, 1988.

82 This is the argument of Jean Baudrillard, who has also shown where such a culture must lead.

83 Hilary Putnam, *Reason, Truth and History*, Cambridge, Cambridge University Press, 1981, p.215. The unavoidability of narratives in the legitimation of such assumptions has been cogently argued by J.M. Bernstein, 'Grand narratives', in *On Paul Ricoeur: Narrative and Interpretation*, ed. David Wood, London, Routledge, 1991, pp.102–23.

84 Jameson, *Postmodernism*, Ch.3, 'Surrealism without the unconscious'.

85 The centrality of cynicism in postmodernism has been revealed by Peter Sloterdijk, *Critique of Cynical Reason*, tr. Michael Eldred, Minneapolis, University of Minnesota Press, 1987 (first published 1983).

86 Henry S. Kariel, *The Desperate Politics of Postmodernism*, Amherst, University of Massachussetts Press, 1989, p.ix.

87 As Jameson argues, in *Postmodernism*, pp.34–8.

2 POSTMODERNISM AND POSTSTRUCTURALISM

1 Andreas Huyssen in 'Mapping the postmodern' argues that 'rather than offering a *theory of postmodernity* . . . French theory provides us primarily with an *archaeology of modernity,* a theory of modernism at the stage of its exhaustion' (Andreas Huyssen, *After the Great Divide,* Houndmills, Macmillan, 1986, p.209).

2 The influence of the marginal position of these academics within France on the ideas they have espoused has been noted by Pierre Bourdieu in *Homo Academicus,* Cambridge, Polity Press, 1988 (first published 1984), especially in the 'Preface to the English edition'.

3 On this aspect of poststructuralism, see Robert Young, *White Mythologies: Writing History and the West,* London, Routledge, 1990.

4 This is argued by Jürgen Habermas in *The Philosophical Discourse of Modernity,* Cambridge, Polity Press, 1987 (first published 1985).

5 One of the best descriptions of this is Stephen Toulmin's *Cosmopolis: The Hidden Agenda of Modernity,* Chicago, University of Chicago Press, 1990.

6 I have described the development and relationship between these ideas and disciplines, and their ideological significance, in *Nihilism Incorporated,* Bungendore, Eco-Logical Press, 1993.

7 See Giambattista Vico, *The New Science of Giambattista Vico,* tr. Thomas Goddard Bergin and Max Harold Fisch, Ithaca, Cornell University Press, 1984 (3rd edn 1744), par.331, p.96.

8 Giambattista Vico, *On the Study Methods of Our Time,* tr. Elio Gianturco, Ithaca, Cornell University Press, 1990 (first published 1709), p.40.

9 Vico, *The New Science,* par.2, pp.3f.

10 Ibid., par.923.

11 Ibid., par.352.

12 Ibid., par.32.

13 Ibid., par.1106.

14 There are other differences between Vico and Hegel not spelt out here. Croce interpreted Vico from an Hegelian perspective, and this interpretation has been criticized by Pietro Piovani in 'Vico without Hegel', in *Giambattista Vico: An International Symposium,* ed. G. Tagliacozzo and H.V. White, Baltimore, Johns Hopkins University Press, 1969; and by Leon Pompa, 'Vico and Hegel', in *Vico: Past and Present,* ed. Giorgio Tagliacozzo, Atlantic Highlands, Humanities Press, 1981, vol.2. The differences noted in these essays are not relevant to my argument.

15 On this see Leszek Kolakowski, *Main Currents of Marxism,* 3 vols, vol.1: *The Founders,* tr. P.S. Falla, Oxford, Oxford University Press, 1981. The basic tenets of neo-Platonism are described in vol.1, Ch.3.

16 G.W.F. Hegel, *Hegel's Philosophy of Nature,* tr. A.V. Miller, Oxford, Clarendon Press, 1970, §247 Zusatz, p.16.

17 G.W.F. Hegel, *Reason in History: A General Introduction to the Philosophy of History,* tr. Robert S. Hartman, Indianapolis, Bobbs Merrill, 1953, p.44.

18 Ibid., p.45.

19 Ibid., pp.67, 78f. and 95.

20 G.W.F. Hegel, *The Phenomenology of Mind,* tr. J.B. Baillie, New York, Harper Colophon, 1967 (first published 1931), pp.234ff. This is developed further in Hegel, *Philosophy of Mind,* tr. William Wallace, Oxford, Clarendon Press, 1971, §433–5.

21 On Nietzsche's relation to Hegel and other post-Hegelian philosophers, see Karl Löwith, *From Hegel to Nietzsche: The Revolution in 19th Century Thought,* tr. David E. Green, London, Constable, 1965 (first published 1941).

22 Friedrich Nietzsche, *The Will to Power*, tr. Walter Kaufmann, New York, Vintage Books, 1968, §12A.

23 Friedrich Nietzsche, *Twilight of the Idols*, tr. R.J. Hollingdale, Harmondsworth, Penguin, 1968 (first published 1889), par.1, p.35.

24 Ibid., par.4, p.37.

25 Nietzsche, *The Will to Power*, §§619ff.

26 Ibid., §715.

27 Friedrich Nietzsche, 'The Philosopher', 46, in *Philosophy and Truth*, ed. Daniel Breazeale, New Jersey, Humanities Press, 1979, p.16.

28 See Friedrich Nietzsche, *Beyond Good and Evil*, tr. R.J. Hollingdale, Harmondsworth, Penguin, 1973, par.261.

29 Friedrich Nietzsche, *The Genealogy of Morals*, tr. Francis Golffing, along with *The Birth of Tragedy*, New York, Doubleday, Second Essay, II, pp.190f.

30 Nietzsche, *The Genealogy of Morals*, Third Essay, XXV, pp.291f.

31 Nietzsche, 'The Philosopher', 150, p.51.

32 Nietzsche, 'On truth and lies in a nonmoral sense', 2, in *Philosophy and Truth*, pp.88f.

33 Ibid., 1, p.84.

34 Nietzsche, 'The Philosopher', 79, pp.30f.

35 Nietzsche, 'On truth and lies', 1, p.81.

36 Nietzsche, *The Will to Power*, §632.

37 Nietzsche, 'On Truth and Lies', 2, p.88.

38 Nietzsche, *The Will to Power*, §619.

39 In Nietzsche, *Philosophy and Truth*, §193, p.134.

40 See Martin Heidegger, *Nietzsche*, 4 vols, tr. David Farrell Krell, San Francisco, HarperCollins, 1991 (first published 1961), vol.1, pp.18ff.

41 Martin Heidegger, 'The age of the world picture', in *The Question Concerning Technology and Other Essays*, tr. William Lovitt, New York, Harper Torchbooks, 1977, p.117.

42 Martin Heidegger, *Being and Time*, tr. John Macquarrie and Edward Robinson, Oxford, Blackwell, 1962, p.63.

43 Martin Heidegger, 'Letter on humanism', tr. Frank A. Capuzzi, in *Martin Heidegger: Basic Writings*, ed. David Farrell Krell, London, Routledge & Kegan Paul, 1978, pp.193–242, p.207.

44 Martin Heidegger, 'The origin of the work of art', in *Poetry, Language, Thought*, tr. Albert Hofstadter, New York, Harper & Row, 1971, p.23.

45 Martin Heidegger, 'The end of philosophy and the task of thinking', in *Basic Writings*, p.374.

46 Martin Heidegger, 'The age of the world picture', pp.115–54, pp.149f.

47 Heidegger, 'The end of philosophy and the task of thinking', pp.375f.

48 Heidegger, 'The question concerning technology', in *The Question Concerning Technology and Other Essays*, p.21.

49 Heidegger, 'The age of the world picture', pp.152f.

50 Heidegger, 'The end of philosophy and the task of thinking', p.377.

51 Heidegger, 'The question concerning technology', pp.12f.

52 Ibid., pp.14, 16.

53 Martin Heidegger, 'The ontotheological nature of metaphysics', in *Identity and Difference*, tr. Joan Stambaugh, New York, Harper & Row, 1969, p.73.

54 Heidegger, 'Letter on humanism', p.199.

55 Heidegger's interpretation of Parmenides' understanding of being is outlined in 'The age of the world picture', p.131.

56 The best effort to situate poststructuralist thinkers in the tradition of philo-

sophy is Vincent Descombes, *Modern French Philosophy*, Cambridge, Cambridge University Press, 1980 (first published 1979).

57 Alexandre Kojève, *Introduction to the Reading of Hegel: Lectures on the Phenomenology of Spirit*, tr. James H. Nichols, Jr, Ithaca, Cornell University Press, 1980, p.71.

58 On this, see Jitendra Mohanty, 'Foucault as a philosopher', in *Foucault and the Critique of Institutions*, ed. John Caputo and Mark Yount, University Park, Pennsylvania State University Press, 1993.

59 For an excellent analysis of the relationship between Derrida and Hegel, and general interpretation of Derrida, see Rodolphe Gasché, *The Tain of the Mirror: Derrida and the Philosophy of Reflection*, Cambridge, Mass., Harvard University Press, 1986. Apart from this the most useful works for interpreting Derrida are *Working Through Derrida*, ed. Gary B. Madison, Evanston, Northwestern University Press, 1993, and Christopher Norris, *Derrida*, London, Fontana, 1987. Ernst Behler, in *Confrontations: Derrida, Heidegger, Nietzsche*, tr. Steven Taubeneck, Stanford, Stanford University Press, 1991 (first published 1988), argues that Derrida's philosophy is essentially a defence of Nietzsche against Heidegger in order to answer the questions raised by Heidegger.

60 See Jacques Derrida, '*Ousia* and *Gramme*', in *Margins of Philosophy*, tr. Alan Bass, Brighton, Harvester Press, 1982 (first published 1972).

61 Jacques Derrida, '*Différance*', in *Speech and Phenomena*, Evanston, Northwestern University Press, 1973, pp.129–60, pp.129f.

62 Jacques Derrida, *Positions*, tr. Alan Bass, Chicago, University of Chicago Press, 1981, p.26.

63 Jacques Derrida, *Dissemination*, tr. Barbara Johnson, Chicago, University of Chicago Press, 1981, p.328. In an interview with Richard Kearney, Derrida denied that he meant that there is no world beyond the text (Richard Kearney, *Dialogues with Contemporary Continental Thinkers*, Manchester, Manchester University Press, 1984, p.123).

64 'Deconstruction' is a very complex notion. For its full explication see Gasché, *The Tain of the Mirror*, Part II.

65 Jacques Derrida, *Limited Inc.*, ed. Gerald Graff, Evanston, Northwestern University Press, 1988, p.93.

66 Derrida, *Positions*, p.19.

67 Jacques Derrida, 'The conflict of faculties: a *Mochlos*', p.56, cited by Richard J. Bernstein, in *The New Constellation*, Cambridge, Polity Press, 1991, p.197.

68 Derrida, *Positions*, p.29.

69 While all poststructuralists oppose efforts to interpret their writings, Lacan is particularly recalcitrant in this regard. In his preface to Anika Lemaire's *Jacques Lacan* (London and New York, Routledge & Kegan Paul, 1977 (first published 1970)) Lacan claims his works are unsuitable for a thesis, and he refused to allow the translator into English of the collected transcripts of his seminars, John Forrester, to include an introduction which would situate his ideas, an introduction which has since been published by Forrester in his *Seductions of Psychoanalysis* (Cambridge, Cambridge University Press), as 'In place of an introduction'. These two works are nevertheless invaluable for making sense of the seminar transcripts. See also Ellie Ragland, *Jacques Lacan and the Philosophy of Psychoanalysis*, Chicago, University of Chicago Press, 1985, and Richard Boothby, *Death and Desire*, New York and London, Routledge, 1991.

70 Jacques Lacan, *Ecrits: A Selection,*, tr. Alan Sheridan, London, Tavistock/ Routledge, 1977 (first published 1966), p.126. Lacan differs from Derrida in postulating an ultimate signifier, the phallus. But although this has been taken very seriously by feminists, it is a highly problematic concept. On this see

Malcolm Bowie, 'The meaning of the phallus', in *Lacan*, London, Fontana Press, 1991.

71 Derrida, *Positions*, p.29.
72 Jacques Lacan, 'The signification of the phallus', in *Ecrits*, pp.281–91, p.287.
73 Jacques Lacan, 'Function and field of speech and language', in *Ecrits*, pp.30–113, p.49.
74 Ibid., p.68.
75 Jacques Lacan, *The Four Fundamental Concepts of Psycho-Analysis*, tr. Alan Sheridan, London, Peregrine, 1979 (first published 1973), pp. 67, 126, 203, 206–7.
76 Jacques Lacan, 'Subversion of the subject and the dialectic of desire', in *Ecrits*, p.300.
77 Lacan's ideas have been taken up and elaborated by others, particularly in feminism and film theory. The best example of this, synthesizing Lacan's ideas with those of others, is Kaja Silverman, *The Subject of Semiotics*, New York, Oxford University Press.
78 For this history of narratology see the bibliographical essay by Khachig Tololyan, 'Telling the event, telling *as* event: the theory of narrative', *Choice*, July/August, 1990, pp.1791–9.
79 Roland Barthes, 'Introduction to the structural analysis of narratives', in *Image, Music, Text*, London, Fontana Press, 1977, pp.79–124.
80 The most well-known example of structuralist narratology is Gérard Genette's *Narrative Discourse*, tr. Jane E. Lewin, Ithaca, Cornell University Press, 1980. See also Shlomith Rimmon-Kenan, *Narrative Fiction: Contemporary Poetics*, London, Methuen, 1983. While developing her own theory, Rimmon-Kenan also reviews the work of other theorists.
81 On Lacan's contribution to narratology see *Lacan and Narration: The Psychoanalytic Difference in Narrative Theory*, ed. Robert Con Davis, Baltimore, Johns Hopkins University Press, 1983; especially the editor's introduction, 'Lacan and narration'.
82 Roland Barthes, 'The death of the author', in *Image, Music, Text*, p.145.
83 Ibid., p.146.
84 Ibid.
85 Again, see Roland Barthes, 'From work to text', in *Image, Music, Text*, pp.155–64.
86 Ibid., p.164.
87 Roland Barthes, 'Introduction to the structural analysis of narratives', p.115.
88 Paul Ricoeur, *Time and Narrative*, 3 vols 1983–4, Chicago, University of Chicago Press, 1984–5, vol.1, Ch.3.
89 Barthes, 'The death of the author', p.147.
90 Roland Barthes, *The Pleasure of the Text*, tr. Richard Miller, New York, Hill & Wang, 1978 (first published 1973), p.47.
91 Jean-François Lyotard, 'Universal history and cultural differences', in *The Lyotard Reader*, ed. Andrew Benjamin, Oxford, Blackwell, 1989, pp.314–23, p.314.
92 Ibid., p.320.
93 Ibid., p.321.
94 Jean-François Lyotard, *Discours, Figure*, Paris, Klincksieck, 1971, p.11.
95 Michel Foucault, *Madness and Civilization*, tr. Richard Howard, London, Tavistock, 1967, p.70.
96 This aspect of Foucault has been most fully explored by Martin Jay in 'In the empire of the gaze: Foucault and the denigration of vision in twentieth century thought', in *Foucault: A Critical Reader*, ed. David Couzens Hoy, Oxford, Blackwell, 1986, pp.175–204.

97 Michel Foucault, *Discipline and Punish*, tr. Alan Sheridan, Harmondsworth, Penguin, 1979, p.193.

98 Foucault expounded these ideas in *The Archaeology of Knowledge*, tr. A.M. Sheridan Smith, New York, Pantheon Books, 1972.

99 Ibid., p.33.

100 Ibid., p.51.

101 Ibid., p.50.

102 Foucault, *Discipline and Punish*, p.27.

103 Ibid., pp.27f.

104 Ibid., pp.202f.

105 Ibid., p.29.

106 Michel Foucault, *The History of Sexuality: An Introduction*, tr. Robert Hurley, Harmondsworth, Penguin, 1978 (first published 1976), p.59.

107 See Gilles Deleuze, *Nietzsche and Philosophy*, tr. Hugh Tomlinson, New York, Columbia University Press, 1983 (first published 1962).

108 Gilles Deleuze, *Bergsonism*, tr. Hugh Tomlinson and Barbara Habberiam, New York, Zone Books, 1991, p.115. This statement is made in an afterword written in 1988.

109 Gillian Rose, *Dialectic of Nihilism*, Oxford, Blackwell, 1984, Ch.6.

110 Gilles Deleuze and Félix Guattari, *A Thousand Plateaus: Capitalism and Schizophrenia*, tr. Brian Massumi, Minneapolis, University of Minnesota Press, 1988 (first published 1980), p.21.

111 Michel Foucault, 'Preface' to Gilles Deleuze and Félix Guattari, *Anti-Oedipus: Capitalism and Schizophrenia*, London, Athlone Press, 1984 (first published 1972), p.xii.

112 Ibid., p.xiii.

113 Deleuze and Guattari, *A Thousand Plateaus*, pp.18f.

114 This is not to say that all Marxists are opposed to poststructuralism. See for instance Michael Ryan, *Marxism and Deconstruction: A Critical Articulation*, Baltimore, John Hopkins University Press, 1982.

115 The obvious exceptions are the ex-analytical philosopher, Richard Rorty, who has embraced Derrida, and John Searle, who has attacked him. For efforts to relate analytical philosophy and poststructuralism, see *Redrawing the Lines: Analytical Philosophy, Deconstruction, and Literary Theory*, ed. Reed Way Dasenbrock, Minneapolis, University of Minnesota Press, 1989.

116 The central figure in this at present is Jürgen Habermas, who has written a controversial critique of the poststructuralists, *The Philosophical Discourse of Modernity*, Cambridge, Polity Press, 1987 (first published 1985).

3 POSTSTRUCTURALISM, MARXISM AND THE ENVIRONMENT

1 Niklas Luhmann, *Ecological Communication*, Cambridge, Polity Press, 1989 (first published 1986).

2 For example Peter Self has recently complained that politics has been invaded by market theories which assume that 'political man or woman' has the same motives and goals as 'economic man or woman', in 'Market ideology and good government', *Current Affairs Bulletin*, September 1990, pp.4–10, p.4. Peter Vintila in 'Democracy and the politics of counterfeit nationhood', in *Markets, Morals and Manifestos*, ed. Peter Vintila, John Phillimore and Peter Newman, Murdoch, Institute for Science and Technology Policy, Murdoch University, 1992, has pointed out that the policies of the New Right based on economic

theory amount to the abolition of politics. An impassioned defence of traditional politics and law against the imperialism of economic thought is Mark Sagoff's *The Economy of the Earth: Philosophy, Law and the Environment*, Cambridge and New York, Cambridge University Press, 1988.

3 On this, see Philip Mirowski, *Against Mechanism: Protecting Economics from Science*, Totowa, Rowman & Littlefield, 1988; Philip Mirowski, *More Heat than Light: Economics as Social Physics*, New York, Cambridge University Press, 1989; and Philip Mirowski, 'How not to do things with metaphors: Paul Samuelson and the Science of neoclassical economics', *Studies in the History and Philosophy of Science*, vol.20, no.2, 1989, pp.175–91.

4 Dieter Groh and Rolf-Peter Sieferle, 'Experience of nature in bourgeois society and economic theory', *Social Research*, no.3, Autumn 1980, pp.557–81, p.569.

5 Quoted by Vandana Shiva, *Staying Alive: Women, Ecology and Development*, London, Zed Books, 1990, p.218.

6 There are now journals devoted to environmental economics, the *Journal of Environmental Economics and Management* and *Ecological Economics*. For a sample of the work of environmental economists, see *Economic Policy Towards the Environment*, ed. Dieter Helm, Oxford, Blackwell, 1991.

7 William D. Nordhaus, 'Greenhouse economics', *The Economist*, 7–13 July 1980, p.20.

8 David Pearce, Anil Markandya and Edward B. Barbier, *Blueprint for a Green Economy*, London, Earthscan Publications, 1989. These authors have attempted to extend the ideas of this book to the Third World and to the world as a whole. See David Pearce, Edward B. Barbier and Anil Markandya, *Sustainable Development: Economics and the Environment in the Third World*, London, Earthscan Publications, 1991, and *Blueprint 2: Greening the World Economy*, ed. David Pearce, London, Earthscan Publications, 1991. Michael Jacobs, in his book *The Green Economy*, London, Pluto, 1991, is more critical of the basic assumption of economics.

9 Pearce, Makandya and Barbier, *Blueprint for a Green Economy*, p.61.

10 See for example Joseph Seneca and Michael Taussig, *Environmental Economics*, Englefield Cliffs, NJ, Prentice Hall, 1984, esp. p.85.

11 Seneca and Taussig are major proponents of tradeable permits.

12 For a general review of what has been achieved see the yearly reports of the Worldwatch Institute, *State of the World*, ed. Lester R. Brown. See also Barry Commoner, *Making Peace with the Planet*, New York, Pantheon Books, 1990 and Donella H. Meadows *et al.*, *Beyond the Limits*, London, Earthscan, 1992. For an analysis of how and why environmental measures have failed, see Sharon Beder, *The Nature of Sustainable Development*, Newham, Australia, Scribe, 1993.

13 See the Organisation for Economic Co-operation and Development report, *The Economic Instruments for Environmental Protection*, Paris, OECD, 1989. See also Robert Hahn and Gordon Hester, 'Where did all the markets go? An analysis of EPA's emissions trading program', *Yale Journal of Regulation*, vol.6, Winter 1989.

14 See Beder, *The Nature of Sustainable Development*, Ch.12.

15 From a leaked document reported in the *New Scientist*, February, 1992.

16 Herman E. Daly and John B. Cobb, Jr, *For the Common Good*, Boston, Beacon Press, 1989, p.37.

17 This is not to say that Western Marxists have enthusiastically taken up the task of presenting an alternative analysis of the crisis. Marxists have not taken any consistent position on environmental issues. For a review of some Marxist or post-Marxist thought (which does not consider Soviet Marxists such as Ivan Frolov, nor Marxists associated with analysing Third World exploitation), see

Robyn Eckersley, *Environmentalism and Political Theory: Toward an Ecocentric Approach*, London, UCL Press, 1992, Chs 4, 5, 6. Only since 1989, with the publication of the journal *Capitalism, Nature, Socialism*, have Western Marxists begun to make a concerted effort to extend Marxism to deal with the environmental crisis.

18 Karl Marx, *Grundrisse*, tr. Martin Nicolaus, Harmondsworth, Penguin, 1973, pp.409f.

19 On this, see Arran Gare, 'Mechanistic materialism and capitalism', in *Nihilism Incorporated*, Bungendore, Eco-Logical Press, 1993, Ch.5.

20 The extent to which Marx himself could be understood as an environmentalist is much disputed. On this see Alfred Schmidt, *The Concept of Nature in Marx*, London, New Left Books, 1971 (first published 1962).

21 See J. Martinez-Alier and J.M. Naredo, 'A Marxist Precursor of energy economics: Podolinski', *Journal of Peasant Studies*, vol.8, January, pp.207–24. While Marx was sympathetic to Podolinski, Engels wrote disparagingly of the proposal, and argued against him in a number of articles. See J. Martinez-Alier, *Ecological Economics*, Oxford, Blackwell, 1987, p.222.

22 Bogdanov's concerns are evident in his novels *Red Star* and *Engineer Menni*. See Alexander Bogdanov, *Red Star: The First Bolshevik Utopia*, ed. Loren R. Graham and Richard Stites, tr. Charles Rougle, Bloomington, Indiana University Press, 1984, with an afterword on the subject of 'Bogdanov's inner message', by Loren Graham. On Bogdanov's significance for the environmental movement see Arran E. Gare, 'Soviet environmentalism: the path not taken', *Capitalism, Nature, Socialism*, vol.4, no.4, December 1993, and 'Aleksandr Bogdanov: *Proletkult* and conservation', *Capitalism, Nature, Socialism*, vol.5, no.2, June 1994. See also Arran E. Gare, *Beyond European Civilization: Marxism, Process Philosophy and the Environment*, Bungendore, Eco-Logical Press, 1993, Ch.4.

23 A.A. Bogdanov, *Tektologia: Vseobshchaya Organizatsionnay Nauka*, vol.1, St Petersburg, 1912; vol.2, Moscow, 1917; vol.3, Moscow, 1922.

24 Aleksandr Aleksandrovich Bogdanov (autobiography), in *Makers of the Russian Revolution*, tr. C.I.P. Ferdinand and D.M. Bellos, Ithaca, Cornell University Press, 1974, p.288.

25 This is argued by George Gorelik, the translator of Bogdanov's *Essays in Tektology: The General Science of Organization* (Seaside, Calif., Intersystems Publications, 1980) in 'Bogdanov's tektology: its basic concepts and relevance to modern generalizing sciences', *Human Systems Management*, vol.1, 1980, pp.327–37.

26 On this, see Zenovia A. Sochor, *Revolution and Culture: The Bogdanov–Lenin Controversy*, Ithaca, Cornell University Press, 1988.

27 Douglas Weiner, *The History of the Conservation Movement in Russia and the U.S.S.R. from its Origin to the Stalin Period*, Ph.D. thesis, Columbia University, 1983, p.348. This thesis formed the basis of Weiner's *Models of Nature*, Bloomington, Indiana University Press, 1988.

28 On this see Ilmari Susiluoto, *The Origins and Development of Systems Thinking in the Soviet Union: Political and Philosophical Controversies from Bogdanov and Bukharin to Present-day Re-evaluations*, Helsinki, Suomalainen Tiedeakatemia, 1982.

29 For a review of the failure of critical theory in this regard see Eckersley, 'The failed promise of critical theory', in *Environmentalism and Political Theory*, Ch.5. On Marcuse in particular, see Fred C. Alford, *Science and the Revenge of Nature: Marcuse and Habermas*, Tampa and Gainsville, University of Florida Press, 1985.

30 See André Gorz, *Ecology as Politics*, tr. Patsy Vigderman and Jonathon Cloud, Boston, South End Press, 1980 (first published 1975).

31 Richard England and Barry Bluestone, 'Ecology and social conflict', in *Toward a Steady-State Economy*, ed. Herman E. Daly, San Francisco, Freeman, 1973, pp.190–214. Gorz's work makes the same points in a more polemical and detailed way.

32 On this see Beder, *The Nature of Sustainable Development*, Ch.14.

33 See for example, Daniel Faber, 'Imperialism and the crisis of nature in Central America', *Capitalism, Nature, Socialism*, no.1, Fall 1988, pp.39–46; and James O'Connor, 'Uneven and combined development and ecological crisis: a theoretical introduction', *Race and Class*, vol.30, no.3, 1989, pp.1–11.

34 Conventional economists *have* addressed the issue of the environment in the Third World, but have ignored the imperatives of the world-system which drives people to this destruction. For instance David Pearce and his colleagues in *Sustainable Development*, pp.101ff. have listed the causes of forest destruction in Indonesia, and have ignored Indonesia's debt. Susan George in *The Debt Boomerang: How Third World Debt Harms Us All*, London, Pluto, 1992, esp. p.10, points out the close correlation between rainforest destruction and international debt (and describes the pressures brought on governments to facilitate this). Indonesia is both one of the biggest debtors, and is destroying more rainforest than any other country apart from Brazil.

35 England and Bluestone, 'Ecology and social conflict', p.199.

36 James O'Connor, 'The second contradiction of capitalism: causes and consequences', *Conference Papers*, Santa Cruz, CES/CNS Pamphlet 1.

37 R.J. Johnston, *Environmental Problems: Nature, Economy and State*, London, Belhaven, 1989, p.188.

38 Ibid., p.199. This is also the argument of Michael Redclift in *Sustainable Development: Exploring the Contradictions*, London, Methuen, 1987, and T. O'Riordan, 'The politics of sustainability', in *Sustainable Environmental Development*, ed. R.K. Turner, London, Belhaven, 1989.

39 Ibid.

40 Stephen Bunker, *Underdeveloping the Amazon: Extraction, Unequal Exchange, and the Failure of the Modern State*, Chicago, University of Chicago Press, 1988 (first published 1985). Bunker's energetic approach to the global system is taken from Richard Newbold Adams, who in turn was influenced by Leslie White. Leslie White's energetic approach to anthropology was probably inspired by Proletkult in Russia. See John Biggart, 'Marxism and social anthropology', *Studies in Soviet Thought*, 24, 1982, pp.1–9, esp. p.4.

41 See for instance the debate between Ted Benton and Reiner Grundmann in *New Left Review* between 1989 and 1992. See also Reiner Grundmann, *Marxism and Ecology*, Oxford, Oxford University Press, 1991, and Ted Benton, *Natural Relations: Ecology, Animal Rights and Socialist Thought*, London, Verso, 1993.

42 Rudolph Bahro, *The Alternative in Eastern Europe*, tr. David Fernbach, London, New Left Books, 1978 (first published 1977); André Gorz, *Paths to Paradise: On the Liberation from Work*, London, Pluto Press, 1985 (first published 1983).

43 See Boris Frankel, *Beyond the State? Dominant Theories and Socialist Strategies*, London, Macmillan, 1983, for a critique of Gorz.

44 For a review of environmentalist Marxist proposals for the future, see Eckersley, *Environmentalism and Political Theory*, Chs 4, 5, 6.

45 Frankel has defended the state as essential to an environmentally sustainable socialism in *Beyond the State?*

46 The seminal works in this regard were Arne Naess, 'The shallow and the deep, long-range ecology movement: a summary', *Inquiry*, vol.16, 1973, pp.95–100;

John Rodman, 'The liberation of nature', *Inquiry,* vol.20, 1977, pp.83–145; and Bill Devall and George Sessions, *Deep Ecology,* Salt Lake City, Gibbs M. Smith, Inc., 1985. For a critical review of deep ecology see Warwick Fox, *Toward a Transpersonal Ecology,* Boston, Shambhala, 1990. The link between environmentalism and postmodernism was first made by Charlene Spretnak in Appendix C, 'The spiritual dimension of green politics', in Charlene Spretnak and Fritjof Capra, *Green Politics: The Global Promise,* London, Paladin, 1985. However Spretnak did not link postmodernism and poststructuralism

47 Jean Baudrillard, *Selected Writings,* ed. Mark Poster, Cambridge, Polity Press, 1988, p.104.

48 While poststructuralists or postmodernists have not referred to Kolakowski, Leszek Kolakowski provides a parallel and more thorough critique of Marxism for these sins. See especially vol.1: 'The Founders' of *Main Currents of Marxism,* 3 vols, tr. P.S. Falla, Oxford, Oxford University Press, 1981.

49 The early deep ecologists turned to Spinoza, Buddhism, Taoism and Native American views to justify their opposition to anthropocentricism.

50 The importance of Nietzsche for environmentalism has been argued by Max O. Hallman, in 'Nietzsche's environmental ethics', *Environmental Ethics,* vol.13, Summer 1991, pp.99–125.

51 See for instance Michael E. Zimmerman, 'Toward a Heideggerean *ethos* for radical environmentalism', in *Environmental Ethics,* vol.5, Summer 1983, pp.99–132. For a later review of arguments surrounding Heidegger and deep ecology see Michael E. Zimmerman, 'Rethinking the Heidegger–deep ecology relationship', *Environmental Ethics,* vol.15, Fall 1993, pp.195–224.

52 René Schérer, 'Le Dernier des philosophes', in René Schérer and Arion Lothar Kelkel, *Heidegger ou l'expérience de la pensée,* Paris, Editions Segers, 1973, p.5.

53 See Peter Quigley, 'Rethinking resistance, environmentalism, literature, and poststructuralist theory', *Environmental Ethics,* vol. 14, Winter 1992, pp.291–306.

54 Hallman, 'Nietzsche's Environmental Ethics', pp.99–127, and more extensively in *The Shattered Self: Self Overcoming and the Transfiguration of Nature in the Philosophy of Nietzsche,* Ann Arbor, University Microfilms International, 1988. Hallman points out the similarity in the argument against Christianity of Nietzsche and of Lynn White, Jr in his famous paper 'The historical roots of our ecological crisis', *Science,* 155, 1967, pp.1203–7.

55 Friedrich Nietzsche, *Twilight of the Idols* and *The Anti-Christ,* tr. R.J. Hollingdale, Harmondsworth, Penguin, 1968, §38, p.150.

56 Ibid., p.135.

57 Friedrich Nietzsche, *The Will to Power,* tr. Walter Kaufmann, New York, Vintage Books, 1968, §765, p.401.

58 Ibid., §245, p.141.

59 Ibid., §303, p.169.

60 Ibid., §556, pp.301f.

61 Ibid., §12B, pp.13–14.

62 Ibid.

63 Ibid., §§1066, 1067, pp.548–50.

64 Ibid., §567, p.305.

65 Ibid., §565, p.305.

66 Ibid., §556, pp.301f.

67 Hallman, 'Nietzsche's environmental ethics', p.117.

68 As Ralph R. Acamporah has pointed out in 'Using and abusing Nietzsche for environmental ethics', *Environmental Ethics,* vol. 16, Summer 1994, pp.187–94, p.194.

69 Martin Heidegger, 'Letter on humanism', in *Basic Writings*, ed. David Farrell Krell, London, Routledge & Kegan Paul, 1978, p.233.

70 Martin Heidegger, *The End of Philosophy*, tr. Joan Stambaugh, New York, Harper & Row, 1973, p.190.

71 See for instance Holmes Rolston III, 'Are values in nature subjective or objective?', in *Environmental Philosophy*, ed. Robert Elliot and Arran Gare, London, Open University Press, 1983, or R. and V. Routley, 'Against the inevitability of human chauvinism', in *Ethics and Problems of the 21st Century*, ed. K.E. Goodpaster and K.M. Sayre, Notre Dame, Notre Dame University Press, 1979.

72 Heidegger, 'Letter on humanism', p.228.

73 Jacques Derrida, 'The ends of man', in *Margins of Philosophy*, Brighton, Harvester Press, 1982 (first published 1972), pp. 111–36, p.136.

74 Genevieve Lloyd, *The Man of Reason: 'Male' and 'Female' in Western Philosophy*, London, Methuen, 1984; Carolyn Merchant, *The Death of Nature: Women, Ecology, and the Scientific Revolution*, London, Wildwood House, 1982 (first published 1980); and Brian Easlea, *Witchcraft, Magic and the New Philosophy*, Brighton, Harvester Press, 1980.

75 See Nicholas Xenos, *Scarcity and Modernity*, London, Routledge 1989.

76 Jean Baudrillard, *The Mirror of Production*, tr. Mark Poster, St Louis, Telos Press, 1975, p.121.

77 Ibid.

78 Ibid.

79 Ibid., p.122.

80 Quigley, 'Rethinking resistance', p.292.

81 Ibid., p.300.

82 Examples of this, together with a long bibliography of such works, are to be found in *Reweaving the World: The Emergence of Eco-feminism*, ed. Irene Diamond and Gloria Feman Orenstein, San Francisco, Sierra Club Books, 1990. For an eco-feminist work which rejects this tendency, see Val Plumwood, *Feminism and the Mastery of Nature*, London, Routledge, 1993.

83 Jim Cheney, 'Nature and the theorizing of difference', *Contemporary Philosophy*, vol.13, no.1, 1990.

84 Derrida is often invoked, probably mistakenly, to justify such relativism (although not by Cheney).

85 In a personal communication, Cheney states that the main influences on him have been Wittgenstein, Kuhn, Rorty and postmodern feminists rather than Derrida and Lyotard, and that he is now sympathetic to the contruction of a new grand narrative.

86 Jim Cheney, 'Postmodern environmental ethics: ethics as bioregional narrative', *Environmental Ethics*, vol. 11, Summer 1989, pp.117–34, pp. 126, 128, 132, 133.

87 Ibid., p.134.

88 On this, see Roy Boyne, 'Conclusion: difference and the other', in *Foucault and Derrida: The Other Side of Reason*, London, Unwin Hyman, 1990.

89 'Intellectuals and power: a conversation between Michel Foucault and Gilles Deleuze', in *Language, Counter-Memory, Practice: Selected Essays and Interviews by Michel Foucault*, ed. Donald Bouchard, Ithaca, Cornell University Press, 1977, pp.205–17.

90 Arne Naess, *Ecology, Community and Lifestyle*, ed. and tr. David Rothenberg, Cambridge, Cambridge University Press, 1989, pp.160 and 161f.

91 See *Ecodefense: A Field Guide to Monkeywrenching*, ed. Dave Foreman and Bill Haywood, Tucson, New Ludd Books, 1987.

92 A range of actions along these lines is described in Roderick Nash, 'Liberating Nature', in *The Rights of Nature*, Madison, University of Wisconsin Press, 1989, Ch.6.

93 Vandana Shiva, *Staying Alive: Women, Ecology and Development*, London, Zed Books, 1989, p.218n. See also pp.67–77 for an account of the development of this movement.

94 Ibid., p.223.

95 Martin Heidegger, *Discourse on Thinking*, tr. John M. Anderson and E. Hans Freund, New York, Harper & Row, 1966, p.51.

96 The best analysis of this absence is Richard J. Bernstein's 'Heidegger's silence? *Ethos* and technology', in *The New Constellation: The Ethical-Political Horizons of Modernity/Postmodernity*, Cambridge, Polity Press, 1991, pp.79–141. See also Stephen K. White, *Political Theory and Postmodernism*, Cambridge, Cambridge University Press, 1991, who at the same time relates Heidegger's work to the poststructuralists.

97 On this, see Thomas McCarthy, 'The politics of the ineffable: Derrida's deconstructionism', and 'Postscript: the politics of friendship', in *Ideals and Illusions: On Reconstruction and Deconstruction in Contemporary Critical Theory*, Cambridge, MIT Press, 1991, pp.97–123.

98 For an excellent critique of this relativism, see Robert Frodeman, 'Radical environmentalism and the political roots of postmodernism: differences that make a difference', *Environmental Ethics*, vol.14, Winter 1992.

99 Nicos Poulantzas, *State, Power, Socialism*, tr. Patrick Camiller, London, Verso, 1978, p.149.

100 A major problem is the incoherence of this argument. For a critique of Cheney, see Mick Smith, 'Cheney and the myth of postmodernism', *Environmental Ethics*, vol.15, Spring 1993, pp.3–17. In a personal communication, however, Cheney has aligned himself with those feminist postmodernists who have defended metanarratives.

101 Jean Baudrillard, 'Symbolic exchange and death', in *Selected Writings*, ed. Mark Poster, Cambridge, Polity Press, 1988, pp.119–48, p.147n.

102 Chistopher Norris, one of Derrida's major interpreters, has attempted to distance him from postmodern appropriation and the relativism of other poststructuralists in 'Deconstruction *versus* postmodernism', in *Uncritical Theory*, London, Lawrence & Wishart, 1992, Ch.2. At the same time this work highlights the way postmodernists have lost their grip on reality. Michael Ryan in *Marxism and Deconstruction: A Critical Articulation*, supports Norris' evaluation of the different poststructuralists.

103 'The earth is not fragile', Lecture at the Shell Symposium, The Hague, June 1991.

104 There has been much soul-searching recently by radical environmentalists at their failures. This is associated with a call to reconsider Marxist analyses of society, despite what are regarded as the deficiencies of Marxists. See P.R. Hay, 'Getting From here to there: reflections on a green praxis', in *Ecopolitical Theory*, ed. Peter Hay and Robyn Eckersly, Hobart, Board of Environmental Studies, University of Tasmania, 1993.

105 Karl Marx, 'The German ideology', in *Karl Marx, Frederick Engels: Collected Works*, vol.5: *Marx and Engels: 1845–47*, tr. Clemens Dutt *et al.*, New York, International Publishers, 1976, p.55.

106 *The Letters of Karl Marx*, ed. and tr. Saul K. Padover, Englewood Cliffs, NJ, Prentice-Hall, 1979, pp.321f.

107 Karl Marx, 'Theses of Feuerbach' (original version), in *Karl Marx, Frederick Engels: Collected Works*, vol.5: *Marx and Engels: 1845–47*, p.3.

108 Bogdanov, *Red Star*, pp.116f.

109 Yrjo Haila and Richard Levins, *Humanity and Nature: Ecology, Science and Society*, London, Pluto Press, 1992; Benton, *Natural Relations*.

110 Ted Benton's distinction between labour which transforms inert material and labour which provides the conditions for natural processes to take place, and from this, his argument that the ideal of 'mastery of nature' makes no sense, captures one of the important insights of Heidegger. See Ted Benton, 'Ecology, socialism and the mastery of nature: a reply to Reiner Grundman', *New Left Review*, no.194, 1992, pp.55–74.

111 On this, see David Harvey, 'The nature of environment: the dialectics of social and environmental change', *The Socialist Register*.

112 This was quoted in the frontispiece of Alec Nove's *The Economics of Feasible Socialism*, London, George Allen & Unwin, 1983.

113 Poststructuralists have been interpreted in terms of systems theory by Anthony Wilden in *System and Structure: Essays in Communication and Exchange*, 2nd edn, London, Tavistock Publications, 1980.

114 R.B. Norgaard has argued for the coexistence of economic theory and ecological theory, with appreciation of the limitations of each, rather than the absorption of one into the other. See 'Environmental economics: an evolutionary critique and a plea for pluralism', *Journal of Environmental Economics and Management*, vol.12, 1985, pp.382–94, and 'The case for methodological pluralism', *Ecological Economics*, vol.1, 1989, pp.37–57.

115 On Japanese management, see Richard Tanner Pascale and Anthony G. Athos, *The Art of Japanese Management*, Harmondsworth, Penguin, 1982.

4 POSTMODERN METAPHYSICS

1 Peter Dews, *The Logics of Disintegration*, London, Verso, 1987, p.231.

2 Aristotle, *Metaphysics*, 1003a21–8.

3 Roy Bhaskar has defended realism in a way which could be modified to refute linguistic idealism. See *A Realist Theory of Science*, Hassocks, Sussex, Harvester Press, 1978 (first published 1975).

4 Friedrich Nietzsche, *The Will to Power*, tr. Walter Kaufmann, New York, Vintage Books 1968, §715, p.380.

5 Aristotle, *Metaphysics*, 1026a25–32.

6 Charles Sanders Peirce, 'The approach to metaphysics', in *Philosophical Writings of Peirce*, ed. Justus Buchler, New York, Dover, 1955. Bogdanov's Tektology is metaphysics in this sense, despite his claim that it was a general science beyond philosophy.

7 Floyd Matson was the first to use the term 'postmodern science' in 1964 in his book *The Broken Image: Man, Science, and Society*, New York, Braziller, although the term 'postmodern physics' had been used in 1962 by Huston Smith. In 1976 the 'postmodern science' was used by Frederick Ferré in *Shaping the Future: Resources for the Postmodern World*, New York, Harper & Row, and Stephen Toulmin in 'The construal of reality: criticism in modern and postmodern science', in *The Politics of Interpretation*, ed. W.J.T. Mitchell, Chicago, University of Chicago Press, 1982, pp.99–117. David Ray Griffin has promoted the development of postmodern science in a series of anthologies. See for instance *The Reenchantment of Science: Postmodern Proposals*, New York, State University of New York Press, 1988. For a history and overview of 'postmodern' science, see Steven Best, 'Chaos and entropy: metaphors in postmodern science and social theory', *Science as Culture*, vol.2, Part 2, no.11, 1992.

8 Jean-François Lyotard, *The Postmodern Condition*, tr. Geoff Benninton and Brian Massumi, Minneapolis, University of Minnesota Press, 1985, p.60.

9 P. Forman's paper, 'Weimar culture, causality and quantum theory, 1918–1927' (in *Historical Studies in the Physical Sciences no.3*, ed. R. McCormach, Philadelphia, University of Pennsylvania Press, 1971), which argued this, has been severely criticized, but not totally refuted.

10 See for instance C.H. Waddington, *Tools for Thought*, Frogmore, Paladin, 1977. Thom described his debt to Waddington and process philosophy in *Structural Stability and Morphogenesis: An Outline of a General Theory of Models*, tr. D.H. Fowler, Reading, Mass., W.A. Benjamin, 1975 (first published 1972), esp. pp.1, 10, 114ff.

11 Ilya Prigogine, *From Being to Becoming: Time and Complexity in the Physical Sciences*, San Francisco, Freeman, 1980, pp.xiif.

12 Ilya Prigogine and Isabelle Stengers, *Order Out of Chaos*, Toronto, Bantam Books, 1984, p.312.

13 David Ray Griffin, 'Introduction', in *The Reenchantment of Science*, pp.15f.

14 See for instance Richard J. Bernstein, *Beyond Objectivism and Relativism: Science, Hermeneutics, and Praxis*, Philadelphia, University of Pennsylvania Press, 1983. For the history of the destruction of logical positivism and the rise of the new philosophy of science, see Frederick Suppe, 'The Search for philosophic understanding of scientific theories', in *The Structure of Scientific Theories*, 2nd edn, Urbana, University of Illinois Press, 1977, pp.3–241.

15 Mark Johnson in *The Body in the Mind*, Chicago, Chicago University Press, 1987, p.102.

16 Alasdair MacIntyre, 'Epistemological crises, dramatic narrative and the philosophy of science', *Monist*, 60, 1977, pp.453–72, 459–60, 467.

17 Jean-François Lyotard, *The Postmodern Condition*, pp.28f.

18 J.M. Bernstein has defended grand narratives along these lines. See 'Grand narratives', in *On Paul Ricoeur: Narrative and Interpretation*, ed. David Wood, London, Routledge & Kegan Paul, 1991, pp.102–23.

19 David Bohm, 'Further remarks on order', in *Towards a Theoretical Biology, 2 Sketches*, ed. C.H. Waddington, Edinburgh, Edinburgh University Press, 1969, pp.41f.

20 On this, see Ivor Leclerc, *The Nature of Physical Existence*, London, Allen & Unwin, 1972.

21 Henri Bergson, *The Creative Mind*, tr. Mabelle L. Anderson, New York, Philosophical Library, 1946, p.174.

22 See Milic Capek, *Bergson and Modern Physics*, Dordrecht, Reidel, 1971, and Victor Zuckerkandl, *Sound and Symbol: Music and the External World*, tr. Willard R. Trask, Princeton, Princeton University Press, 1969.

23 Alfred North Whitehead, *Process and Reality*, corrected edn, ed. David Ray Griffin and Donald W. Sherburne, London, Collier Macmillan, 1978, pp.14, 17.

24 Alfred North Whitehead, *Modes of Thought*, New York, The Free Press, 1968 (first published 1938), p.154.

25 Alfred North Whitehead, *Science and the Modern World*, New York, Mentor Books, 1948 (first published 1925), p.58. See also pp.52 and 179.

26 Whitehead, *Process and Reality*, p.4.

27 Ibid., p.21.

28 Ibid., p.7.

29 Alfred North Whitehead, *Adventure of Ideas*, New York, The Free Press, 1967 (first published 1933), p.236.

30 Alfred North Whitehead, *Concept of Nature*, Cambridge, Cambridge University Press, 1964 (first published 1920), p.14.

31 Whitehead, *Process and Reality*, p.41.

32 Whitehead, *Modes of Thought*, p.92. Whitehead argued that when we say 'twice three is six' we are not saying that 'twice three' and 'six' are tautologies, but are describing the process which issues in the form of 'six' which is then a potential for other processes beyond itself. On Whitehead's view of mathematics see Murray Code, *Order and Organism*, New York, State University of New York Press, 1985.

33 Whitehead, *Adventure of Ideas*, p.157.

34 Ibid., p.199.

35 Especially Ivor Leclerc's *The Nature of Physical Existence*, London, Allen & Unwin, 1972 and *The Philosophy of Nature*, Washington, Catholic University of America Press, 1986.

36 Whitehead, *Process and Reality*, p.20. On Whitehead's concept of creativity, showing its relationship to the concept of energy, see Dorothy Emmet, 'Creativity and the passage of nature' and Friedrich Rapp, 'Whitehead's concept of creativity and modern science', in *Whitehead's Metaphysics of Creativity*, ed. Friedrich Rapp and Reiner Wiehl, New York, State University of New York Press, 1990.

37 For an elaboration of a conception of order in terms of similarities and differences see David Bohm, *Wholeness and the Implicate Order*, London, Routledge & Kegan Paul, 1980, pp.115ff, and David Bohm and F. David Peat, *Science, Order, and Creativity*, Toronto, Bantam, 1987, pp.104–91. Whitehead has defined order differently, and I have not used his concept.

38 Whitehead, *Process and Reality*, p.23. What I have called 'process' corresponds roughly to what Whitehead called 'the concrescence of an actual entity or occasion', although I am rejecting Whitehead's atomism in favour of Capek's notion that becoming is 'pulsational' (also argued for by Leclerc), and of Leclerc's inclusion of compound actualities as primary beings (in accordance with Aristotle's metaphysics).

39 This makes sense of what Whitehead had claimed (inconsistently with his ideas in *Process and Reality*) in *Science and the Modern World*, that 'the plan of the *whole* influences the very characters of the various subordinate organisms which enter into it', *Science and the Modern World*, p.76. On this, see also Whitehead's *Adventure of Ideas*.

40 Whitehead, *Process and Reality*, p.23. Whitehead argued: '"potentiality for process" is the meaning of the more general term "entity" or "thing"', ibid., p.41.

41 *The English Works of Thomas Hobbes*, ed. Sir William Molesworth, London, John Bohn, 1939, vol.1: *Elements of Philosophy Concerning Body*, Ch.9, p.121.

42 Edward Pols, 'Power and agency', *International Philosophical Quarterly*, vol.11, 1971, pp.293–313, p.297.

43 As Whitehead put it,

in every act of becoming there is the becoming of something with temporal extension; but . . . the act itself is not extensive, in the sense that it is divisible into earlier and later acts of becoming which correspond to the extensive divisibility of what has become.

(*Process and Reality*, p.69.)

44 The fullest elaboration of time and space in terms of an auditory analogy is provided by Zuckerkandl, *Sound and Symbol*, Chs 12–18.

45 An argument somewhat along these lines has been made in relation to time by J.T. Fraser in *The Genesis and Evolution of Time*, Amherst, University of Massachusetts Press, 1982.

46 The best account of this is David Bohm's *Special Theory of Relativity*, Redwood City, Calif., Addison Wesley, 1989 (first published 1965).

47 The most up-to-date and coherent formulation of this is contained in D. Bohm and B.J. Hiley, *The Undivided Universe: An Ontological Interpretation of Quantum Theory*, London and New York, Routledge, 1993.

48 On this, see Milic Capek, 'The myth of frozen passage: the status of becoming in the physical world', in *Boston Studies in the Philosophy of Science*, vol.2, New York, Humanities Press, 1965, pp.441–63.

49 See David Bohm, *Wholeness and the Implicate Order*, London, Routledge & Kegan Paul, 1980, Chs 5, 6.

50 A. Baracca, D.J. Bohm, B.J. Hiley and A.E.G. Stuart, 'On some new notions concerning locality and nonlocality in the quantum theory', in *Il Nuovo Cimento*, vol.28B, no.2, 11 August 1975, pp.453–65, p.458.

51 See G. Nicolis and I. Prigogine, *Self-organization in Non-Equilibrium Systems*, New York, Wiley, 1977. For a summary of the work on this subject see also Ilya Prigogine, 'Order through fluctuation: self-organization and social system', in *Evolution and Consciousness*, ed. Erich Jantsch and Conrad H. Waddington, Reading, Mass., Addison Wesley, 1976, pp.93–133.

52 On this see James Gleick, *Chaos*, London, Cardinal, 1987.

53 See for example H. Harken, *Synergetics: An Introduction*, 3rd edn, Berlin, Springer, 1983; *Synergetics – From Macroscopic to Microscopic Order*, ed. E. Frehland, Berlin, Springer-Verlag, 1984; Giorgio Careri, *Order and Disorder in Matter*, tr. Kristin Jarratt, Reading, Benjamin/Cummings, 1984; and Paul Davies, *The Cosmic Blueprint*, London, Heinemann, 1987.

54 Prigogine and Stengers, *Order Out of Chaos*, p.125.

55 David Bohm, 'Some remarks on the notion of order', in *Towards a Theoretical Biology, 2 Sketches*, ed. Waddington.

56 C.H. Waddington, 'Cellular oscillations and development', in *Towards a Theoretical Biology, 2 Sketches*, ed. Waddington, pp.179–83, pp.180f. For more recent work in this area see Brian C. Goodwin, 'Changing from an evolutionary to a generative paradigm in biology', in *Evolutionary Theory: Paths into the Future*, ed. J.W. Pollard, Chichester, Wiley, 1984, pp.99–120.

57 Humberto R. Maturana and Francisco J. Varela, *Autopoiesis and Cognition: The Realization of the Living*, Dordrecht, Reidel, 1980.

58 Ted Bastin, 'A general property of hierarchies', in *Towards a Theoretical Biology, 2 Sketches*, ed. Waddington, pp.252–65, p.256.

59 See B.C. Goodwin, *Temporal Organization of Cells: A Dynamical Theory of Cellular Control Processes*, London, Academic Press, 1963, pp.20f, and *Analytical Physiology of Cells and Developing Organisms*, London, Academic Press, 1976, Chs 1, 2, 3 and pp.190f.

60 A.S. Iberall, 'New thoughts on bio-control', in *Towards a Theoretical Biology, 2 Sketches*, ed. Waddington, pp.166–77.

61 For recent developments of this area see Leon Glass and Michael C. Mackey, *From Clocks to Chaos: The Rhythms of Life*, Princeton, Princeton University Press, 1988, and Stuart Kauffman, *The Origins of Order: Self-Organization and Selection in Evolution*, New York and Oxford, Oxford University Press, 1993.

62 See Robert P. McIntosh, *The Background of Ecology*, Cambridge, Cambridge University Press, 1985.

63 Richard Levins and Richard Lewontin, 'Dialectics and reductionism in ecology', in *The Dialectical Biologist*, Cambridge, Mass., Harvard University Press, 1985, pp.132–60, p.136.

64 The best overview of the Gaia hypothesis is contained in *Gaia: The Thesis, the Mechanisms and the Implications*, ed. Peter Bunyard and Edward Goldsmith,

Camelford, Cornwall, Wadebridge Ecological Centre, 1988. This contains a history of the concept by Jacques Grinevald, 'Sketch for a history of the idea of the biosphere' and a number of contributions by Lovelock and Margulis.

65 Jacob von Uexküll, *Theoretical Biology*, London, Kegan Paul, Trench, Trubner & Co., 1926, p.176.

66 See Konrad Lorenz, *Behind the Mirror: A Search for a Natural History of Human Knowledge*, tr. Ronald Taylor, London, Methuen, 1977; W.H. Thorpe, *Animal Nature and Human Nature*, London, Methuen, 1974; and Donald R. Griffin, *The Question of Animal Awareness: Evolutionary Continuity of Mental Experience*, New York, Rockefeller University Press, 1976, and *Animal Thinking*, Cambridge, Mass., Harvard University Press, 1984.

67 R.W. Sperry, 'A modified concept of consciousness', *Psychological Review*, vol. 76, 1969, pp. 532–6; Gerald Edelman, *Bright Air, Brilliant Fire: On the Matter of the Mind*, New York, Basic Books, 1992.

68 Richard N. Adams, *Paradoxical Harvest*, Cambridge, Cambridge University Press, 1982, p.17. Adams has further developed his ideas on this in *The Eighth Day: Social Evolution as the Self-organization of Energy*, Austin, University of Texas Press, 1988.

69 See for instance Jane van Lawick-Goodall, 'The chimpanzee', in *The Quest for Man*, ed. Vanne Goodall, London, Phaidon, 1975.

70 Jena Lectures of 1803–4 and 1805–6. These lectures have been critically examined by Jürgen Habermas in 'Labour and interaction: remarks on Hegel's Jena *Philosophy of Mind*', in *Theory and Practice*, tr. John Viertel, London, Heinemann, 1974 (first published 1971), pp.142–69. The threefold division derives ultimately from the Pythagorean division between lovers of wisdom, lovers of honour and lovers of gain. It was subordinated to the division between subjective spirit, objective spirit and absolute spirit in Hegel's later work, but was never totally abandoned.

71 Georg Simmel, 'The conflict in modern culture', in *George Simmel on Individual and Social Forms*, ed. Donald N. Levine, Chicago, University of Chicago Press, 1971, pp.375–93, pp.375f.

72 Kent V. Flannery, 'The cultural evolution of civilizations', *Annual Review of Ecology and Systematics*, vol.3, 1972, pp.399–426, based on the work of Rapaport. This notion has been further developed by Stephen Bunker in *Underdeveloping the Amazon: Extraction, Unequal Exchange, and the Failure of the Modern State* (Chicago, University of Chicago Press, 1988 (first published 1985)) and used to characterize the core zones of Western capitalism. It could equally be applied to the Soviet bureaucracy.

73 The importance of spatio-temporal order has long been recognized in geography and architecture. Recently Anthony Giddens has developed ideas on this subject. See Anthony Giddens, *The Constitution of Society*, Cambridge, Polity Press, 1984, Ch.3.

74 F. Braudel, *The Mediterranean and the Mediterranean World in the Age of Philip II*, 2 vols, vol.1, tr. S. Reynolds, London, Collins, 1972, p.16. See also Fernand Braudel, 'History and the social sciences', in *On History*, tr. Sarah Matthews, Chicago, Chicago University Press, 1980, pp.25–54.

75 Braudel, *The Mediterranean and the Mediterranean World*, pp.16f.

76 Fernand Braudel, *Civilization and Capitalism 15th–18th Century*, 3 vols, vol.3: *The Perspective of the World*, tr. S. Reynolds, London, Fontana, 1985, 'Divisions of space and time in Europe', pp.21–88.

77 *Kierkegaard's Concluding Unscientific Postscript*, tr. David F. Swenson and Walter Lowrie, Princeton, Princeton University Press, 1968, p.112.

78 G.W.F. Hegel, *The Philosophy of History*, tr. J. Sibree, New York, Dover, 1956 (first published 1899), p.457.

79 *Kierkegaard's Concluding Unscientific Postscript*, p.84.

80 Søren Kierkegaard, 'The sickness unto death', in *Fear and Trembling and The Sickness Unto Death*, tr. Walter Lowrie, Princeton, Princeton University Press, 1968, p.146.

81 Postmodernism amounts to the abandonment of a culture which promoted the development of mind and its replacement by a culture which severely suppresses its development.

82 Paul Ricoeur, *Time and Narrative*, 3 vols, Chicago, University of Chicago Press, vol.1, p.ix.

5 TOWARDS A NEW WORLD ORDER

1 See for example Fredric Jameson, *The Political Unconscious: Narrative as a Socially Symbolic Act*, Ithaca, Cornell University Press, 1981; David Carr, *Time, Narrative and History*, Bloomington, Indiana University Press, 1986; Paul Ricoeur, *Time and Narrative*, 3 vols, Chicago, Chicago University Press, 1984–8; and Donald E. Polkinghorne, *Narrative Knowing and the Human Sciences*, New York, State University of New York Press, 1988.

2 Mikhail Bakhtin, *Problems of Dostoyevsky Poetics*, Minneapolis, Minnesota University Press, 1984; Julia Kristeva (expounding Bakhtin's notion), 'Word, dialogue and novel', in *The Kristeva Reader*, ed. Toril Moi, New York, Columbia University Press, 1988, pp.35–61, p.47.

3 Eric Wolfe, *Europe and the People Without History*, Berkeley, University of California Press, 1982. See also Johannes Fabian, *Time and the Other: How Anthropology Makes its Object*, New York, Columbia University Press, 1983.

4 This has been described by Edward Said, *Orientalism*, Harmondsworth, Peregrine, 1985.

5 Joseph Needham and his colleagues have made a major contribution to this by analysing the achievements of Chinese civilization from the perspective of the new cosmology in their multi-volume *Science and Civilisation in China*, Cambridge, Cambridge University Press, 1954.

6 As I have argued in *Beyond European Civilization*, Bungendore, Eco-Logical Press, 1993, p.236.

7 Alasdair MacIntyre, *After Virtue*, 2nd edn, Notre Dame, University of Notre Dame Press, 1984.

8 See for example Partha Chatterjee, *Nationalist Thought and the Colonial World: A Derivative Discourse*, London, Zed Books, 1986. For a critique of the work of subaltern studies see Rosalind O'Hanlon, 'Recovering the subject', *Modern Asian Studies*, vol.22, no.1, 1988, pp.189–224, and Rosalind O'Hanlon and David Washbrook, 'After orientalism: culture, criticism, and politics in the Third World', *Comparative Studies in Society and History*, vol.34, no.1, 1992, pp.141–67.

9 Dudley Seers, *The Political Economy of Nationalism*, Oxford, Oxford University Press, 1983.

10 Denis Goulet, 'Looking at Guinea-Bissau: a new nation's development strategy', Occasional Paper no.9: Overseas Development Council, March 1978, p.52, cited by Charles K. Wilber and Kenneth P. Jameson in 'Paradigms of economic development and beyond' in *The Political Economy of Development and Underdevelopment*, ed. Wilber, 3rd edn, New York, Random House, 1984, pp.4–25, p.22.

11 James J. Lamb, 'The Third World and the development debate', *IDOC – North*

America, January–February 1973, p.20, cited in Wilber and Jameson, 'Paradigms of economic development and beyond', p.23.

12 On the success of Zimbabwe see Paul Harrison, *The Greening of Africa*, London, Paladin, 1987, pp.87–97.

13 Stephen Bunker, *Underdeveloping the Amazon:Extraction, Unequal Exchange, and the Failure of the Modern State*, Chicago, University of Chicago Press, 1988 (first published 1985), p.253.

14 As shown by Susan George's *The Debt Boomerang: How Third World Debt Harms Us All*, London, Pluto, 1992.

15 The best-worked-out defence of this is Herman Daly and John Cobb Jr's, *For the Common Good: Redirecting the Economy toward Community, the Environment, and a Sustainable Future*, Boston, Beacon Press, 1989. See especially Ch.9 and Ch.11.

16 John Maynard Keynes, 'National self-sufficiency', *The Yale Review*, vol.22, 1933, p.758.

17 This definition is developed by James Anderson, in 'Nationalism and geography', in *The Rise of the Modern State*, ed. James Anderson, Brighton, Wheatsheaf, 1986, pp.115–42, p.116.

18 Benedict Anderson, *Imagined Communities: Reflections on the Origin and Spread of Nationalism*, London, Verso, 1983, p.14.

19 John Breuilly, *Nationalism and the State*, Manchester, Manchester University Press, 1985, p.382.

20 See ibid.

21 This development was recognized by Rudolf Hilferding. See *Finance Capital*, tr. Morris Watnick and Sam Gordon, London, Routledge & Kegan Paul, 1985 (first published 1910), esp. p.335.

22 On this see Peter Katzenstein, *Small States in World Markets*, Ithaca, Cornell University Press, 1985.

23 Michio Morishima, *Why Has Japan 'Succeeded'?*, Cambridge, Cambridge University Press, 1982, p.197n.

24 Anderson, *Imagined Communities*, p.136.

25 G. Therborn, 'The working class and the welfare state', 5th Nordic Congress of Research in the History of the Labour Movement, Murikka, Finland, August 1983, p.20.

26 Cited ibid., p.23.

27 'The Alva Myrdal report to the Swedish Social Democratic Party: the need for equality', excerpts reprinted in *Philosophy Now*, ed. Paula Rothenberg Struhl and Karsten J. Struhl, 3rd edn, New York, Random House, 1980, pp.385–91, pp.386f.

28 In 1974 the top 5 per cent received only three times as much disposable income as the bottom 5 per cent compared to 5.7 times in the Soviet Union and 12.7 times in the USA (from Michael Ellman, *Socialist Planning*, Cambridge, Cambridge University Press, p.189).

29 On the Swedish effort to address environmental problems see Peter Bunyard, 'Sweden: choosing the right energy path?', *The Ecologist*, vol.16, no.1, 1986, pp.24–8. In 1988 laws were passed to phase out battery hens, and to improve the living conditions of cattle and pigs.

30 See Peter Katzenstein, *Small States in World Markets*, Ithaca, Cornell University Press, 1985.

31 Chatterjee, *Nationalist Thought and the Colonial World*.

32 Jacobo Schatan, *World Debt: Who is to Pay?* London, Zed Books, 1987, p.110.

33 On this see *The Economist*, 28 January–3 February, 1989, p.65.

34 The distinction between shareholders and stakeholders is drawn by Andrei

Sheifer and Lawrence Summers in 'Breach of trust in hostile takeovers', in *Corporate Takeovers*, ed. Alan Auerbach, Chicago, University of Chicago Press, 1988.

35 Dudley Seers, *The Political Economy of Nationalism*, Oxford, Oxford University Press, 1983, p.105.

36 For an illuminating study of education and its problems and what is required to overcome these problems and to induct students in this way see Basil Bernstein, 'On the classification and framing of educational knowledge', in *Class, Codes and Control*, St Albans, Paladin, 1973, pp.227–56.

37 Clifford A. Hooker, 'Scientific neutrality versus normative learning: the theoretician's and politician's dilemma', in *Science and Ethics*, ed. David Oldroyd, Kensington, New South Wales University Press, 1982, pp.8–33, p.17.

38 Rom Harré, *Personal Being*, Oxford, Blackwell, 1983, p.24.

39 Some steps in this direction have been made by Herman E. Daly and John B. Cobb, Jr in *For the Common Good*, Boston, Beacon Press, 1989; and Stephen Bunker, *Underdeveloping the Amazon*, esp. Ch.1. See also André Gorz, *Critique of Economic Reason*, tr. Gillian Handyside and Chris Turner, London, Verso, 1989.

40 Daly and Cobb, *For the Common Good*, Appendix.

41 James O'Connor, *Accumulation Crisis*, Oxford, Blackwell, 1984, p.vii.

42 This is the form of psychology argued for by Rom Harré in *Social Being*, Oxford, Blackwell, 1979, and *Personal Being* – anticipated to some extent by L. Vygotsky.

43 The study of money-making and spending – chrematistics – must be placed in a broader context and evaluated in terms of this broader context.

44 Such an ecological social science has been in the making for over a century without gaining institutional recognition. See Juan Martinez-Alier, *Ecological Economics*, Oxford, Blackwell, 1987. A milestone in its development was Nicholas Georgescu-Roegen's work, *The Entropy Law and the Economic Process*, Cambridge, Mass., Harvard University Press, 1971. Other relatively recent works have been produced by Herman E. Daly (*Steady-State Economics*, San Francisco, Freeman, 1977), Narindar Singh (*Economics and the Crisis of Ecology*, 2nd edn, Delhi, Oxford University Press, 1976), and Richard Newbold Adams (*The Eighth Day: Social Evolution as the Self-organization of Energy*, Austin, University of Texas Press, 1988).

45 Michel Foucault, *Power/Knowledge*, tr. Colin Gordon *et al.*, Brighton, Harvester Press, 1980, p.114.

46 Karl Marx, 'Theses on Feuerbach' (2), in *Karl Marx, Frederick Engels: Collected Works*, vol.5: *Marx and Engels: 1845–1847*, tr. Clemens Dutt *et al.*, New York, International Publishers, 1976, p.3.

INDEX

191